RIDE *the* CAMEL

exploring the path less traveled

TAUNI CREFELD

MILSPACE BOOKS

an imprint of W. Brand Publishing

NASHVILLE, TENNESSEE

Copyright ©2025 Tauni Crefeld

The views and opinions expressed in this book are those of the author and do not necessarily reflect the official policy or position of W. Brand Publishing.

All rights reserved. No part of this publication may be reproduced, distributed or transmitted in any form or by any means, including photocopying, recording, or other electronic or mechanical methods, without the prior written permission of the publisher, except in the case of brief quotations embodied in critical reviews and certain other noncommercial uses permitted by copyright law.

j.brand@wbrandpub.com
W. Brand Publishing
www.wbrandpub.com
Cover design by JuLee Brand / designchik
Illustrations by Brian Serff

Ride the Camel / Tauni Crefeld —1st ed.

Available in Paperback, eBook and Kindle formats.

Paperback ISBN: 979-8-89503-030-1
eBook ISBN: 979-8-89503-031-8
Library of Congress Control Number: (applied for)

CONTENTS

The Early Years

Chapter 1 Bolivia: Life's Little Luxuries 1
Chapter 2 Colombia: Objects on a Map 13
Chapter 3 Bogotá, Colombia: Scammers Gonna Scam 19
Chapter 4 Guatemala: Yay! A Parade 25
Chapter 5 Ecuador: Life Lessons 29
Chapter 6 Nepal: Choose Your Travel Partner Well 39
Chapter 7 Korea: A Saturday Drive 55

Family Travel

Chapter 8 Germany: No Regrets 67
Chapter 9 Puerto Rico: The Peril of Using Points 77
Chapter 10 Puerto Rico: No Rules 83
Chapter 11 Spain: Not Your Mother's Spain 92

Work & Solo

Chapter 12 Peru & Honduras: Mission Trips 103
Chapter 13 U.S.: The 50 115
Chapter 14 Belgium & the Netherlands:
             There May Not Be a Later 121
Chapter 15 Denmark / Sweden: Between the Cities 131
Chapter 16 India: It Wasn't the Food 141
Chapter 17 Singapore: Weekend Vacation 153
Chapter 18 Wales: But It Should Be 161
Chapter 19 Milan: The Apocalypse 165

Travel Buddy

Chapter 20 Monaco, Liechtenstein and . . .
             How about Timiosora? 171
Chapter 21 The Baltics: Mother Russia 181
Chapter 22 Balkans: Reemerge and Restore 193
Chapter 23 Caucasus: Hidden Gems 205
Chapter 24 Albania: What Happens in Albania 217

The Later Years

Chapter 25 Saudi Arabia: When in Rome, but Not at Home 231
Chapter 26 Jamaica: Weekend Adventure 239
Chapter 27 Slovenia & Croatia: Unexpected Adventures 243
Chapter 28 Japan: Snow Monkeys and Hedgehogs 253
Chapter 29 The Pyrenees: Who You Travel With 261
Chapter 30 Slovakia & Poland: In Search of Ukraine 271
Chapter 31 Jordan: Golden Triangle 283

On To the Next Phase

Chapter 32 Portugal & Morocco: Mini-Sabbatical 299
Chapter 33 Kashmir: Where Are We? 313
Chapter 34 India: Back to India 325
Chapter 35 Sri Lanka: The Best Part of Travel 335
Chapter 36 What's Next? 351

About the Author 353
Other Books by Tauni Crefeld 355

THE EARLY YEARS

CHAPTER 1

BOLIVIA:
LIFE'S LITTLE LUXURIES

"There is a sacrifice in the mine tonight."

What?

My friend Tera and I were eating the most heavenly banana ice cream, made with real bananas, in a dinky hotel restaurant in Flores, Bolivia, a tiny town with brick houses clustered together in the Yungas jungle. The polished brown tile floors reflected the late afternoon light streaming in from the windows. We were at one of only four tables in the room, and the others were empty.

A middle-aged man dressed in dark polyester pants, a button up shirt, and a sweater thrown over his shoulders like he was a preppie from Connecticut, spoke with another man, who I presumed to be the owner of the hotel. The room was so empty and quiet that I couldn't help but overhear them.

I translated for Tera, who didn't speak Spanish. She said, "A sacrifice? Of what?"

"I don't know. Let's see if we can go!"

"You want to go to a sacrifice?" she asked.

"When else are we ever going to see a sacrifice?"

"Could we die this way? Cool!" Tera said. She didn't think we would actually die—nor did she want to—but if we *could* die doing it, that made it seem so much more interesting. It wasn't the first time she'd said that on the trip, nor would it be the last.

It was the early '90s; we were twenty-one years old and had been friends since we met in junior high in Minot, North Dakota. Tera had just graduated from the University of North Dakota. I graduated from the United States Air Force Academy, and I had 60 days of leave before I had to show up to my first duty station as a new lieutenant.

I wanted to spend as many of those days as possible traveling through South America and practicing my Spanish. I traveled to Spain in high school for a class trip and got hooked on Spanish. I kept studying it throughout high school and during my four years at the Academy.

Tera was game to travel with me for the first six weeks.

We flew into La Paz, the capitol of Bolivia. La Paz is built in a valley, with the main street at the bottom and houses ringing the hillsides. There were eucalyptus trees lined up along the top of the valley like tall, skinny soldiers guarding the town. Whenever we got lost, we just had to walk down, and we could re-orient once we hit the main street.

We were eager to explore the city; it was so vibrant and interesting. Many of the local women wore indigenous clothing—full skirts, two long braids, and bowler hats perched on top of their heads. Shops sold everything from coca leaf tea and candies to—believe it or not—llama fetuses, to be used as good luck charms. But Tera spent the first few days there feeling sick, with a headache and nausea. I felt fine.

It took us a while to realize that Tera had altitude sickness. At almost 12,000 feet, La Paz is the highest capital in the world. I had spent the previous four years at The Air Force Academy, which is over 7,000 feet above sea level, while Tera had been living in North Dakota, where the elevation is effectively nil. Once we realized why she felt so terrible, we decided to travel to a lower elevation.

We arrived in Flores on a bus from La Paz earlier that afternoon, having paid for a tour to "Las Yungas." At the time, there were no neatly packaged tours from Tripadvisor with multiple Instagram-friendly activities like ziplining and selfie stops in front of waterfalls. For our tour fee, we got a round-trip bus fare, a hotel, and two days to explore on our own.

Before leaving for Las Yungas, the bus driver poured alcohol on the floor of the bus and said a prayer. The road wound through the mountains from La Paz down into the jungles on what should have been a one-way road—but wasn't. Low-hanging clouds and mist lingered in the air. The steep sides of the mountains were covered in dark green vegetation with red dirt spotted throughout. In front of us were trucks piled high with boxes and bags of goods, with women dressed in traditional bowler hats and wide skirts perched on top of everything. Trucks wound down the mountain, sometimes teetering so much on a turn that it looked like the women would be tossed out and roll down the hillside.

There were multiple times a car or another loaded-up truck had to reverse to make room for us to pass, and multiple times I thought one of us wouldn't make it.

There are probably YouTube videos of that pass now because of how dangerous it is, and I highly doubt the roads have improved much since. The road was on the side of a mountain; they would have had to blast away significant portions of the mountain to widen it at all.

The hotel in Flores didn't have more than 6-8 rooms, but it was clean, whitewashed, and seemed safe. After we checked in, we walked to a waterfall outside of town, following the description in our Lonely Planet *South America on a Shoestring* guidebook. Through the town, we passed banana plants, children using sticks to roll hoops in the street, and women selling spices, grains, and vegetables from sacks on the sidewalk.

For lunch, we bought a sandwich from a woman with one arm who cut the meat (beef maybe?) by holding a huge butcher knife under her arm and sliding the meat over it before piling it into hard rolls.

It was late afternoon by the time we made it back to the hotel, and we couldn't resist the banana ice cream.

When the two men finished talking, I approached the mine owner. "I heard you talking about the sacrifice," I said. "Could we come?" I wasn't sure how to more tactfully ask to go to a sacrifice, so I just said it.

"I will need to ask the *brujo*, the witch doctor," he said. "If he says it's ok, we'll come get you and you can come with us."

At first it seemed odd that the mine owner would have to ask the *brujo*. He *owned* the mine; shouldn't he get to decide? But then I realized that the ritual meant something to the mine owner. And he didn't want a couple of gringo tourists to mess it up.

We waited while the man went to pick up the *brujo* and buy the supplies needed for the sacrifice. On the balcony of our hotel room, we could see over the whole valley. The clouds still hung low and cast shadows over the jungle-covered mountains.

When the man came back, he informed us that the *brujo* didn't mind us coming, so we hopped into the back of the jeep.

There was a little piglet squirming in a burlap sack at our feet, only his head visible through the opening. I assumed he was tonight's special guest. I was told the *chanchito* or piglet had to be "young, male, and red" for the ceremony to work. I felt sick to my stomach thinking about it. It was one thing to talk about sacrifices while eating banana ice cream; it was another entirely to see the animal that wouldn't make it through the night.

I stared at the *brujo*, who was wearing cheap light-blue polyester dress pants with his zipper down, and a jean jacket like the one Tera was wearing. I don't know what I expected, a grass skirt? A necklace made of bones? A headdress with feathers? Definitely not this very short, middle-aged man in light-blue polyester slacks. His zipper being down really bothered me and made him appear less professional. Less competent? Did those words even apply to a *brujo*?

We bumped along the dirt road through town and kept going until the town was no longer visible—we were surrounded by jungle. And then we kept going. The trees closed over the road and enveloped us.

It was at that point we realized we never asked where we were going, how long the sacrifice was going to last, or who would get us back to the hotel. No one knew where we were; and of course we had no cell or satellite phones and no Google maps. This was the '90s. We were at the mercy of the mine owner and the *brujo*, and it was getting dark.

We hadn't brought much with us. I didn't have anything *to* bring—my bags never made it to Bolivia from Miami. I was already four days in—and counting—with no luggage and nothing but my guidebook and money belt. Tera had brought a messenger-style bag with a notebook and camera, but neither of us had anything sensible like a change of clothes or a toothbrush.

We'd been driving at least an hour, maybe more, when the jeep finally stopped. It was pitch black by then, and we were ushered into one of several Gilligan's Island-style bamboo huts in the mining compound. The hut was rectangular and had a long table with benches around it. Surrounding the table were about ten to twelve people, who I guessed were the miners and their families. The table took up all the space in the hut, so we sat on the benches and leaned against the bamboo walls. There were a few candles burning on the table to push back the dark.

The sacrifice was going to be made to the Mother Earth, or *Pachamama* that night. The goal was to pay Her so that the small, gold-mining operation on the river would produce in the coming year. Judging by the huts around us, they weren't getting much gold out of the river.

The ceremony started with no fanfare. The *brujo* simply sat in the middle of one of the benches at the table and passed out cigarettes to everyone. I didn't smoke, but since I was there as a guest and didn't want to upset the miners or *Pachamama*, I politely mimed smoking the cigarette, not even drawing in air through it, much less inhaling.

Tera, on the other hand, started smoking in college. She smoked during parties and when we were out but wasn't a pack-a-day type smoker. "It gives me something to do with my hands," she'd told me as her reasoning, to which I'd rolled my eyes. She took a cigarette and smoked it.

Once we had all smoked (or not smoked!) our cigarettes, the *brujo* took each cigarette in turn and read out the fortune of the individual smoker. When he got to me, I dutifully passed over the butt of my burned-down cigarette.

He analyzed it as he had done the others and pronounced, "There is nothing here." He held out his hand for the next person's cigarette.

Up to that point I'd thought of the evening as somewhere between pure entertainment and a sociological observation, but I admit it shocked me and freaked me out a little that he couldn't discern a fortune. Maybe the *brujo* was a legit fortune teller and witch doctor? I also admit that I would have liked to hear his fortune for me, but maybe I should be glad I didn't.

There was a huge pile of coca leaves—several inches high—covering most of the table, and the miners were methodically chewing them during the fortune-telling and throughout the night. One of the miners showed us how to take a pinch of chalky white lime and a handful of leaves, bundle them together, put them in our mouths, and chew them like gum—adding a leaf or two at a time to the bundle after that.

They assured us chewing coca leaves is nothing like taking cocaine, as the coca leaves have to be super refined to become cocaine. Chewing raw coca leaves is more like drinking a Coke in terms of effect; at most it just numbed our cheeks slightly. In Bolivia and Peru, coca leaf tea is popular for altitude sickness and other ailments like nausea and headache. Tera was already feeling better at the lower elevation of the Yungas. Maybe if we'd had a huge pile of coca leaves in La Paz we could have tested their efficacy on her altitude-induced nausea, but I doubt we would have been brave enough to try coca on our own. What a random drug test in the military might say about coca leaves was a different question, but one I never had to face as I didn't get hit with testing until many months had passed.

The *brujo* then took a set of plastic charms which looked like wrapped pieces of candy (and about the same size), tiny llamas, baby dolls, etc. He was doing more fortune-telling of some sort, but it was hard to follow the details, and I'm not sure anyone else was paying much attention either.

In addition to the coca leaves, a bottle was being passed from hand to hand around the circle, with each person taking a swig and passing it on. It was *aguardiente*, or firewater—straight alcohol that burned its way down. It felt like it could bore a hole straight through my stomach. I took enough of a sip so as not to offend *Pachamama* but avoided it after that.

Finally, after what must have been three hours, the *brujo* bundled up all the charms, cigarette butts, and remaining coca leaves into a cloth. We all followed him outside to a spot near the river. It was pitch black, and we were surrounded by trees so thick that even if it were high noon, it might still have felt like evening.

The young, male, red *chanchito*, still very much alive in his burlap sack, was placed in a hole dug into Mother Earth. All of the paraphernalia from the *brujo's* ceremony was placed in the hole on top of him. Several miners grabbed shovels and started filling the hole back up with dirt. In only a few minutes, the hole was filled in, the piglet buried beneath. Everything was quiet.

A fire was started on top of where the pig was buried, and as the fire was fed and built up into a bonfire, I kept waiting for the piglet to be dug up. Would they eat him? Would they pull his heart out? I held my breath while watching the flames, wondering what would happen to the little pig.

But nothing did. Everyone stood around the bonfire, drinking more aguardiente, and the air was festive and fun. People were celebrating and laughing. I kept holding my breath and watching the pit where the *chanchito* was.

Then I realized . . . that was it. The piglet's job had been to pay the Mother Earth. They meant that in as literal of a sense as possible. It was buried in the earth, and the ritual was complete. They wouldn't eat him; they wouldn't dig him up.

We were all perched around the lip of the pit that the

bonfire was burning in and stayed that way for at least another hour, talking, joking, and drinking.

At one point—I don't quite know how—I started to fall into the pit. It was so dark, and the night had been so long. To keep myself from falling, I vaulted over the bonfire and landed on the other side. To cover my embarrassment, I did what any former gymnast would do. I did a "present," throwing my arms into the air, like a silent ta-da!

When the fire started to die down, the mine owner took us to one of the small bamboo huts and said we could sleep there until the morning. There were bamboo platforms and not much else. Tera and I climbed onto one that was about as wide as a twin bed. We didn't have sleeping bags or blankets or anything. I tucked my arms into the alpaca wool sweater that I'd bought in La Paz to fight the chill in the air. Tera's jean jacket was probably even less warm.

In the middle of the night, a man started to climb up into our bamboo platform bed. My arms were pinned to my body inside my sweater. Tera leaned over me and started hitting the man as I struggled to get my arms unstuck. By the time I started adding my punches to Tera's, the man decided we weren't worth the trouble and stumbled away into the night.

I wondered later if the man was just drunk and climbing into his own bed (which we had been given for the night), or if he was lost getting to his own bed in the dark because of all of the aguardiente floating in his system. Or worse—if he really was intent on attacking us. In retrospect, I have to believe one of the former options because he went away and didn't come back. However, I may also be protecting myself by ignoring how ridiculously stupid we were to be out there alone without doing anything to protect ourselves.

The next morning, Tera said, "I can't believe they killed that little pig. How horrible! How could they do that?"

I rationalized, "Right or wrong, they were doing what they believe is necessary. Paying Mother Earth allows them to earn enough from the mine to feed their families. How is that any worse than us feeding our families bacon in the morning?"

She didn't disagree with my logic. "Well, then I'm never eating meat again."

I came from a family of hunters and ranchers who had raised me to believe that we were part of the cycle of life. I said as much to Tera, then added, "The only difference is we actually witnessed this animal's death. I don't see why that means we should drop everything and stop eating meat."

I should have known what a hollow argument it was and agreed with Tera from the outset. I was never a huge fan of meat, in spite of, or perhaps because of my family's hunting and ranching. My father hunted deer, elk, antelope, geese, duck, and whatever else he could get a license for. I hated all of it. I would chew it, but I couldn't force myself to swallow it. There were many late nights spent sitting in front of my uneaten food, and a few spankings when I refused to eat it.

During military survival training at the Air Force Academy, we had to learn how to kill, skin, and cook a rabbit. I made myself useful cutting the vegetables we were provided with for the stew. I couldn't touch the rabbit. Meanwhile, my fellow students argued over who got to eat the rabbit's eyes, which was seen as a badge of courage. When it came time to eat the rabbit stew, I took one bite and gagged. I gave my stew away, endearing myself greatly to my hungry survival partners. I just couldn't eat it.

You'd think this little piggy would have tipped me right over the line into vegetarianism, but it didn't. Not then anyway.

A year later, I was eating TCBY frozen yogurt overlooking San Antonio's Riverwalk—a concrete canal with wall-to-wall restaurants and tourists, as far from a natural environment as possible—when I realized how ridiculous my "cycle of life" argument was.

Those miners believed that the piglet would help the mine produce and enable them to feed their families. Any meat I was eating was purely because I wanted to eat it. I didn't need meat to survive. For me, eating meat was pure luxury. And if I was eating meat just for fun, I was worse than that *brujo* and those miners.

I was a vegetarian from that day forward, about a year after that sacrifice. I'm still a vegetarian today, over 30 years later.

Tera has allowed some meat back in her life and might be what I'd call a flexitarian, but for both of us, watching that one piglet die changed our relationship with meat forever.

CHAPTER 2

COLOMBIA:
OBJECTS ON A MAP . . .

Tera and I managed to make it out of the Yungas of Bolivia alive and flew from La Paz into Caracas, Venezuela. We bought a package deal from AeroPerú that let us travel from the U.S. to South America, fly a few intracontinental flights, and return to the U.S.—all for one price. While the package deal was great for two college grads with tight finances, customer service was south of abysmal. We called AeroPerú *AeroPeor*—WorstAir. I finally got my duffel bag en route to Venezuela after I'd spent eight days in Bolivia with nothing but my guidebook and money belt. I'd never been so happy to see wrinkled shirts and underwear!

We spent a week or so in Venezuela, starting in Caracas.

It was a big city, gray and lifeless, at least compared to what we'd seen in Bolivia.

After a day or two in Caracas, we knew we had to go find something fun. We found an excursion to the Isla de Margarita. It was a tropical Caribbean paradise, with shimmering white-sand beaches and a nightlife that was as vibrant the sun-filled days.

Neither Tera nor I were big drinkers. I ordered Kahlua and cream whenever we were out at night. In La Paz, I found a place serving a drink with Kahlua, Coke, and chocolate ice cream, which was just my speed. I tried to replicate it whenever I could. Tera was a little more adventurous and would order a cocktail or her trusty Jack and Diet Coke.

The best part about the nightlife in Isla de Margarita was the dancing. The nightclubs were open-air, on the beach, and filled with salsa and merengue music—none of which we'd ever heard before. Some young men took us out on the dance floor and taught us merengue. We tried salsa but couldn't quite get the hang of the rhythm. However, I loved merengue and could have danced all night to that.

When we were planning our trip to South America, we didn't know what to expect because we had never traveled on our own before. We'd always traveled with school groups, like my trip to Spain, or on family trips. We read the *South America on a Shoestring* guide over and over, but what you read doesn't always translate to real life. I imagined being in rainforests, all but having to machete my way through hanging vines. I bought waterproof hiking boots, and they were the only shoes I brought with me. I didn't have any sandals or flip flops, and I certainly didn't have any dancing shoes. Never in my wildest dreams did I imagine I'd be doing the merengue on a Caribbean island off the coast of Venezuela.

I danced in my hiking boots. Since Tera had left most of

the planning to me, she only brought hiking boots too and was doing the same.

Despite the boots, dancing the merengue in that beach club felt like freedom. It felt like I was catching up on some of the fun I'd missed out on by going to the Air Force Academy and not doing the "normal" college thing. It was glorious.

After the Isla de Margarita, we took a boat back to the mainland and then a bus to Maracaibo. We planned to travel overland from Venezuela to Cartagena, Colombia, since we had a limited number of flights with *AeroPeor* and the distance was relatively short. On the map, it made total sense.

We found a taxi in Maracaibo that would take us over the border to Colombia. There were two other passengers in the taxi with us—British backpackers, also in their early twenties though they probably had a few years on us, also traveling through South America.

The taxi was a beat-up sedan. Tera and I sat in the front with the two British guys in the back. The journey would take several hours—reaching the border, getting through it, and then continuing on to the first town in Colombia: Maicao.

Because of how we were situated in the car, we didn't talk to the British guys much. Tera, being the more outgoing of the two of us, turned around and asked them a few standard traveler questions. *How long are you traveling? Where have you been? Where are you going? Where are you from?* They'd been traveling a lot longer than us, and what felt like an epic journey to us was just a drop in the bucket compared to their plans.

After we got through the border, we drove into Colombia. The road was surrounded by jungle, dense and green, unbroken by towns or villages. By the time we got to Maicao, it was dark. Pitch black. There were no streetlights. Any light from the stars or moon was swallowed up by the jungle.

The taxi deposited us in the center of town. The main street was a dirt road, and on both sides were street vendors cooking over open fires. There were tons of people on the street, but it didn't feel festive. It felt threatening, and we immediately felt unsafe. The British guys looked just as uncomfortable. We knew that Colombia was a hotbed for both drugs and guerrillas, but only in theory—like reading news clips about someplace far away. It happened, but it didn't seem real. And it definitely didn't seem like anything we'd ever encounter.

We didn't know anything about Maicao in particular, but we could feel it—feel that we shouldn't be there.

In the back of my mind, I also kept thinking, *I'm an active-duty Air Force officer; I should definitely not be in the middle of a narco-guerilla war zone.* If anyone there knew I was U. S. military, would I be a target? Would they kidnap me? I didn't have any secrets or anything, but maybe I'd be good for ransom?

We asked around for buses. We all hoped that we could catch a bus out of Maicao right away—to anywhere, really, though ideally toward Cartagena. But there were no buses leaving until the morning. We were still standing huddled in a group with the British guys, none of us quite sure what to do next. None of us were at all comfortable with our situation.

One of the guys asked, "Do you want to get a hotel room together?"

"Yes," we both said without hesitation. We walked across the street to a small hotel and asked for a room for four. They only had a room for three, but since the guys had their own hammocks, we agreed to it and split the minimal cost between us.

We got up to our room, and the two guys started getting their hammocks rigged. Tera and I claimed two of the three beds.

"What are your names?" Tera asked. "We have a policy of never sharing a room with anyone without knowing their names." We all laughed nervously and exchanged names. We knew they weren't hitting on us; there was nothing remotely romantic in the air in Maicao. We all just knew we needed to stay together.

One of the guys asked if we wanted to get dinner together, and we all agreed immediately.

We found a restaurant a few doors down from the hotel rather than a fire on the street. It served chicken and rice. Despite Tera's newfound vegetarian stance, she was perfectly happy to eat chicken with the rest of us.

The guys slept in their hammocks. We didn't doubt our safety with them at all, especially compared to the streets of Maicao! We managed to fall asleep.

The next morning, we got on separate buses, ours going to Santa Marta en route to Cartagena. I don't know where theirs was headed. We didn't plan on staying in touch; we just knew we needed to stay together that night.

After we'd been on the bus for a while, I asked the driver how far it was to Santa Marta. He said we'd missed the stop. Except the bus hadn't stopped in Santa Marta. The driver said we had to get off the bus, right on the side of the two-lane highway, and wait for a bus going the other way. He said if I told the driver of the next bus what happened, they'd let us on for free.

If we were smarter, we would've just stayed on the bus and gone straight to Cartagena. It wasn't a brilliant idea to be plopped on the side of the road in the middle of Colombia waiting for a bus, especially not when we knew we were in drug trafficking and guerrilla land. But we got off the bus, waited, and another bus came along. The driver didn't let us on for free, but we didn't argue and handed over the small fare to take us to Santa Marta.

Santa Marta was fine, but not nice enough to justify getting off the bus in the middle of Colombia.

Maybe we should have paid for an extra flight from Venezuela to Colombia. It looked close on the map, but we could have been kidnapped or killed a few times over in that "short" distance.

CHAPTER 3

BOGOTÁ, COLOMBIA:
SCAMMERS GONNA SCAM

Tera had to get back to her job, but I had a couple more weeks before reporting to my first duty station, and I wanted to keep traveling.

I decided to go to Bogotá, Colombia, and I had a long layover in Lima en route. I was reading and eating some Soft Batch cookies I'd found in a shop. They tasted like home after traveling for six weeks.

Though I'm normally the introverted type who will sit at the airport and never say so much as a hello to anyone—that type of chit-chat was always Tera's role—a family sat near me and started asking the typical questions: *Where are you from? Where are you going?*

They were from Bogotá and had been visiting friends in Tucson, Arizona. They pronounced it "Took-Son," which made me smile.

Somewhere in our conversation, they asked if I would mind going through customs with them when we landed in Bogotá. They were over on baggage, and if I only had one bag, going through together would count as two bags per person. If I didn't mind, they would give me a ride into Bogotá.

Looking back on this, there were so many red flags. I was twenty-one at the time, and my friend just left, so I was alone for the first time. But they seemed nice. I didn't know anything about Bogotá, so a ride sounded helpful.

We got on and off the flight, then went through customs together. I didn't have to carry any of their luggage; I was just bundled into their family unit. Once we were through, we loaded all of the luggage into a black sedan, and they drove me to the hotel I was staying at—just like they promised.

The thing is . . . nothing came of it. I wasn't "caught" for being a mule. Maybe I helped them smuggle in drugs or bundles of money—it was '90s Colombia after all. Or maybe it was just a normal family trying to avoid customs fines. I'll never know. After they dropped me at my hotel, they waved and smiled as they drove off.

I didn't even think about the interaction again until years later when TSA and airlines started asking questions on that topic. *Did anyone else pack my bag?* No. *Did anyone else ask you to pretend their bag was yours?* Uh. . . well, maybe. Those questions started in South America long before they started being the norm in the U.S.

I was in Bogotá for a week by myself. I climbed Mount Monserrate and looked over the city, a vast set of buildings tucked into the green hills.

I called the Compassion charity where I'd been sponsoring

a child since I was a sophomore at the Air Force Academy. I had gotten to meet the little girl and see the Compassion program when I was in Bolivia. I was so impressed, I asked to sponsor a few children from Colombia and asked if I could meet them while I was there. A few days later, I had the awkward pleasure of meeting three teenagers who I would sponsor until their graduation from the program.

I went to the theater and saw a Spanish version of La Cage aux Folles, which was fun and as crazy as it sounds. I didn't know what it was about before I went, and it definitely tested my Spanish. Since it was live theater, there were no subtitles or people to explain to me what I missed.

I normally tried to be in my hotel by nightfall, but that night, it was already dark after the theater let out. I considered getting a taxi, but I will never accept a taxi that approaches me or honks at me. I prefer approaching a taxi that is sitting and waiting for the next rider. It feels like they're more likely to be honest and take me to my stop. Unfortunately, every other theater goer was getting a taxi too, so there weren't any waiting for passengers.

I decided to start walking toward my hotel and keep an eye out for a taxi. When I had walked over halfway to my hotel, I saw a policeman up ahead. I thought if I could just make it to the cop, I'd definitely be safe, since my hotel was only a few blocks after that. The cop was like a lighthouse in the dark.

As I approached him, he whistled at me.

I felt so deflated. I couldn't trust the cop any more than I could trust anyone else. My illusion of safety shattered. I quickly walked the last couple of blocks to my hotel. I made it safely, but the experience reinforced my need to be in the hotel before nightfall.

My hotel was small, basic, and tucked in on a back street. It probably only had a few rooms. There were no frills—nothing really besides a bed with a thin blanket and a small bathroom. There was a club nearby that played salsa music every night. It was far enough away that I couldn't hear the music, but I could hear the "ting, ting, ting" of the cowbell, which carries forever. That is the sound of Colombia to me. Even though I had learned to dance merengue and a little salsa, I never got the nerve to go to the club by myself. I don't think it was an Isla de Margarita kind of club, and I would probably have fit in as well as a cat at a rodeo.

On one of my last days in Bogotá, I was approached by a middle-aged local woman asking for my help. She said she'd just been robbed. She was still explaining to me what happened when a man came by, claimed to be with the police, and offered to help her. He started asking me a lot of questions and offered to help me out as well. He wanted to register my money to make sure I wouldn't be scammed or robbed.

I knew it was a scam. The woman had initially seemed trustworthy, but the man definitely didn't. By then it was obvious that they were working together. I knew it... but I didn't quite know how to get away from them. I should have just said no and walked away. But I didn't. The man wasn't physically imposing, so I'm not sure why I didn't. Was I worried about being rude?

The only thing that really saved me from anything worse was that I had very little cash on me. I hadn't exchanged money in a while, and all I had was a single traveler's check worth twenty dollars. What few traveler's checks I had left were in the hotel, and because I was nearing the end of the trip, I was down to almost nothing. I ended up giving them eight dollars in cash and the twenty-dollar traveler's check, just to get away. I called AMEX when I got back to the hotel and canceled the travelers check. Later, I laughed at how much effort they spent to get the eight dollars' worth of pesos from me.

Bogotá was the first place I ever traveled solo and it might not have been the safest choice. But I learned a lot there like how to recognize scammers, say no, and keep myself safe. And despite being in the capital of a country enduring a drug war and beset by guerrillas, I felt generally safe—most of the time. I was very, very fortunate that all my lessons came with minimal impact. It could have been a LOT worse.

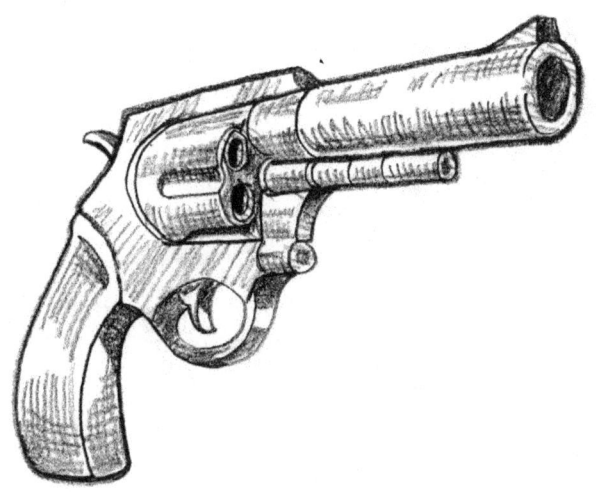

CHAPTER 4

GUATEMALA:
YAY! A PARADE

A year after my travels in South America with Tera, I was ready for my next adventure. I was stationed at Grand Forks, Air Force Base in North Dakota, working as a Security Police Officer.

I didn't want to go back to North Dakota after the Air Force Academy. I wanted to go anywhere *but* my home state, but the Air Force had a different idea. After a year there, I needed to go exploring again.

Tera wasn't up for traveling this time though, so I decided to go solo. Because I had loved Bolivia so much, I thought that another country with a lot of history and native culture would be interesting. I settled on Guatemala. I was twenty-two, and I had ten days of leave.

In many of the South American countries we visited, there tended to be two main cities—one that served as the business hub, and the other that was the cultural capitol. That was true of Ecuador—Guayaquil for business and Quito for culture. In Peru—Lima for business and Cuzco for culture. And in Guatemala, Guatemala City was the business hub, and Antigua was the cultural capitol. I spent a day in Guatemala City before heading to the bus station to visit Antigua.

It was near Easter, and in Antigua there is a tradition of creating beautiful *alfombras* (carpets) for Easter—ornate mosaics made from flower petals that cover the streets. The carpets will often include images of the Virgin Mary, Jesus, and crosses, or form images of flowers with flowers. I was so excited to see the *alfombras*, and Antigua was supposed to be a gorgeous city in the mountains near Lake Atitlán.

As I walked through Guatemala City, I was focused on getting to the bus station and what I'd see when I got to Antigua. I hadn't expected to see a massive parade with spectators lining the sidewalk.

It was May 1, not a day that I would have anticipated a parade. I learned that in Guatemala, like many other countries, May 1 is Labor Day, or International Worker's Day. I had a few extra minutes, so I stopped and watched the parade, happy that I was lucky enough to stumble onto it.

If you're from the U.S. and I say, "Labor Day parade," you probably picture floats, marching bands, clowns, and people throwing candy. That was not what happened in Guatemala.

These floats were designed to send a message, and the message was generally: *the government is evil, the U.S. is an evil puppet master, and both deserve death and destruction.* I watched each float go by, reading the messages—too fascinated and too naive to be properly afraid. Then there was an Uncle Sam character, and he was being hung.

I suddenly became very aware that I was carrying a big army-green backpack with a giant "U.S." stamped on it in black ink. I bought it at the Air Force Academy the year prior for fifteen dollars and thought it was a great deal. I bought one for Tera too, and we carried them all through South America. Now, it was making me a huge target.

And then a man saw me—and the backpack.

"Are you from the United States?" he asked.

I knew better than to tell him I was a U.S. Air Force officer. I replied, "I am a teacher from Canada." My Mom was a teacher, so I thought I could fake that pretty well. And being from North Dakota, well, it's almost Canada.

I don't think my cover story convinced him. He pulled out a pistol and aimed it at my head. "Bang," he said and laughed.

I blinked, started breathing again, hurried down the parade route, and reached the bus station.

If I had been male, there would have been no question that I'd been military, and then who knows what would have happened. Women in the military was barely a thing in the U.S. at that time. It was 1992, I'd only graduated the year before, and I'd been in the 11th class with women at the Air Force Academy. Women in the military was definitely NOT a thing in Latin America.

I knew that Guatemala and some of the countries in Latin America were not fans of the U.S., but I hadn't really understood the depth of their anger until then.

At that time, Guatemala was still in the middle of a civil war, and various leftist groups fought the government. The U.S. was seen as having instigated it because in 1954, there was a coup d'état backed by the U.S., which installed a right-wing military regime. The civil war started a few years later as a leftist reaction to that regime.

Since I didn't want to end up like Uncle Sam on the float, I hightailed it to the bus station and made my way to Antigua.

CHAPTER 5

ECUADOR:
LIFE LESSONS

While I was still stationed at Grand Forks Air Force Base, I was deployed to Ecuador for a few months in support of the war on drugs because I was fluent in Spanish. Our mission was to set up a small radar unit in the jungles of Ecuador to watch the drug planes fly from Colombia.

I had been to Ecuador with Tera as part of our South America trip, but we'd only been to the mountainous regions, including Quito and Otavalo—areas that were friendly to tourists, filled with traditional crafts, little cafés, and hikes to gorgeous waterfalls. The part of Ecuador I was in with the military was fewer than 200 miles from Quito, but it was deep in the jungle and not set up for tourists. It was an entirely different world.

We landed in our military aircraft on an airstrip adjacent to a small town. There was no commercial airport, and even using the word "airstrip" seemed like a stretch. It was a patch of asphalt in the middle of the jungle. Saying "jungle" also seemed like an overstatement. When I think of jungle, I think of wildlife documentaries with triple canopy trees and constant rain. This wasn't like that. It was dry and hot, and although we were surrounded by green trees, they were low and sparse. It didn't even feel like Bolivia's Yungas, where the trees and vegetation were so tightly packed it was dark even in the afternoon sun. It felt more like being in Florida or California than what I had imagined a real jungle would be like.

We set up our site on a hill near the airstrip. There was nothing on it except long, weedy grass, which we had to cut back with machetes to make it a workable plot of land. There were no trees, no cover, no buildings. Just grass.

As the Security Police Officer, my job was to work with the local Ecuadoran Army post to keep the site secure. After we landed, my sergeant and I went straight to the Army base to meet up with my Ecuadoran Army contact, Lieutenant Flores. My sergeant, Sgt. Roberts, was in his thirties or forties, with salt-and-pepper hair. We met at the start of the deployment, and he seemed like he'd be good to work with. He didn't speak any Spanish though.

My contact was a lieutenant, the same rank I was. As soon as Lt. Flores came out of the barracks, I stepped up and introduced my sergeant and me in Spanish. Sgt. Roberts shook the lieutenant's hand but didn't say anything. I thanked Lt. Flores for supporting our mission and began explaining what we needed.

Lt. Flores listened, but whenever he responded, he would look at Sgt. Roberts.

Sgt. Roberts wasn't saying anything and only understood what I translated for him. I was the ranking officer, and it was my job to coordinate what we needed for security with the lieutenant.

I spoke, and Lt. Flores addressed Sgt. Roberts when he responded.

It took me about two responses to realize what was happening. I was a woman. There were no female military personnel in Ecuador, and apparently Lt. Flores believed that was the way it should be. By that point, I'd been in the military for over a year, had led troops, and felt capable and strong.

Despite my qualifications, the moment he treated me that way—or refused to deal with me at all—I felt as small as I must have looked to him. I was twenty-two, five feet four inches tall, slim, and looked like I was being swallowed by my Battle Dress Uniform (BDU). The BDU camouflage cargo pants and multi-pocket button-up shirt was made for men. While it had been shrunk to kind of fit women, it had clearly never been designed with women in mind or adapted for women.

Despite Lt. Flores' attitude and lack of respect, I kept pressing our needs and forced him to listen until everything was agreed to. He continued to only address Sgt. Roberts throughout the conversation.

Lt. Flores continued on the job for several months. After a few weeks, he begrudgingly listened and talked to me, mostly when I didn't have my sergeant with me. However, our relationship was never cordial.

Eventually, Lt. Flores rotated out to a different assignment, and I was given a new contact, Captain Alvarez. The first time I met him, I said, "*Mucho gusto*"—nice to meet you.

He looked directly at me and responded with, "*El placer es mio*"—the pleasure is mine. He was a breath of fresh air compared to what I had to endure with the first guy.

During our mission in Ecuador, we lived in a local hotel and worked on the hill, which we turned into an operational radar site. We built it up to protect it and make it more comfortable.

The hotel had a large, grassy courtyard, and all of the hotel rooms were arranged around it. Our team filled most of the rooms. I'm not sure who else would stay there. It wasn't a town that was ever going to be high on the tourist circuit. It was mostly an oil town—there was an oil company operating nearby that the town had grown to support. Maybe some of the oil company executives stayed at the hotel occasionally.

We worked in 12-hour shifts, seven days a week, so there wasn't much downtime. But since there wasn't a great deal to see in town, it didn't matter much.

Every time I got back to my room after my shift, there was always one cockroach waiting for me, regardless of how many I had killed. These were giant cockroaches—two inches long, longer if you include their antenna. I named them all Waldo because I knew there was always one; I just had to find Waldo each day. The worst place, and the most common, was on the lamp where I would have to reach under the lampshade to turn it on. I never let myself relax until I finished my "Where's Waldo?" search.

There were also spiders that were as big as the palm of my hand. Those were less frequent visitors, but they freaked me out way more than my Waldos. Those would take a few boot throws to get them to vacate or die. I didn't mind stomping Waldo, but I couldn't stomp on those spiders. Especially because they were usually on the walls and the thought of squishing them was too disgusting.

We usually ate dinner at the hotel restaurant, which was decent, but there were limited options for me as a vegetarian. Most nights I'd get the American breakfast for dinner, which was scrambled eggs, bread with jelly, and instant coffee.

Sometimes, a few of us would venture into town to find a different place to eat. I found one place that made ramen noodles with vegetables, but options for vegetarians were limited in town, too.

Some of the more adventurous soldiers would get kebobs from the street-side vendors, but there were definitely no vegetarian options at those. Once, I saw one of the vendors with a slab of meat waiting to be butchered. It looked weird, round, and nothing like the meat I'd seen my dad butcher after his hunting trips. I asked her what it was.

"*Perro*," she said. Dog.

Yeah, nope. I wasn't eating meat regardless, but no way was I eating *anything* from a street-side vendor.

Every once in a while, we had to go to the oil company for supplies or to coordinate with them. If we were really lucky, we would get to go to the oil company cafeteria for lunch when we were over there. They had a nice cafeteria with a ton of options, and all of it looked well-prepared and clean. You could tell the oil company had money.

There was another young officer on the deployment who also spoke Spanish. His parents were from Spain, so his Spanish sounded very different from the Ecuadorians' we worked with. It sounded highbrow, like the difference between the Queen's English and American English. Once, when we were at the oil company cafeteria, he put the whole bowl of salsa on his plate and started walking to our table. When we told him that the salsa was for everyone to use, he said, "Oh, I thought it was gazpacho"—which is a cold Spanish soup made of tomatoes and onions. We were definitely not in gazpacho territory.

At the beginning of the deployment, he and I were assigned to drive the tanker truck over to the oil company and get it filled with diesel. Since the site was literally on top of a hill, there was no electricity, and everything ran on diesel generators.

Neither one of us knew the word for diesel. We tried explaining it, "like gasoline (*gasolina*), but not gasoline." That only confused our oil company contact, for obvious reasons. Neither one of us had brought a dictionary over to the oil company, and obviously this was well before the days of Google translate or even cell phones. We were all getting frustrated when finally, my colleague wrote the word "diesel" down on a piece of paper.

The oil company contact immediately said, "Ah, diesel!"—but pronounced it with a Spanish accent: "Dee-AY-sal." We both felt stupid for not trying that earlier. Finally, we got our diesel. After that first time, the oil company knew what we needed and filled it up whenever our tanker was running low.

After we had the site set up and I had built a relationship with the Ecuadoran soldiers working for me to secure it, a couple of them offered to take Sgt. Roberts and me on a hike in the jungle. That sounded amazing to me, so we got permission to take a morning off. I was hoping for real jungle, not the scrubby vegetation and trees that surrounded the site.

When we got to the path in the jungle, the soldiers handed us machetes, which made the hike even more exciting. Would we have to chop through the dense forest, go where no one had been before? Tera's voice echoed in my head, "*Could we die like this? Cool!*" I grabbed the machete by its handle, and we walked into the jungle following our troops.

There was a pretty clear path, and the jungle wasn't that dense, so we were mostly just walking. It was honestly rather disappointing.

I felt a sharp sting on my left wrist.

I looked down, and there was a slice about an inch long across my wrist, so deep that I could see the fat layers beneath the skin. It hadn't started bleeding yet. I kept staring at it, wondering what had happened. I stopped walking, and one of the Ecuadoran troops finally came back to see why I stopped. I was too surprised to talk.

I had been wearing a bandana as a headband to keep my hair out of my face. I pulled it off my head, and someone wrapped it around my wrist as a bandage.

We walked back out of the jungle.

While we were walking back, our Ecuadorian troops told us that you aren't supposed to hold a machete by its handle when you walk. The machete is so long that you can cut your wrist with your natural arm swing. This is apparently true. They told us that you're supposed to hold the top of the blade, just below the handle, gripping it between your first and middle fingers, which shortens the blade and lessens the chances you'll cut yourself.

What a fantastic tidbit of trivia! If only I'd learned it at the beginning of the hike.

Usually, I faint at the sight of blood and have done so all my life. No amount of military training or injury has ever cured me of it. Maybe I was saved by the fact that it hadn't started bleeding yet when it got covered up. Or, maybe I knew that passing out in the middle of the jungle wasn't a great idea. Regardless, I kept it together until we got to the truck. Sgt. Roberts drove us to the oil company, where we went to their clinic.

I earned six stitches for my bravery and stupidity. The oil clinic medic patched me up, but he was no artist. Having a ragged, inch-long scar on your wrist makes for an interesting conversation starter.

Once the site was fully up and running, we only received a supply aircraft once a week. It would bring anything the commander ordered for the site and send and deliver any mail. Since we were in a classified, secret location, the Armed Forces Post Office (APO) address was the only way to reach us. Of course, snail mail was the only form of mail at the time, so that weekly aircraft was a lifeline to home.

The pilot of the plane also offered to shop for us on the U.S. airbase where he was bringing our supplies from. I desperately wanted new envelopes for letters home, and I added a few treats to my list. Pop-Tarts and Soft-Batch cookies were at the top of my list. I'd order one of each, every week.

The days started blurring together—the continuous cycle of the 12-hour shift—especially since we had no days off and there was nowhere else to go.

The week before I was due to rotate back to my base in North Dakota, there was an uprising in the local town. Initially, I was worried about our site, but the truth is that the local population barely noticed it.

The uprising was focused on local Ecuadorian politics, taxes, inflation, and low wages. The people burned tires in the street and barred traffic. We decided to limit transportation between the site and the hotel, locking everyone down at whichever location they were at until the uprisings calmed down.

It was only a day or two before we were able to resume normal operations; the uprising ended and didn't amount to much, at least from our perspective.

Shortly after, it was time for me to fly back with the pilot when the weekly resupply plane came.

It was a very different adventure than when I'd been in Ecuador the first time with Tera. I honed my Spanish, learned to work with a-holes who didn't believe that women should be in the military, and learned how to carry a machete. Admittedly, I never needed to use the how-to-carry-a-machete skill again, but the other lessons I used for the rest of my life.

A few years later, I was the lead Security Police instructor at a school in Texas called the Inter-American Air Forces

Academy. We taught military skills to Latin American officers in Spanish.

    Lt. Flores ended up in one of the classes I was leading. I enjoyed watching him squirm realizing I was the boss and that he was in my world now. Unlike him, I treated him with professional respect and courtesy, and I let him deal with his own guilt.

CHAPTER 6

NEPAL:
CHOOSE YOUR TRAVEL PARTNER WELL

Jon and I met at the Air Force Academy, but he was two years behind me, and we never dated at school. After I graduated, we kept in contact through letters and eventually started "dating." I was stationed in North Dakota; he was still in Colorado Springs, so most of our dating was long-distance.

I knew that if we had any chance of making it work, we needed to spend some time together. Traveling during his 60-day graduation leave would be a great test of our ability to get along.

I had learned that traveling with someone was a better gauge for knowing the person as they truly were after traveling to Mexico on another Spanish class trip. My roommate for that trip was a girl who seemed fun and interesting in our Spanish class. However, when I had to live with her, she turned out to be rude, sloppy, and constantly late—we nearly missed the bus every day.

I thought that if Jon and I could travel well together, it would be a good test of whether we could be together.

Jon had been to Nepal as a teenager on a mission trip, and he told me about it on one of our phone calls. Even though he'd only been in Kathmandu and hadn't gone to the mountains, as soon as he mentioned Nepal, I was fixated on the idea of going there. It sounded impossibly remote and adventurous. Ever since I was a little girl growing up in the Black Hills of South Dakota, I had loved being in the mountains. The Himalayas were the pinnacle of mountain ranges, so of course I wanted to go.

I begged for thirty days of leave from my North Dakota duty station. The only reason my boss let me go for that long was because I told him I was going to Nepal, and he'd always wanted to see Kathmandu. He said I could go as long as I brought him back a picture of Kathmandu. That seemed like a pretty good deal to me.

Jon and I left in July. He had sixty days until he had to report to his first assignment—the same sixty-day leave I'd had after the Academy when Tera and I traveled through South America two years earlier.

We decided to do the Annapurna circuit, a twenty-one-day trek around Annapurna that promised the most varied scenery, from lowland rhododendron forests to above-the-tree-line moonscapes. We also liked that the trek was a loop, unlike treks like Everest Base Camp, where you go up and then double back down the same path.

In Kathmandu, we hired a trekking guide and had a day before we left for the trek. Though the guidebook said there would be tea houses or guest houses along the way, we weren't sure if we would always be able to stay in one, so Jon brought a tent and a camping stove. *How many were there? How far apart were they?* Plus, the guidebook said sometimes they'd fill up.

We went to the market and bought the food we thought we'd need for the hike: rice, potatoes, oatmeal, and granola which we could cook on the little stove. Since I had a lot of pockets in my backpack, I shoved a lot of the food into my pack. We also had bota bags (like wine skins) that we could carry water in and iodine tablets to purify our water. There were no Nalgene bottles at that time, and bota bags actually kept the water cool in the sun.

The next morning, we took a bus from Kathmandu to Pokhara with our guide Ramish. Then we loaded onto the back of a big truck—almost like a dump truck—to take us the final distance to the trailhead. We sprawled out on the bags of rice and potatoes the truck was loaded with. It reminded me of the over-laden trucks I'd seen in Bolivia on our trip over the mountains to the Yungas, with the traditional women in bowler hats resting on bags and boxes. This time, we were the ones perched on top. Though the road was bumpy, there weren't too many twists and turns, so we never felt like we would topple out.

We drove past rice paddies, watching people standing and working in the flooded fields. I'd never seen a rice paddy before. It was all so different from the huge fields of potatoes, sunflowers, and wheat in North Dakota that farmers planted and harvested with enormous, air-conditioned John Deere tractors. In Nepal, the rice paddies were divided and sub-divided. There were little raised paths between a patchwork of paddies, and everyone was working manually, bent over their sections.

After about an hour, we got down from the truck and started to walk.

And oh, I didn't know how I was going to do 140 miles. Jon seemed to be doing fine—enjoying himself, even. I had walked with my pack on some hikes through North Dakota to get ready for the trip, but let's be honest . . . North Dakota is flat as a pancake, and I only did a few hikes with the pack. Frankly, to use a military expression, I was sucking wind.

Fortunately, we only had two hours or so to walk until we got to the first tea house where our guide Ramish planned for us to stay. We were given a small room. It was about eight by eight feet and held two plywood cots, each with a thin cushion for a mattress. That was it. We had to use our sleeping bags on top of the cushions. There was no running water or electricity, and there was an outhouse behind the tea house.

I knew I had to repack to lighten my load or I wasn't going to make it. As we started unpacking our bags, we realized that I had tucked at least two-thirds of the food in my pack. When that included things like potatoes and rice, it was weight that I couldn't carry.

We also talked to the guide, who assured us that we would be stopping at guest houses like this along the entire route. It was off-season, so there wouldn't be many others on the trail with us, and the guest houses would have plenty of space. We wished we'd realized that before we set out on the trek, but we didn't know enough to ask the right questions. Ramish probably assumed we knew, so he didn't tell us.

I brought too many clothes, most of it cotton and heavy. I off-loaded a sweater and a pair of jeans. Jon left behind a few of his older T-shirts and planned to wear a few of mine that I didn't want to get rid of. My T-shirts were all unisex and baggy on me, so they fit him well.

We brought all the food that we'd bought in Kathmandu down to the dining room and bartered with the owners of the tea house. Room and dinner or, "Lodging and Foodging" as we saw on multiple signs, would have normally cost around four dollars, but we paid two—so we saved a couple of dollars. We also gave the guesthouse owners the extra clothes we couldn't carry.

Ramish had a small backpack, the size of a kid's elementary school backpack. I think he wore the same clothes the whole time, with a few layers that he could add on for warmth. He also mostly wore flip-flops. While I don't think I could have managed the hike in flip-flops, I wish I'd known how little clothing I actually needed and left the rest either at home or in Kathmandu. I envied his tiny pack.

On Day Two, we started the hike with lighter packs and a much better idea of what to expect. We were still at lower elevations—around 2,500 feet—hiking through fields and along hillsides terraced with rice paddies. We saw one field with plants that looked like cannabis. I'm no expert, but I was pretty sure. It was broad and green and lush. Since we were both in the military and knew we would be subject to random drug tests back in the U.S., we stayed clear of it—like I should have with the coca leaves in Bolivia.

The trail was only a foot path. When we started on the trail, it was approximately a 140-mile-long circle, and there was no real way to quit. If I didn't think I could do the trek, my only option was to turn around and go back. Every day I went on the trail was another day of walking back. And once I got six or seven days into the trek, there was no way I was turning around. I was near enough to the midpoint that I wouldn't have quit, no matter how hard it got.

The thing about the circuit is that over the course of the 140 miles, there is an elevation gain from roughly 2,000 feet to almost 18,000 feet at Thorong La Pass, which is basically at the midpoint of the trek. This means that you go up for about ten days, and then back down for the next ten days.

The path on the way up goes alongside a river, and the elevation gain isn't constant. It's up and down, then more up and down, and then up and more up. It's a lot, I'm not going to lie.

The landscape changed with the elevation, starting out with rice paddies climbing the foothills, and everything was a bright spring green. As we got higher, the palette shifted to the darker green of pine and rhododendron, with the rocky faces of mountains looming over us. The Marsyangdi River was our constant companion, rushing down the mountains while we plodded upward. Then, the dark greens gave way to browns as we rose above the tree line where only scrubby vegetation grew.

Since there was only a foot path on the route, all of the guesthouses served locally grown food like rice, or food that was literally carried up the mountain. There were donkey-trains with eight-to-ten donkeys, each with two baskets hung on their flanks. We were forced to shift to the side of the path to let them pass. They carried everything from potatoes to bottles of Coke—yes, you could buy Cokes in the guesthouses, but the price was outrageous: two dollars a bottle, when our entire dinner and night's stay cost only four. And yes, we indulged in them a few times after particularly hard days.

There were also human porters carrying huge baskets on their backs, balanced by a tumpline on their foreheads. Most of the porters wore flip-flops like Ramish did. I was wearing the same super waterproof hiking boots I'd bought for my South America trip, and I was glad I had them.

We could have hired porters to carry our backpacks from guesthouse to guesthouse, but that just didn't feel right to us. Maybe it was our military be-tough mentality, but we decided we'd carry our packs. It was doable once we'd lightened them (especially for me).

Jon had jokingly referred to the trek we were doing as a 'lollipop trail,' after getting the impression from the guidebook that it was so well-traveled it would be like a walk in the park. Every time he said it, I got angry because I was working so hard to keep up and keep pushing. He was definitely in better shape than I was. Two years working in the Air Force in North Dakota had not helped my fitness level, but I didn't think I was THAT out of shape. Ten days straight of straight "up" is tough.

Part of it was a difference in our hiking styles. I am a plodder and will keep a steady pace like a mule, especially on the super steep inclines. Think of the longest staircase you've ever seen, then triple or quadruple it, and replace the steps with uneven rocks, and you've got much of Nepal. Jon, on the other hand, will rush to the top of an incline and then rest at the top, like a horse. Which was fine—except Jon always wanted to start walking again as soon as I reached the top, but I wanted a break too. Sometimes I'd continue on, but most of the time I refused to budge until I had rested—also like a mule.

Our guide, Ramish, was an eternal cheerleader. Ramish was the first guide we'd ever traveled with, and his phrases still get used as family jokes whenever we go hiking. "Just a little further," he'd say, regardless of how far it really was. Just a "little bit up," regardless of how much *up* was coming.

Side note: I've heard that since our trek, parts of the Annapurna circuit have been paved for vehicular traffic, allowing trekkers to start at different points and potentially shorten the route, but that was not an option for us back then.

We fell into a steady rhythm, hiking for a few hours, then stopping for lunch and tea. We'd pore over the map at lunch and figure out where we were and what was coming up. Then we'd hike a few more hours until dinner. We walked around eight miles a day, which doesn't seem like much, but when those miles are all up and down, it's a lot!

The guesthouses were always empty except for Ramish, Jon, and I. I don't think we passed another set of trekkers the whole way up. Ramish told us it was because it was off season. The high season for trekking is September and October, when the skies are clearest. Even if we'd known that, it wouldn't have made a difference. Jon only had leave in June and July and would have to be at his duty station in the fall.

Most of the guesthouses were similar—a dining area lit by candles, a few picnic tables and benches on the main floor, and guest rooms on either an upper floor or in the back.

The menus were generally simple, with only a few options to choose from. There was always dal bhat—a vegetarian meal consisting of rice and lentils and the staple diet of the Nepalis. I think Ramesh had dal bhat for every meal. There were often egg-fried potatoes, apple pancakes, and a ramen-type noodle soup. There was usually a variant of vegetarian pizza, which we often ordered just to see what it would be. It ranged from a piece of bread with fried onions on it to a fried bread crust with potato curry—and nearly everything in between. Never once did it taste like pizza. I don't think I ever saw anything that looked like tomato sauce or cheese, but it was generally hearty and tasty.

Almost everything had curry powder in it. The first couple of meals we thought it was delicious, but we found out that curry powder at lunch was especially hard on us. After lunch, we still had another four or five miles to trek, and the curry powder gave us heartburn that wouldn't quit. My favorite thing was the chai tea—it was always available and always delicious, so we ordered it with every meal. It was milky, spicy, and had just enough sugar. Coffee wasn't really an option, and Coke was far too expensive, so tea became the drink of choice.

The outdoor clothing industry wasn't where it is today, so I didn't have any of the light synthetic hiking pants and shirts that I'd definitely wear if I did the hike now.

On the first couple of days of the trek, I tried various combinations of clothing to find something that worked. I tried hiking in a loose skirt that I bought in Kathmandu because the guidebook recommended it as a comfortable option. I don't know who wrote that, but I don't think it was a woman. It was awful. Most of the time we were hiking up stone steps, and I felt like I was always holding the skirt up.

Then I tried hiking in jeans. I felt like they were weighing me down, and I kept having to tug at the knees where they were binding me. I had brought a few pairs of tights from my gymnastics days at the Academy, which I ended up wearing almost exclusively during the trek. They were light, breathable, and effective when nothing else was.

After one of our mornings in the higher elevations, we stopped for lunch. As we were waiting for our meal, we sat outside in the sunshine at a picnic table. We suddenly started shivering and not feeling well. We hurriedly put on our jackets but still felt sick until our hot chai tea and noodle soup came.

We realized that when we were hiking, we were warm enough with just our T-shirts because of our levels of exertion. But as soon as we stopped, the day felt surprisingly chilly—and with sweat evaporating off us, we could easily get hypothermia if we weren't careful. We were very diligent after that, and the moment we stopped, even if only for a 10-minute water break, we put on our jackets or thermal layers, to be removed only once we started moving again.

After dinner, we sat in the main room of the guesthouse near the fire, talking, writing in our journals, or reading. Jon spent time learning a few words in Nepali from Ramish. At night, we massaged each other's sore muscles or cuddled in our sleeping bags for warmth. Then we would go to sleep and start again the next day.

We made it to Manang, at the base of Thorong La Pass. The pass is 18,000 feet, and we would have to hike up and over it. Manang was one of the larger towns we came across. It sat high on a plateau, above the tree line, and it was windswept. We had a rest day in Manang because to hike over Thorong La, we needed to start early—like 4:00 a.m. early—to make it up and over with enough time to come back down before dark.

It was going to be a big push, and we were exhausted from the previous ten days. Me probably more than Jon, but we both were. My muscles, especially my thighs and calves, were so tight and sore that it was hard to stand up and walk after sitting for a few minutes.

In Manang, it was just the three of us again. We slept in, ate breakfast, and enjoyed a few hours in the lodge reading and catching up on our journals. Our muscles cramped up, so we walked through the town.

Because Manang was above the tree line, all the homes were made of small stones piled up like bricks. Stone walls lined the narrow streets of the town, giving it a uniform light-brown color—interrupted only by Nepali prayer flags: small, square flags in yellow, red, blue, and green strung across the streets, flapping in the wind that whipped through the mountains.

Manang was also ringed by mountains that still seemed to tower over us, even though we were at over 11,000 feet. The green hillsides and rice paddies had given way several days ago, and at this elevation, all we saw were dark, rocky mountains, topped with dazzling white snow. It was starkly beautiful in a barren, windswept way. We didn't see any people, trekkers or locals, and with little else to do, we returned to our guesthouse.

That afternoon as we were sitting in the dining room of the lodge reading, Jon said, "After we get back to the U.S., I want to see other people."

I'm sorry, what? I don't know if I actually said anything or if I just stared at him, uncomprehending.

We were ten days into a circular 21-day hike. We had not seen a single other hiker along the way. It was just Jon, Ramish, and I out there. And the next morning we would get up at 4:00 a.m. to do what was supposed to be an incredibly difficult hike going over an 18,000-foot pass. And NOW he decides to tell me he wants to break up? *NOW?*

After ten incredibly physically taxing days, we were still getting along. It was going great—or so I'd thought. Our biggest point of frustration was when he wouldn't wait for me to rest at the top of a hill.

"I just graduated," he said. "I don't want to go from one institution into the next." I knew he meant: going from the Academy to marriage. But we had never talked about marriage. This whole trip was designed to see if we *liked* and could be with each other, since we'd started "dating" remotely.

I walked out of the room, crying. I didn't want to be anywhere near him at that moment.

He followed me.

"Leave me alone," I said.

"No, I don't want you to be alone right now."

"I just need to go to the bathroom," I said, but I just wanted to get away.

He kept following me, so I walked to the outhouse—there was no real bathroom.

Our lodge in Manang had one of the worst outhouses we'd been to, which said something after ten days of only using outhouses. This outhouse was the same squatty-potty style as the rest—a simple hole in the floor with no "toilet" or bench. The difference was that this outhouse had a pipe that allowed waste to drain out the side of the hill it was perched on. Maybe its designer assumed that it would be less smelly or more sanitary. The reality was that wind blew *up* the pipe, so squatting was like spitting in the wind—except it wasn't spit.

I was in this cold, windy outhouse, with my boyfriend—or maybe-not-boyfriend—waiting for me outside. I was trying to get myself under control, to stop crying and pull myself together. I couldn't decide which was worse, staying in the outhouse or going back out where he was.

When I finally came out of the outhouse, he tried to give me a hug. I pushed him away, saying, "You don't get to be nice."

Back in our 8x8 room, huddled in our sleeping bags against the chilly air, I asked, "So what happens for the rest of the trip?"

"We just keep going like before," he said.

Like nothing ever happened, I thought. Right. *But it had.*

Sleep was hard to come by that night. I was miserable—tired, cold, and still upset.

Our guide came and woke us at 3:00 a.m. It was freezing and still dark. Plus, we didn't have headlamps back then, just flashlights. We started to hike.

"It's a little bit up," Ramish told us.

Within about fifteen minutes, I felt like I couldn't breathe and had to sit down. It was all uphill. There was no up and down like we'd experienced alongside the river. With the elevation, the lack of oxygen and sleep, and my foul mood, it was hard.

I mostly stayed silent and plodded ahead like a mule. Even Jon couldn't race to the top and wait for me; the summit was far too far away. His footsteps were more measured that day, too.

I told Ramish never to tell anyone, "A little bit up," again. I insisted he tell them, "It's a big damn hill," instead.

Somehow, we made it to the top. There were some clouds—not the pristine blue skies that trekkers in prime season might get in September and October—but it was still amazing. Even though we were at 18,000 feet, there were still mountain peaks looming above us. And there were endless valleys below, all of them rocky and bare. The mountains seemed to go on forever, making it feel like we were the only people in the world—yet still such small, insignificant specks compared to the whole of creation. It was at once humbling and exhilarating.

We shared a celebratory Snickers bar that we bought at one of the tea houses for the exorbitant price of two dollars. It was frozen solid and crunchy, but still worth it.

Then Ramish pushed for us to start down. It's not good to stay at that altitude for long, and it was super cold. You don't want to stand still up there and invite hypothermia in addition to hypoxia.

We started down the other side of the mountain. Down is also hard. I won't say it's harder than going uphill, but the strain on your calves shifts to strain on your knees and thighs. We didn't have trekker's poles. I'd never used them before and never wanted them until that day. That day, having something to lean on would have been amazing.

Finally, after hours of nothing but hiking downhill, we were on the other side and at the next guesthouse.

We still had ten more days of trekking ahead; it would take that long to get back down to the lower altitudes. The rest of the way was very similar to the way up—days spent hiking in the morning followed by lunch at a teahouse and dinner at yet another guesthouse. Since it was still just the three of us, Jon and I were forced to be together. Despite his pronouncement, we still got along. He would occasionally throw out an "I love you" as we hiked along, which only frustrated me, and I refused to respond.

The ten days passed, and then we hopped on a bus to Pokhara. What had seemed endless at times felt like it was over too quickly. I didn't know if I was ready to go back to real life.

The trip still had a few curveballs to throw at us. The monsoon had wiped out the road between Kathmandu and Pokhara, so we had to fly instead of taking the bus. And then our flight home got delayed in Cairo for a day due to maintenance issues, so we had to stay the night there. By that point, we were so exhausted and spent all of our money, so we didn't leave the hotel. We didn't even see the Pyramids.

After we landed at JFK, we separated. I flew back to North Dakota to resume my duties in the Air Force, and Jon went to Columbus, Georgia, where he was starting an Army Infantry Officer's Course.

He called every weekend for a few weeks to "check in," but it was too frustrating. I couldn't handle the emotional anticipation of thinking he might change his mind only to be disappointed when it was just another "friendly call." Based on my friend Tera's recommendation, I told him not to call me again unless he wanted to get back together. In or out!

A friend of his in Infantry school asked him what the heck he was thinking. He found someone who would hike through Nepal with him, and he was going to let her go?

After a long four weeks, he called again. He was in.

We got married a year later.

We decided to go back to Nepal for our 20th anniversary and bring our son with us. We went over Christmas, and our son Jono turned eighteen while we were there.

Before we left, I told a friend we were heading to Nepal to celebrate our 20th anniversary. My friend said, "You're going to Nepal? Where your husband broke up with you? To celebrate your anniversary?"

From an outsider's perspective, going back to Nepal would seem like the last thing we should do. But the whole goal of going to Nepal in the first place was to see if it would make or break us. In our case, it broke us *and* made us stronger. We both look back on Nepal fondly, and that's where we fell in love—even if I wanted to poke Jon's eyes out after he broke up with me there.

The second time, though we only had time for a three-day hike to Poon Hill, it was as difficult and as awe-inspiring as before.

Jono got sick from eating a cucumber immediately after declaring, "I have a cast-iron stomach." He didn't, and he suffered for the first two days of the journey, passing out on his bed with 7Up and crackers each night. I had been working in an office for the past fifteen years and was WAY less in shape than the first time, so the stone steps took it out of me, leaving me breathless and sore. I still managed to bring too much, even though it was only three days—and I dang well knew better. We still chose not to use porters. Still too self-sufficient and hardheaded.

Thankfully, Jono was feeling better the morning we climbed to the top of Poon Hill. We were able to leave our backpacks at the lodge because we'd hike back down the same way. We left at 6:00 a.m. so we could be at the top of the hill by sunrise.

It was straight up, an endless stone stairway. Jon still was a faster hiker than me, and I was still a plodder. I told him to go ahead and that I'd catch up, but this time he refused and stayed by my side. "We've made it twenty years. We're going to make it to the top together."

I probably went faster than I wanted to, and he definitely went slower than he normally would have. We made it to the top just as the sun rose over the crest of the peak. We were surrounded by mountains, and Annapurna loomed over us.

It was gorgeous, indescribable, amazing.

I sat down and puked.

Once I'd caught my breath and my stomach settled, we took as many pictures as we could. We took jumping pictures, looking like cheerleaders leaping in front of the backdrop of the mountains, and reveled in the beauty of the sunrise.

Then we headed back down to the lodge. Going downhill was still a challenge, but not as bad as going uphill. I still didn't have hiking poles, but I definitely should have brought them this time.

After eating breakfast and gathering our stuff, we set out again for the remaining day and a half of the hike. Our guide promised us it was, "All down now," and then we promptly had to climb up for about three more hours. What is it with guides, anyway?

Would I go to Nepal again? Absolutely. *Would I do the Annapurna circuit again?* Maybe, if I had time to train and brought WAY fewer things in my pack.

Would I go with Jon again? Absolutely. I married Jon for love and adventure, and though it hasn't always been an easy road, when is adventure ever easy?

CHAPTER 7

KOREA:
A SATURDAY DRIVE

After Jon and I patched things up after our breakup in Nepal, we were both stationed in Korea in 1993 to 1994. We knew that if we picked Korea, we could both get stationed there. Korea was considered a "remote" location, which meant a one-year tour of duty where service members can't bring their families. Being remote could be a hardship, especially for families with kids. For us, it was an "easy" way to be stationed near each other—despite not being married (a prerequisite for the military to station people together), and despite being in two different branches: me in the Air Force, Jon in the Army.

I was stationed at Osan Air Force Base, south of Seoul.

Jon was going to be at Camp Casey up north near the DMZ. As an Air Force officer, I had the privilege of owning a car. I bought a 1983 Hyundai Pony for three hundred dollars from another lieutenant who was finishing his one-year assignment and leaving Korea. When I finished my year, I would sell it to the next lieutenant, who would sell it when they left, and so on—until it finally fell apart. It was already on its last legs when I had it. When I closed the door, the blue paint came off on my fingers. And even though I got the heater coil replaced, when I drove to Camp Casey in the winter, I'd travel with a thermos of hot tea and a blanket on my lap because the cold air would stream straight through the frame.

It was a 2-hour drive with no traffic between our posts late at night, or it could be fifteen hours if I tried to drive on a Saturday, which I learned very quickly not to do. On Saturdays when everyone had time off, if you braved travel, you could be stopped dead on the road for hours. Vendors would walk in between the lines of cars and sell bottles of juice or water, or my favorite: dried squid. I watched the locals tear into dried squid with gusto, gnawing on its thin, spindly legs. I called it squid jerky. If the vendors came out, you knew you were dead in the water, and the traffic wasn't going anywhere.

At the time, Korea was booming and everyone was buying cars, but the road infrastructure had not kept up. There wasn't much in the way of mass transit yet. There would be six lanes of black sedans filling a 4-lane highway (everyone had black sedans, for some reason). And in the middle of Seoul, there might be three major roads coming together, controlled by a single traffic light. If a road was closed, there was no detour, it was just closed—I had to figure it out. I learned to be bold and push through traffic jams. The best part of having a crappy car was that I was not worried about it getting scratched.

I also learned not to stop at a stoplight late at night on the highway—you slow and treat it like a yield, otherwise cars coming behind you are likely to ram into you. I also learned to stay calm.

When Jon was flying to Korea a few months after I arrived there, I drove to Gimpo Airport to meet him. We hadn't seen each other for a few months, so I was super anxious to get there. A lieutenant friend who had done the trip from Osan to the airport before came with me. It should normally have taken sixty to ninety minutes from Osan, but it was a Saturday. We left four hours early because I was so anxious. It took six hours. Jon's flight landed late, so we ended up getting to Gimpo only a little late. That was the first time I'd driven off-post and the first time I was confronted with Saturday traffic.

When I drove to Camp Casey the first time, it was nerve-wracking. Not yet having learned the advantages of driving late at night, I left after work, and it was a 4-hour drive through heavy Seoul traffic. Then I had to drive onto the Army base, which was confusing—and by then it was already dark. There were not many cars on the roads in the Army base because the Army officers were not allowed to own cars. It felt eerie and empty as I drove through the post.

I knew I was at the right spot, and I almost started crying when I saw candles lined up outside one of the barracks—like a beacon welcoming me home.

At the time, Korea was not a tourist destination. There were not that many people in Korea who spoke English, many of the signs were only in Korean, and getting around could sometimes be challenging. It was extremely frustrating for me because I'd mostly traveled to Spanish-speaking countries before and was used to being able to communicate.

Once, I stopped at a gas station en route to Camp Casey and asked for the bathroom, restroom, toilet, water closet—trying any word that might be understood. Finally, in desperation, I crossed my legs like I was 'holding it.' The gas station attendant laughed and pointed to the restroom.

Even though it was not the best of cars, the Hyundai gave us freedom. Jon and I named it Boogadie after an article we read where a pet rabbit named Boogadie was saved from drowning in a pool by a little boy in Australia. Boogadie enabled me to visit Camp Casey whenever I had time off. If both Jon and I had a free day, we would go to Bukhansan park to rock climb, or into Seoul to see the temples.

I was still a vegetarian because of the Bolivian pig sacrifice, and while Korea may be better for vegetarians now, at the time, it was challenging at best. The only dish I could count on to be vegetarian was bibimbap—a bowl of rice, veggies, and chili paste with an egg on top. If that wasn't on the menu, it was often difficult to order anything, especially because the menus were in Korean and had no pictures.

After a couple of unsuccessful eating adventures, I asked the translator who worked with us at my Security Police unit in Osan to write, "I don't eat meat or fish," on a piece of paper so that I could give it to servers in restaurants. He was happy to help and wrote it on a small scrap of paper that I carried in my wallet.

On one of our days off, Jon and I went to Incheon. We were focused on seeing the battlefield and monuments from the amphibious landing during the Korean War, so I didn't consider that Incheon (forty years after that battle) would be a seaside port city. We stopped at a restaurant to get lunch. The menus were entirely in Korean, and we were the only foreigners there. Jon picked something off the menu at random, pointing his finger at an entry. I smiled and handed the server the note the translator had written for me.

She took it from me, read it, and nodded. Then she turned the piece of paper over, bent down to our table, and wrote on the back of it in Korean. She gave the note back to me, and it was entirely indecipherable to me. I laughed. Maybe she thought I could read Korean but just not speak it? I never asked my translator what she wrote, but I'm pretty sure the gist was something like, "No food for you," or "Why are you in a seafood restaurant if you don't eat fish?"

Jon's food came in a tray with multiple compartments, like a cafeteria tray. There was a compartment with rice (they could at least have given me a bowl of rice!) and some kimchi. The other compartments each held a different sea creature—a sea cucumber, a baby octopus, a squid. I watched him eat and stole a few bites of his rice. Even if I wasn't a vegetarian, there's no way I could have eaten his meal, just not my thing!

How nice would it have been to have Google translate, where I'd hover over the menu and be able to understand it. It would still all have been seafood, but maybe I could have at least ordered rice.

We got engaged just before we were shipped off to Korea. We each had a one-year tour of duty there. Since we hoped to be stationed together at our next duty stations, we'd have to get married in Korea. The military wouldn't even *try* to station people together if they weren't married.

We could have just walked over to the American embassy at any point and signed the paperwork to be legally married. But I didn't want that. I didn't want a "paper wedding." If we were going to get married, I wanted to do it right.

We decided to get married and have a small ceremony in Seoul, followed by a "Homecoming" reception in New Jersey, where Jon is from. My family and friends are scattered, so getting them all in one place would have been hard regardless.

We decided to have the wedding at The Dragon Hill Lodge, a military hotel at Yongsan Army Base in Seoul. They set up a gazebo, decorated it with flowers, and set up a small buffet for the reception. The cost was super reasonable. They only balked when I asked for white flowers for the gazebo.

"White, are you sure?" the florist asked. White is the color of death and funerals in Korea, she told me. Traditional Korean wedding dresses are red and very colorful. Despite this, even then we saw brides in various temples taking pictures using both red Korean traditional *hanbok* dresses and white western bridal gowns.

We found a local photographer to take pictures. Jon got a local tailor to make a tuxedo for him. I cut a tiny picture out of a magazine and brought it to a tailor near Osan, who made me a dress like it from scratch. I wanted it to be simple, and he delivered. It only cost me about two hundred dollars, a steal even at the time.

Jon's parents and my mother flew in for the wedding. I had to pick up Jon's parents from the airport and drive them to the Dragon Hill Lodge. By that time, I had a lot of experience driving through Seoul, so I was driving "normally" for Korea. Jon's mom was white-knuckled and all but screaming in the back seat. I think Jon's father—used to driving in New Jersey and New York City—was impressed.

The day before the wedding ceremony, we had to go to the Embassy. It was the only way to be legally married in the U.S. Jon's parents and my mother accompanied us to the Embassy and watched as we signed our names on the paper. Our marriage certificate is in both Korean and English, which is cool, but it can also be confusing. The last time I used it was at the DMV to renew my license when they needed 85 forms of ID. I finally had to put my marriage certificate away and use other forms of ID because they couldn't read the Korean on it (even though it was also in English).

In addition to our parents, two of my buddies from the Academy flew to the wedding on military space-available flights—one from Japan and one all the way from Panama. The journey took him nearly a week to get there. A female sergeant from my North Dakota duty station who I'd gotten very close with was also stationed in Korea, so I asked her to be my bridesmaid. Her nickname was "Gunny." I told her she had to wear a dress but that she could pick it out. You'd think I'd told her she had to drown a puppy; she was so distraught at the idea of wearing a dress. She ended up with a white lace antique-looking dress that she threw away right after the ceremony. I thought it suited her.

My uncle was an Army Colonel who also happened to be stationed in Korea, so he stood in for my father to give me away. His daughter—my niece—was my flower girl. She wore a little white dress, completing our all-white wedding party of death! His wife—my aunt—helped me with dress fittings and helped me keep my wits about me. We had an Army chaplain from Jon's post do the wedding ceremony, and we invited all our troops.

On the day of the wedding, most of Jon's troops couldn't make it because the Army is more restrictive than the Air Force, but I had about twenty of my Air Force troops and colleagues there in addition to our parents, my uncle, and my two Academy buddies.

It was small and beautiful, exactly the kind of wedding I wanted. Neither a "paper wedding" nor a huge ceremony that probably would have overwhelmed me.

Unfortunately, we planned the wedding on a Saturday, so after the wedding, my troops went back to Osan on a bus and were stuck on the road for hours.

Service members who do a remote tour to a place like Korea can do a 30-day leave, designed to allow them to return home and see their families. But Jon and I came to Korea at different times, so it was hard to get our leaves to line up, and thirty days seemed like a very long time to leave our troops.

We ended up taking a three-day honeymoon to Mt. Sorak (Soraksan). We camped for a night and then stayed overnight in a beautiful hotel at Soraksan.

In the hotel, there were two rooms for breakfast—one for foreigners and one for the locals. I thought that was weird, and I decided I wanted the 'real' local experience. They were serving varieties of fish soup. Jon probably would have eaten there, but it was a definite nope for me. We went back to the breakfast room for foreigners and ordered pancakes.

Since we were now married, we put in to be assigned together. We also put in for our dream jobs. My dream job was to go to Texas to the Inter-American Air Forces Academy. There were a lot of Army posts in Texas, so that still seemed like a reasonable place for Jon.

Jon put in for a Ranger post in Tacoma, Washington. There was an Air Force base there, so that would also have been reasonable for me.

Fortunately and unfortunately, we both got our dreams. I was shipped to Texas, and Jon was destined to go to Washington in a few months when his rotation in Korea ended.

Korea had been good to us though. We explored a lot of the country, driving around in my crappy 1983 Hyundai Pony, which I sold to an incoming officer for two hundred dollars. We had a lot of time to be together, and we got married. We just hadn't quite managed to get a joint assignment out of it. But that wasn't Korea's fault. We both requested and got selected for our dream jobs, and we were in two different branches of the service. There was only so much the military could do for us.

It was another two years before we were finally able to live together, after I'd finished serving my five-year commitment.

FAMILY TRAVEL

CHAPTER 8

GERMANY:
NO REGRETS

A couple of years later, in 1996, I got out of the military and moved from my assignment in Texas to join Jon in Tacoma, Washington, where he was stationed at Fort Lewis with the Ranger Battalion. We'd already been married for two years, but this was the first time we were able to live together. I was also expecting our first child, so it wouldn't be long before our family expanded.

Of course, because Jon was in the Ranger Battalion, he was deployed frequently. I set up the crib with a Leatherman by myself one day when the due date was approaching. Jon was deployed again, and I started panicking that we didn't have anything ready for the baby.

Fortunately, Jon was able to be home when our son, Jono arrived. However, it wasn't long before he was sent to Germany and Hungary for six months to support NATO during the Bosnia-Herzegovina crisis and the blockade of Sarajevo.

While Jon was gone, I took videos of Jono and sent him videotapes so that he could see Jono's progress—from lying on his back and kicking, to crawling, then starting to walk. We didn't have social media then, so sending videotapes was the best I could do. Instant Message had just started, and we instant-messaged a few times when we were both online at the same time (via dial-up). But mostly I just had to wait for Jon's weekly call to hear how he was doing and give him updates about Jono.

The six-month deployment stretched, as they often do, which meant that Jon wouldn't be home for Christmas as we'd originally expected, but he could get a few days of leave. We decided that Jono and I would go and visit him in Germany.

I got a passport for Jono and booked our tickets. Jono would have his first birthday on the trip.

We had flown with Jono domestically a few times, to New York for a wedding, and to New Jersey to see Jon's family. I had done a few of those flights without Jon because he was deployed, and Jono had always done well. Since those were 6-hour flights, I thought flying to Germany wouldn't be that much harder.

It was exponentially more challenging. The 6-hour flight to the East Coast felt long, and then we had a layover in Pittsburgh for several hours. I found a play area for Jono where he could get some of his energy out, but we still had another 7-hour flight.

Jono had done reasonably well on the flight, but he was a baby. Since I was traveling alone, that meant that I had to keep him entertained, fed, and changed. I was on my last legs by the time we landed in Frankfurt. It was late morning there, but according to Tacoma time, it was still the middle of the night.

And, the journey wasn't over yet. I still had to drive to Heidelberg where Jon was stationed. I went to the car rental counter to pick up the car I'd reserved. I had the car reservation print-out ready. When I stepped up to the counter, the agent said something to me in German.

After spending a year in Korea, where very few people spoke English, and traveling in South America, where they also didn't speak English, all I thought was I didn't speak German—it never occurred me to ask if he spoke English. English hadn't been spoken *anywhere* I'd traveled before, why would it be useful in Germany?

I was exhausted, and I felt crushed. I dropped my head and put my hands over my eyes to keep from crying.

The agent said, "Do you have a reservation?" in perfect English. I was so relieved. He walked me through the rental process and gave me the keys and a map.

I reviewed the map, figured out that I needed to head South, and struck out for Heidelberg.

I panicked almost immediately because the road signs didn't say north or south—they said Munich or Düsseldorf. I had only glanced at the map. I chose the Munich direction and prayed I got it right.

I drove the hour to Heidelberg after that, holding on a bit longer until I could sleep.

Jon was not yet back from work by the time we got to the base, so I went to the Visiting Officer's Quarters (VOQ), like an on-base hotel, and got a room and a crib for Jono.

I put Jono in his jammies, fed and changed him, and then lay down. He stood up in his crib and bounced up and down, wanting to play, but I was wiped out. I slept.

I woke up to check on Jono, and he was asleep in his crib. He was probably exhausted after the long journey, too.

We met up with Jon the next day after he was back from his mission, but he still had to work. Jono and I were on our own to entertain ourselves for another day. Jono and I had both slept, so we were ready to go.

Jon recommended Rothenberg ob Der Tauber, a quaint little town with medieval architecture—classic Tudor-style buildings with wood frames crisscrossed with timbers. Everything was decorated for Christmas: lights, trees, and a market with dozens of booths offering food, drink, and trinkets.

I don't think I'd ever seen anything so festive. I bought some chocolate and was surprised by the hazelnut flavor. That wasn't a taste I had acquired yet. Back then, I'd never heard of Nutella. We called hazelnuts "filberts" and either picked them out of the mixed-nut jars and tossed them—or just left them, so there'd be a final layer of just filberts and Brazil nuts at the bottom. I kept trying to find chocolate or a chocolate pastry I liked, but I couldn't find anything without the hazelnut flavor.

Finally, Jon was released from work, and we had a few days together. I had spent a lot of time preparing for the trip, but it was mostly focused on getting us there. I hadn't spent a lot of time or energy researching the sights we might be able to see. Frankly, I wasn't traveling to see Germany—I was traveling to see Jon so that we could be together as a family at Christmas. If he had been on the Moon, we would have gone there instead, but it would've been a longer flight.

Jon had thought through some places to visit, so we headed further South for a few days.

As we started driving, I pointed to a sign for Heidelberg castle and asked Jon if he'd had a chance to go there yet. 'Castle' was written in German as Schloß. I pronounced it as "schlob." Jon studied German in high school. He wasn't fluent, but he could converse and knew the basics. He laughed and explained that what I'd taken to be a "B" was actually a double "S." Schloss not schlob, I never forgot the German word for castle again.

Jon taught me some of the basic words in German, but everyone we met in Germany could speak English. So much so that it was almost, *almost* disconcerting. We'd go into a McDonald's, where I could get Jono some chicken nuggets, and I'd ask for *kaffee mit milch* (coffee with milk) for myself. They would reply, in perfect English, "Would you like sugar with that?"

We quickly got used to how easy it was to get around and how nice it was not having to worry about the language.

We visited Ulm, which had a huge cathedral with a towering spire that we climbed up and could see the whole of the city. Then we went to Neuschwanstein Castle—the fairy-tale white castle that at least partly inspired the Disney castle. We only had a couple of days to explore before we headed back to the base.

The next day was Christmas, and Jon's Commander invited us to his home. It is a tradition in the military community to invite single or unaccompanied soldiers to join in for holidays. It was extremely kind of them to extend the invitation to our family.

Jono seemed fussier than normal, but we assumed he was just tired. It had been a lot of travel, and as much as we tried to keep his schedule normal with nap times and meals, it was definitely not normal. Especially since, for the past six months, it had been just Jono and me in our small, quiet apartment, following a pretty structured routine.

We were at their house for only a little while before it was apparent that Jono wasn't feeling well. He threw up the food we gave him—not baby spit-up. He was sick.

We took him back to Jon's quarters and lay him in his crib, thinking that he would be fine after he slept.

But he had a restless night, and in the morning, he wasn't

any better. We took him to the hospital on base. It was Christmastime, so we couldn't book a normal doctor's appointment; the only option was the ER.

The doctor saw him, listened to his heart and his lungs, and said, "Give him plenty of fluids."

We did, but Jono didn't seem to get any better.

Our flight home was the next day, and I wasn't sure whether taking him on another long flight was a good idea. We went back to the ER. A different doctor saw us. I told him that we were there the day before and that Jono still wasn't feeling well. I asked him if I should I stay or take Jono home.

The doctor said, "He should be fine to fly. Just make sure he's getting plenty of fluids."

Jon had to get back to work. My mother was going to visit us in Tacoma, and I was hopeful that getting Jono back in his own environment would help him. I drove us back to Frankfurt, and we got on the plane.

I cannot tell you how awful the flight home was. What I *can* tell you is that there is nothing worse than watching your child suffer despite trying everything possible—from standing in the aisle and rocking him, to letting him sleep on my lap or my shoulder, to giving him juice, water, and milk—knowing that nothing was making a difference.

The people around us grumbled because Jono was so fussy, but I didn't care about them. I was focused on Jono and too stressed out to care.

As soon as we landed, I got Jono in his car seat, and I drove straight to the ER at Fort Lewis. It was still holiday time, so we had to see an ER doctor again, not a pediatrician.

The doctor seemed to be reading from the same script as the first two and told me for a third time to "make sure he was drinking enough fluids."

I knew it wasn't right. I knew something was wrong, but I wasn't a doctor, and I didn't have all the right words to tell them what was wrong. The doctor didn't believe it was anything more than a typical "give him fluids" situation. I told him again that we'd been in Germany, that my son had been sick for several days. But he just repeated himself, patronizing me with that "Who's the doctor here?" smile.

I took Jono home to let him rest for a while. Then I had to bundle him back into the car to pick my mom up from the airport. She was going to stay with us for the remainder of the holiday break.

Jono wasn't getting better. That night, no one got any sleep. I called a tele-nurse service, and I was told the same thing. Fluids, fluids, fluids.

In the morning, I told my mom we were going to the hospital. I knew—I just knew something wasn't right.

On the fourth visit to the hospital, I didn't have to say anything. The nurse took one look at Jono and whisked him away from me. They put me in a separate waiting room and kept my mother in the main waiting area.

Several nurses came by to ask about Jono's condition and how long he'd been showing symptoms. I told them we'd been in Germany, that I'd gone to the Army hospital there, and that I'd already been to the ER in Tacoma. "This is my fourth visit," I told them, my voice tight with frustration, anger, and the threat of tears. They calmly wrote things down on their clipboards, and then someone else would come in and ask me more questions. I was frantic. *Where was Jono, how was he, what were they doing to him?*

Finally, after what must have been two hours, I was taken out of the room to meet my mom, and we were taken to see Jono.

Jono had an IV attached to his head. He was so dehydrated by the time we came in that the only vein they could use was the one at this temple.

I found out that I had been separated from Jono and

questioned because they suspected me of negligence in letting his illness get so far down the road. What kind of mother was I not to have noticed the symptoms? What kind of mother was I not to have brought him to the doctor sooner?

Later, they told us that Jono had rotavirus. Although he had been taking in fluids, he was losing them all. Not one of the previous three doctors asked how full his diapers were. And I knew they were full—but he was drinking so much fluid—how would I know that the input and output didn't add up?

They kept him in the hospital for three days. My mom and I took turns sitting up with him, but he slept a lot of the time. The poor little guy was exhausted and depleted.

They released us after Jono recovered and after they determined that *I* wasn't the negligent one.

I made a lot of decisions in my life by asking myself if I would regret not doing it. That question stemmed from one of my biggest regrets at the Academy: staying on the gymnastics team for a third year. I had wanted to quit and join the parachuting team, but my coach begged me to stay. Don't get me wrong—I wasn't such a rock star gymnast that she needed my skills on the beam or bars. The Academy was hosting the NCAA Division II championships that year, and she wanted my leadership and organizational skills. She wanted to keep me on as a student assistant to help organize for the tournament. I gave in to the flattery and the pleading, and I stayed.

And I have regretted it ever since. I wanted to parachute. Not organize for a tournament.

Usually, asking myself, "Would I regret not doing it?" led me down the more adventurous path, and I was always happy I chose it.

After our trip to Germany, I was very close to regretting my decision to go in the first place. Fortunately, Jono recovered and was back to being the happy, healthy baby he was before. But from then on, I had to consider whether I would regret if I *did* something, not just regret if I *didn't*. When your family and child are involved, sometimes taking the less-adventurous path is the right one.

Jon came home a month or two later when the Army finally released him—eight months into his six-month deployment. Typical Army math. By then, Jono was walking and starting to talk. I was glad Jon got to see him over Christmas, since he had already missed so much of Jono's first year.

It would be a while before I felt comfortable taking Jono overseas again.

How long would it be before the regret of *not* traveling outweighed the risk of traveling with him? I didn't know if I could risk his health and possibly watch him get sick again.

CHAPTER 9

PUERTO RICO:
THE PERIL OF USING POINTS

After Jon got out of the military, we moved to New Jersey, his home state. Jono was a toddler by then, and we wanted to be near his grandparents.

We bought a house, and I joined a technology consulting firm. I started at the company at the entry level because I didn't have any relevant business skills after toting guns for five years. With a house, a toddler, and a starting salary designed for 21-year-olds straight out of college, money was tight, way too tight for international adventures. And of course, I wasn't sure if it was a good idea to travel internationally with Jono yet, either.

The only traveling we did during the first few years was

exploring the Northeast and visiting family in South Dakota and Colorado.

As a consultant, I worked wherever my clients needed me. My first travel job was six months in Washington, D.C. At first, Jon and I were grateful for the policies of the civilian world where I'd get to come home every weekend. Compared to Jon's 8-month deployment to Germany and Hungary, coming home every weekend seemed like an incredible luxury. *At first!*

However, the consulting lifestyle is demanding and never-ending. When our son was ten, I started to work with a client in Philadelphia. I ended up working there for seven years while still living in New Jersey, spending many nights away from my family in hotels.

At the time, my preferred hotel in Philadelphia was a Crown Plaza. It was close to the client's office, and there was a Starbucks across the street—my two main criteria. I stayed there two or three nights a week.

The only upside to all that travel was earning a lot of hotel points. Because I had chosen the Crown Plaza, that meant I had points with International Hotel Group (IHG), which includes Crown Plaza, Holiday Inn, and InterContinental Hotels.

We started traveling internationally again when Jono was about ten—old enough, we felt, to appreciate and learn from the adventures, and old enough to stay healthy. By then, I had gotten a couple of promotions, so we were no longer financially sinking—but we were still very careful with costs. Hotel points were a major factor in making it possible for us to travel again. Our first trip abroad was to Italy, and I had been able to book almost all of our hotels at Holiday Inns, making our hotel budget close to zero. I was impressed by the Holiday Inns in Europe—they were surprisingly modern and well-designed. They're also in smaller, more remote locations where other hotel chains aren't usually found, which worked well for us.

After that first trip to Italy using points, I was hooked on points. If you can book a whole vacation using hotel points and not spend any money, why wouldn't you?

One year, when our son Jono was about eleven, we had a JetBlue voucher after a flight to visit my family in Denver was very delayed. JetBlue had a limited set of destinations at the time, and all flights were either within the U.S. or to the Caribbean.

I wasn't excited about going to the Caribbean. To me, the Caribbean meant beaches and oceans—neither of which I had much experience with. I grew up in North and South Dakota, where oceans aren't a thing.

My first experience with the ocean was when I was a sophomore at the Air Force Academy. We did a two-week training deployment in Hawaii. We were on base most of the time, but when we had a free weekend, we drove around the island and went to the North Shore.

The North Shore in Hawaii. Known for big waves for surfing. That is the first place I walked into the ocean. Brilliant. Everyone else just seemed to walk into the waves and then dive in. I tried to do the same. I didn't realize they were diving *under* the waves. I dove in, and within seconds, I was tumbled and tossed by the waves and was afraid I'd never come back up. My earrings were ripped from my ears, and it's a miracle that was the worst of it. I came up for air and scrambled back to the shore. I didn't bother going back in. I was not qualified to tackle those waves.

Of all the places JetBlue flew, Puerto Rico looked like the best. Although there were beaches, there were a lot of other things to see—including mountains and rain forests. Plus, they speak Spanish, and I'm always happy to go anywhere I can practice. They also had a couple of Holiday Inns, which meant that in addition to free flights, our hotel expenses would be minimal. Free hotels clinched the deal, and I booked the flights.

We flew into Ponce on the island's southern coast (home to a Holiday Inn) and then circled up the east side toward San Juan, where we would catch our flight out. We explored the coast—snorkeling, hiking, and listening to the ever-present chorus of coquí frogs. There was so much to do that didn't involve beaches!

One morning, we were eating breakfast at a cafe. We were still on the eastern side of the island but were heading for San Juan and would stay there that night. The cafe had newspapers for sale, and the front page showed a large photo of the Holiday Inn in San Juan with a line of police tape across the front entrance. The headline read: *"Estrangulacion in San Juan."* My husband doesn't speak Spanish, but there was no doubt what that meant. Strangulation? Yikes!

"Is that where we're staying tonight?" my husband asked, knowing we stayed at Holiday Inns wherever possible.

"I'll have to double check," I said, 99.999 percent sure that was exactly where we were staying.

We put it out of our minds and spent the day exploring more. We found the best hamburgers on the island in a little stand at Luquillo. Ok, Jon and Jono found the best burgers. I ordered a "veggie burger," which ended up being a burger-less burger. It was just the bun with lettuce, tomato, onion, pickles, and ketchup. I rolled my eyes. One star. Jon and Jono polished off their burgers, which were piled high with brisket—because burgers need even more meat, right? I stole some of their fries after eating all of mine.

We made our way to San Juan. As we approached the Holiday Inn, I had been worried that I booked us in some sketchy part of town, but the neighborhood we drove through looked ritzy. It was near the beach, and there were a lot of nice hotels and high-end stores like Coach. It didn't look like a murdery neighborhood.

We got to the Holiday Inn. It looked exactly like it did in the picture, except the police tape had been taken down. I don't know if we expected to see the doors locked or blood on the driveway, but it was almost more disconcerting that there was no indication of what had happened. If we hadn't seen the newspaper, we might not have known.

Normally at hotels, I run in to handle check-in since the reservations are in my name, while Jon and Jono wait in the car. This time, we weren't sure what to do. Eventually, I ran in.

The lobby looked as calm as it did on the outside. I gave the hotel clerk my name for the reservation, then paused. How was I supposed to ask, "Hey, so what's going on with that murder?" Finally, I asked in Spanish, "I saw what happened last night . . . is it ok?"

The clerk responded, "*Todo tranquilo.*" All calm. He started processing our check-in.

Jon and Jono joined me in the hotel because Jon wasn't satisfied with staying in the car this time. I told Jon the clerk had said everything was calm.

"Wait a minute," Jon said to the clerk. "What happened? How do I know you're not booking us in the same room?"

"The whole floor where it happened is closed off while the investigation happens. From what we know, a man and a woman went in, and only the man came out."

It made us feel better that it wasn't a madman running around strangling people. It also horrified me that a man killing a woman was "normal" enough for the hotel to continue operating—and that it would make us feel more "comfortable" knowing what happened.

Though neither of us were entirely satisfied, we ended up staying. We had the booking, and it was free. We were a bit more on edge and listening for odd sounds the whole time. Ghosts? Or murderers? All in all, I'll give credit to the Holiday Inn. It was a nice hotel, and they treated us well. And it was a nice neighborhood.

Shortly after that trip, the Crown Plaza in Philadelphia changed over to a different hotel chain that didn't have a points program. No way was I going to spend that many nights away from my family and not get any points out of it. I shifted to a Courtyard a few blocks farther away, but still within walking distance of the client's office and Starbucks. Courtyard is part of Marriott, so I have been a firmly committed Marriott Bonvoy member ever since.

Since then, I've used my Marriott points all over the world—from Azerbaijan, Moldova, and Albania to Serbia. They may not be in the smaller cities where I might have found Holiday Inns, but after I eventually used all of my IHG points—and probably because of the strangulation—I'm OK if I never go to a Holiday Inn again. I'll stick with Marriott.

CHAPTER 10

PUERTO RICO:
NO RULES

We liked to travel over the Christmas holiday. It was one of the few times I could travel and not have to worry about work because everyone else took time off too. But things had been so busy that we didn't have time to plan. Jon suggested Puerto Rico, since we liked it the last time we were there. And because it's part of the U.S., it's easy. You don't need a passport, and they use American dollars.

We hadn't noticed this the first time we traveled there, but on the second trip, it quickly became clear that some of the rules that we follow in the continental U.S. don't necessarily apply in Puerto Rico. For example, after we landed, we realized that Jono was developing pink eye, so we went to a pharmacy. They gave us over-the-counter medicine. In the continental U.S., that would have been a trip to the doctor and a prescription.

Jono was going to turn fifteen on the trip. Having a birthday between Christmas and New Year is tough because it's easy for your birthday to get lumped in with Christmas or overlooked altogether. To combat this, we always tried to do something special when we traveled on his birthday.

For some reason, Jono kept talking about wanting to go hang gliding. I don't know where he got the idea, but it kept coming up.

On his birthday, we woke him up early and told him we were going on a long hike. We drove out to a remote hill outside of town, definitely somewhere we could actually hike. Even when we pulled up and Jono saw the hang glider, Jon tried to play it off.

"Hey, cool! Look a hang glider," he said, wanting to draw out the surprise as long as possible.

Jono was so surprised! I don't think he realized he was really going to get to hang glide until he was suited up and being briefed on takeoff procedures. Since he would be flying tandem with an experienced pilot, it seemed safe enough when we booked it.

As Jon and I watched the takeoff drills and looked out over the valley that they would be hang gliding into, we both thought, *Oh, what have we done?* The valley looked far, far below the hill we were standing on.

Once they finished their takeoff drills, it was a waiting game to see when the weather was suitable for flight. They stayed hooked into the hang glider, with Jono strapped in so he hung next to and slightly above the instructor. The wind had to be right, along with the clouds and the rain—I don't know exactly what conditions qualified as suitable, but there was nothing we could do except wait until they were or reschedule if not.

Then all of a sudden, the magic window opened, and the pilot told Jono, "Run, run, run."

They ran, and then they were in the air.

We watched them go up and out before slowly gliding into the valley. The pilot's partner waved for us to follow her in our rental car as she drove their pickup down to meet the hang glider. We drove around the hills, and it was frustrating not to be able to see Jono in the air anymore, but there was nothing we could do except follow the truck.

By the time we got to the valley, Jono and the pilot were down, and Jono was taking his suit off. It had been a short ride because of the wind and air conditions, but he was exhilarated. This was definitely going to make the list of most memorable birthdays. Flying fifteen!

Since we hadn't had that much time to plan for the trip, we had several days around San Juan without an itinerary. Jon decided scuba diving would be fun.

In the U.S., scuba diving requires training that starts in nice, calm, warm swimming pools. In Puerto Rico, well, who needs rules?

We signed up for "Discover Scuba" with no experience necessary. They turned on a 30-minute video that we watched on a tiny 8-inch screen in the waiting area of the scuba shop, and then they started fitting us with gear. And then they put us on a boat. And then the boat went out into the ocean... could this really be happening to me? I had imagined a pool first, then maybe some training on the shoreline where I could stand up if I needed to. Then, maybe nothing more. That would have been more than enough discovering.

Jon wasn't scuba certified at that point either, but he had at least taken a few scuba classes at the Air Force Academy, in the gigantic pool which is eighteen feet deep because we all had to jump off a 10-meter board in our water survival courses. Plus, Jon likes the ocean. He's not a lay-on-the-beach guy—he's more into water adventures, or what he calls "Waterfront Ops." That could mean scuba diving, snorkeling, jet skiing, sailing, deep-sea fishing, stand-up paddleboarding, spearfishing—you name it.

Jono grew up in New Jersey and so is comfortable with the beach and ocean adventures, but he had no experience with scuba diving, either.

We rode the boat for fifteen or twenty minutes. The sea was choppy, and I started feeling seasick. I was nauseous, and I thew up over the edge of the boat. I kept thinking that if the boat would just stop and I could get under the water, it would be calm under there. Jon said I was "chumming the waters," which did not make me feel any better.

The last time we were in Puerto Rico, I had gotten a little bit more comfortable with the ocean. We had done some snorkeling and scrambled around the rocky shore. I felt like I might be able to handle the ocean better on this trip.

A few days earlier, we drove by a beautiful beach, and Jon wanted to get in the water. We already had our swimsuits on—because duh, Puerto Rico. Yes, it was beautiful, but there was coral and waves.

Despite thinking I could handle the waves better this time, my prowess with oceans had apparently not improved since I was a cadet in Hawaii. I got thrown around by the waves, and while I wasn't pulled under, I was dragged across the coral, opening gashes on the backs of my thighs and on my forearms and knees. I clambered out of the water and sat silently bleeding until Jon and Jono finished romping in the waves. I should have known I wasn't qualified for this scuba diving experience. My thighs and arms were still scratched up from the coral, but at least I was no longer bleeding, so I wasn't going to attract sharks with my blood, too. Did they have sharks in Puerto Rico?

The boat finally stopped, and the instructor helped us get fitted. We had regulators in our mouths as he led us to the stairs. Jon and Jono went in first, and I followed. *What am I doing? I'm not qualified for this*, I thought.

I couldn't believe they were just going to put tanks on us and let us in the water. The only thing that made it "Discover" scuba diving, as opposed to just plain scuba diving, was that we'd have an instructor with us the whole time. One instructor dedicated to the three of us.

Jon and Jono both disappeared beneath the surface, and I sat bobbing in the ocean like a rubber duckie in a bathtub.

"Are you ready to go down?" the instructor asked. I nodded my head like a good little adventurer, and he counted down from three. He knew I was scared. "Three ... two ... one ..." And nothing. I stayed floating.

"Are you ready?" he asked again. I dutifully nodded my head, and he counted down once more. "Three ... two ... one ..." And I didn't move. I wasn't going down there.

This was not the instructor's first time with a highly unprepared tourist. He had told us that he had been in the U.S. Army, and that made me feel better. I could trust someone who served.

The next time he didn't ask if I was ready. He knew I wasn't. He took both of my hands in his and started the count down again. "Three ... two ... one ..." and then he kept hold of my hands and brought me down with him. I honestly don't think I ever would have gone down there on my own.

It was only about twenty feet deep, and I could see Jon and Jono swimming around nearby, which made me feel better. The instructor stayed with me as we went down, and then I was hovering, floating on my own.

The seas were not calm down there. I'm not sure what led me to believe that it might be calm below when there were choppy waves above—besides pure ignorance. The waves were moving me back and forth, and the nausea from the seasickness didn't get any better.

The instructor went to check on Jon and Jono, leaving me alone for a minute. When he came back, he wanted me to do one of the little exercises that you have to do to "pass" Discover scuba diving, which is to take the regulator out of your mouth and then put it back in. *No sirree! No way!* I shook my head. No countdown was going to get me to do that. He realized I was a lost cause on that one and backed off.

I have no idea how long we stayed down there, but it probably wasn't more than ten to fifteen minutes total. Most likely, Jon and Jono were underwater for fifteen minutes and I was under for three. They got us back on board and motored to the next location.

They offered us drinks and snacks, but I was so nauseous by that time that even the idea of eating tortilla chips almost had me chumming the water again.

At the next stop, the instructor again made sure we were properly outfitted and then pointed to the ocean. That time, I went under the water without him having to hold my hands—a minor victory! It was beautiful, but it still wasn't calm.

I swam around for a bit, watching the schools of fish drift through the currents, then I floated to the surface. I looked up and saw the boat. The boat had a lovely little ladder which was too tempting to pass up. I climbed out of the water and onto the boat. I realize now that probably wasn't the safest idea, since the instructor and my family had no idea where I'd gone. The instructor bobbed up and spotted me before swimming back down to focus on my family. I just couldn't anymore.

Jon has since been scuba certified and has told me many times that we should go scuba diving again. I'm all for traveling to a place that HE can scuba dive. I'll snorkel. I'm good at snorkeling. By "good," I mean able to float on the surface and look at fish in the water without feeling anxious or freaking out.

Jon is, of course, an advanced snorkeler—which I define as "going underwater with a snorkel to get a closer look at fish or coral, then clearing the water out before being able to breathe again." I don't understand why anyone would do that. The whole point of a snorkel is to let you breathe air—it's literally an air tube. Don't get water in my air tube. Also, I can see the fish just fine from the surface, thank you very much.

Jon still wants to get me scuba certified and has promised me instructors who won't just toss me in the ocean with an oxygen tank. I'm not convinced. But if I ever *do* want to learn scuba diving, it will be in a proper class, with a proper teacher, in a proper pool. A warm pool. No ocean, no boat, no tortilla chips.

Puerto Rico allowed us to have some adventures we may not have been able to in the continental U.S. . . . but then again, I think rules exist for a reason. No sane scuba instructor would have thought I was a good candidate for ocean adventures. And, I'm not convinced that any sane parents would have put their fifteen-year-old on a hang glider, either.

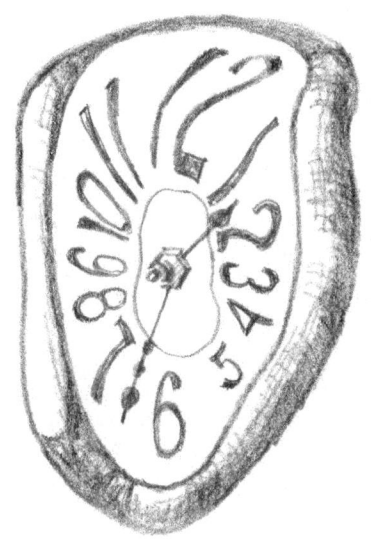

CHAPTER 11

SPAIN:
NOT YOUR MOTHER'S SPAIN

Later that same year, Jono was still fifteen when we traveled to Spain during his spring break. I hadn't been back since I was a teenager traveling with my Spanish class, and I was eager to see how much it had changed (probably a lot!) and how it lived up to my memory of it.

My class trip had been a two-week bus tour that started in Madrid and passed through most of the major cities in southern Spain, followed by a week living with a family in Madrid.

Since I'd already seen a lot of southern Spain, I wanted to go north. Though in reality, it had been so long, I would probably have enjoyed seeing the southern part just as much.

Jon found some climbs in the Pyrenees he wanted us to do, which clinched our decision to travel in the northern half of Spain. We flew into Barcelona and stayed at a Holiday Inn—of course—using the majority of my remaining IHG points.

Jono's spring break fell on Easter that year, so on Easter morning, we went to mass at the Cathedral of Barcelona in the Gothic Quarter of the city. We aren't Catholic, but there's something special about celebrating Easter in an ornate, beautiful cathedral—decked out with Easter lilies and flowers—with all the pomp and formality: the spicy, cloying scent of incense wafting through the air from gilded braziers, and acolytes waving banners and lighting candles. The service was all in Spanish, of course, but the ceremony was standard enough that my family followed along without me needing to translate much.

I loved hearing the Spanish accent from Spain again. It was so smooth and sweet compared to the Latin American accents I'd been listening to for years. Ironically, the people I spoke to in Spain said I had a Latin American accent, while the people in Latin America always told me I had an accent from Spain—probably from my weeks in Spain as a teenager.

After the service, we walked through Barcelona. It seemed to be an infinite maze of small streets, shops, tiny cafés, and beautiful plazas with more cathedrals. We spent the afternoon wandering and exploring.

In the afternoon, we went to the W Barcelona Hotel. A friend had told us that his favorite spot in all of Barcelona was the bar on the twenty-sixth floor. We were there early enough in the afternoon that Jono was allowed in. The expansive view took in the shoreline and the beach, as well as the city sprawling out across the inlet. I could see why it was his favorite spot—the view was worth the ridiculous prices we paid for drinks, including a frothy, fruity smoothie with a tiny umbrella for Jono. There was no one in the bar that early, so we were able to pull seats over to the windows and drink in the views while we nursed our beverages. Barcelona didn't feel like a beach town to me, but that view didn't lie.

The next morning, we planned on heading to the Pyrenees, but since we hadn't gone to La Sagrada Familia the day before, I didn't want to leave Barcelona without at least seeing it. The iconic cathedral that Antonio Gaudi designed—and which has been in construction since 1882, now slated to be finished in 2026—sits far to the north of the part of town we'd spent the day in. Jon drove our rental car to La Sagrada Familia, and we circled it. Though I'd seen it in pictures for years, it was so much more incredible in person, even from the car! It was so ornate and different from all the other cathedrals we'd seen in Europe, like the Gothic-style one where we'd celebrated Easter.

There was a Starbucks near La Sagrada Familia, so I asked to do a quick stop there before we got on the road. It was hard to get the sheer volume of coffee that I'm used to in Spain. Everywhere in Europe only seemed to serve little espresso cups or Americanos, which were still only about half of a "normal" mug of coffee. I needed that venti-sized cup of steaming-hot black coffee.

I had also started collecting Starbucks mugs, and Starbucks became one of my first stops in any new city or country. I bought my first Starbucks cup while I was on a work trip to Mexico City. It was green, white, oversized, and I just loved it. That got me hooked on collecting them in each location. I was disappointed in Italy the year before because Starbucks hadn't opened there yet.

As elated as I was with my coffee, and with my cups from Spain and Barcelona (two cups!), being in Starbucks also drove the point home that Jono's experience of Spain would be vastly different from mine at almost the same age. I had been fourteen when I traveled with my class.

First of all, that trip to Spain was the first time I left the U.S. except for crossing into Canada from North Dakota in the Peace Gardens, which barely counts. Seeing plazas in Sevilla, Moorish palaces in Grenada, Roman ruins in Merida, and orange trees in Valencia were mind-blowing to me. But Jono had already traveled so much more than I had. He'd seen plazas in Puerto Rico and Peru, the Colosseum in Italy, and stood on the Eiffel Tower in France. Spain was interesting to him, but it wouldn't be as life-changing as it was for me.

Secondly, Spain had changed, globalizing and modernizing along with the rest of the world. They were part of the European Union and used the Euro, not the *pesetas* as I remembered.

Back in the '80s, there were no chain stores—everything was local. This time, beyond Starbucks, we saw McDonald's everywhere. We also saw multiple Zaras, the Spanish clothing chain we had in the mall at home.

Back then, most of the people we met only spoke Spanish, and I struggled to get basic points across with my first-year Spanish. This time, while Spanish was always preferred, most people we encountered in Barcelona spoke enough English that Jon and Jono could order meals or buy things in shops without needing me to translate.

Traveling with my class, I felt so far away from my family, like I was totally on my own—especially when I stayed with the host family in Madrid, who I could barely communicate with. I sent postcards and letters home, most of which arrived after I did. This time, we were on Wi-Fi and the internet, and stayed connected to the rest of the world the whole time.

Such is the way of progress. It was good, but it wasn't the same.

We drove to the Pyrenees, where Jon had found an interesting *via ferrata* route. *Via ferrata* is like rock climbing but easier—or at least safer. A steel cable is bolted into the rock, and you are attached to the cable with a harness that has two cords, each with one clip at the end. You can unclip and move one cord at a time, which leaves you always clipped with the other.

The steel cable routes had originally been built for soldiers in WWI to allow them safe travel in the mountains, especially in Italy and Austria. Now, people are restoring and expanding *via ferratas* for adventures.

We had done *via ferrata* once before in Italy and bought the equipment there, since it's still more of a thing in Europe than in the U.S. When we did it in Italy, we were able to climb a route that took us along a ledge high above Lake Garda. The climb itself was easy, a super beginner route. Without the *via ferrata* equipment though, we would have never walked across the ledge. One slip and we would have plummeted hundreds of feet to Lake Garda. The routes were absolutely worth it for the spectacular views. The equipment also gave Jono some freedom to venture ahead of us. We trusted him to stay clipped in, and he was able to move at his own pace.

The *via ferrata* Jon planned for us to climb in Spain was a little more technically challenging than the one in Italy had been, but all I cared about was whether the views would be just as spectacular. The route itself was a challenge to find, since it was pre-Google Maps. The routes weren't well-marked, as they had been used during the war. After driving around for a while looking for it, we stopped in a town to ask for directions.

It might've been more of a village than a town. It was in the heart of the Pyrenees, and it seemed like time didn't exist there. Brick buildings huddled together on streets too narrow for cars against a backdrop of snowcapped mountains. There were a few shops in town. Most were outdoor gear shops, small grocery stores selling snacks and provisions for hikers and adventurers like us, or small restaurants. The town was so far off the beaten path, I couldn't help but wonder who lived there. *How did they survive so far removed from the rest of the world? Were there enough adventurers to keep the town afloat?*

That town was more like the Spain I remembered, and it was one of my favorite stops on our trip. Jon asked about the *via ferrata* in one of the outdoor stores, and we bought snacks in one of the small grocery stores.

The route was only a few miles away, and with our new directions, the route was easy to find. It started as a normal hiking path that wound alongside a river, up toward cliffs with raging waterfalls. We followed the path to the base of the cliff, then put on our *via ferrata* gear—including our rock-climbing helmets, since rockfall could be a problem—and started climbing above the waterfall.

We climbed above the waterfall, walked across a raging river on top of logs, all while being anchored to the steel cables. When the route was vertical, there were ladders made of more steel cables that you could clip to as you climbed. We got views of the valley and little villages below. All around us were the same snow-capped mountains we'd seen before we'd found the route.

I would climb a *via ferrata* route anywhere and everywhere. To me, you get the benefits of rock climbing with the views, and the adventure of being off the beaten track, with the least amount of effort and danger. Of course, Jon would prefer more challenge, more adventure.

Jon needed to get back home in time for an event on the weekend, but Jono and I were able to stay for a few more days. I would happily land back in New York late on Sunday evening and go to work Monday morning, exhausted and jet-lagged, just to squeeze in as much time away as possible—especially when we were traveling internationally.

We dropped Jon off at the airport, and then Jono and I drove north, aiming for the Dali Museum in the town of Figures. While Jon is not a huge fan of museums (preferring mountains and outdoor adventures), Jono and I have spent many Saturdays in New York City museums, going to the Metropolitan Museum of Art, the Museum of Modern Art, or the Museum of Natural History since New York City is only an hour drive from our house in New Jersey.

Dali and Picasso—coincidentally both Spanish—have always been my favorite artists, so we took advantage of the extra days in Spain to hit the museums. We took our time getting to the Dalí Museum, driving along the rocky coastline and stopping in a couple of small towns along the way. It was spring, so the coastal towns weren't hopping yet. We stopped in one town that reminded us of a Jersey Shore boardwalk, with carnival rides, arcade games, and a party atmosphere. Since it was off-season, the town was still pretty deserted. We aren't really Jersey-Shore-boardwalk-type people anyway, so we wandered through the town before hiking along the rocky shoreline.

Once we made it to the museum, as much as I would have considered myself a fan of Dali, it was clear I had only seen a small fraction of Dali's work The entryway showed a classic Dali-style painting with a mosaic of yellow squares. "Is that Abraham Lincoln?" I wondered out loud. The painting is called *Lincoln in Dalivision*. So, yes. Duh! *How had I never noticed that? Had I never seen that painting before, just bad copies or ones similar to it? Or was I just really, truly seeing it for the first time?*

We must have stood in the entryway to the museum for five minutes taking it all in before Jono finally nudged me to move on. Dali's work was so much richer and bigger than

I'd realized, and we spent the afternoon wandering through the museum.

We stayed overnight in a small town along the shoreline. On the map, it had seemed close to Figures. In reality, I had to drive a winding, narrow mountain road through a pass to get to the shoreline. The road was barely wide enough for two lanes, with a mountain on one side and a sheer drop on the other. I kept my eyes glued to the road and a tight grip on the steering wheel the whole time.

The town wasn't bustling, still with that off-season springtime vibe. But it seemed like a place where the rich and famous might vacation in the summer because it was so isolated. It was perfect!

We headed back to Barcelona the next day, and I had a list of things I didn't want us to miss—including Parque Guell and Casa Batllo, the park and house designed by Antonio Gaudi. After seeing the outside of La Sagrada Familia, I didn't want to miss the other things he'd designed!

We walked much of the time, partly because things always seemed close on the map, and partly because I like to explore on foot as much as I can. Jono was game to see it all, too.

Our last stop was the Picasso museum, which was tucked inside a district with small walking streets. The museum covered the evolution of Picasso's art over his lifetime, starting with early sketches that were more life-like and then ended with the more radical abstract style he was famous for.

I'd always admired that Picasso had the ability to paint realistically but chose not to—and that he was always innovating. I'd gone to a Picasso sculpture exhibit in New York City and had been fascinated by it. He broke all of the rules of sculpture the same way he'd broken the rules of painting, and it was so uniquely Picasso. Jono and I were as mesmerized by the Picasso museum as we were by the Dali museum.

After the museum, we explored the walking district and

got lost in the small streets, diving into shops and exploring more. Afterward, we were sitting in a cafe having drinks (me a Rioja, him a Diet Coke) and I was poring over a tourist map of Barcelona. I pointed out a small district and said, "We missed this street!"

Jono groaned. We'd been walking all day, and he was wearing his Converse sneakers. His feet hurt, and he was beat. He grinned when he got my joke—we'd seemingly walked the entire city *except* for that one tiny spot. I was just as tired as he was.

Spain is no longer the Spain of my childhood, and I knew Jono didn't have the same experience I did. My first trip to Spain had such an impact on my life. I fell in love with Spanish and speak fluently because of that trip.

I was also hooked on travel, and I wanted to experience the rest of the world the way I'd experienced Spain—understanding the culture and the history, living with families, learning as much as I could. I came back from Spain that first time a different person. The world was bigger than I ever imagined. My eyes had been opened to it, and I wanted to experience as much of it as possible.

In some ways, my trip to Spain had a major influence on Jono's life as well. Because I loved travel so much, he was able to travel much more than I had when I was his age, and he was far more perceptive and compassionate because of it.

Jono and I got to see some amazing parts of Barcelona and northern Spain that we would have missed if we'd flown home with Jon. But the best part of those last few days, for me, was spending quality time with my son. That was one of many moments that I could sit back and appreciate the intelligent, creative person Jono was becoming and watch him marvel at the world around us.

We had an amazing time exploring by ourselves, and we made it *our* Spain.

WORK & SOLO

CHAPTER 12

PERU & HONDURAS: MISSION TRIPS

When our church bulletin asked for Spanish speakers to help translate on a medical mission in Honduras, I was immediately interested. Our son, Jono, was only six or seven at the time, and Jon and I thought it would be a worthwhile trip—a way for me to give back. It was also a way to keep up my Spanish and to travel to places I would never go otherwise. Jon stayed home with Jono.

I started having serious doubts after I signed up. I faint at the sight of blood. I had to lie down whenever my son lost a tooth. What in the world was I thinking volunteering for anything medical?

I called the coordinator and begged to be let out of the trip, but he calmed me down and said it was more like going to a doctor's office than an ER—I was unlikely to see any blood. I went, but I really wasn't sure what I was walking into.

The first day of clinic, we were out in the jungle of Honduras, surrounded by pineapple fields. We drove down a seemingly endless gravel road to get to the community center where we would host the clinic. The community center had cement floors, a tin roof, and walls built with bricks that had an ornamental pattern like a flower that let the air flow through the petals.

The doctor I was assigned to translate for, Dr. Doug, said he knew Spanish and told me to go work with the team responsible for providing reading glasses.

Dr. Doug's first patient was an elderly woman in her 70s or 80s. He sat with her for a minute before yelling my name and asking me to help him with her. Her speech was mumbled, she only had a few teeth left, and she was going through a litany of aches and pains and not stopping to take a breath. She was hard to understand, but I had kept up with my Spanish and was still able to speak fluently, though I was probably a little rusty.

I broke the flow of her complaints and asked her a few questions like, "How long have you felt that way?" and "Where does it hurt?" and translated her answers. The doctor gave me a few additional questions to ask.

The doctor prescribed her some pain medication and gave her some advice on proper diet and hydration. Dr. Doug sent me back to work at the glasses station.

He took the next patient and, shortly after, called me back, shaking his head. I jumped in again and asked questions, translating what the doctor said. We got through another patient. He sent me away a second time.

After he had to call me back for the third patient, he finally realized his high school Spanish wasn't going to cut it in the jungle of Honduras. Many of the patients we met with were not educated. They may have learned a native language other than Spanish and didn't speak in nice, crisp sentences the doctor could understand.

Older patients were especially difficult. They tended to mumble and weren't clear in their answers. When you asked them how long they'd had an ailment, they'd just say a long time, waving their arms as if to indicate an infinite timeline. I had never had a reason to learn medical words in Spanish, so I had to look up some terms, but my level of fluency was much better than the doctor's.

Each new patient provided a new puzzle to solve—I had to understand what they were saying and then the doctor had to determine how to help them. By the end of the day, the doctor and I were working as a great team, and not only did he not send me back to the glasses team, he wouldn't let me leave his side.

I had a headache that wouldn't quit though, and it seemed to get worse throughout the day. I kept drinking water, thinking I was dehydrated in the hot, humid jungle, but the water didn't help.

It wasn't until I returned to our hotel that night and ordered a Diet Coke with dinner that I realized I was in caffeine withdrawal. I normally drank coffee in the morning and Diet Coke throughout the day, but being so far removed from my normal work routine, I hadn't had any caffeine. After that, I made sure to drink several cups of coffee each morning prior to the clinic to make sure I didn't have a repeat of that headache. And no, I never considered cutting down on my caffeine intake; I just made sure it was always available.

After that first trip to Honduras, I signed up whenever the medical mission team from our church traveled to a Spanish-speaking country.

The next trip was to Lima, Peru, and we set up a clinic in a different neighborhood each day, always in the *pueblos jóvenes*—young towns. Those are shantytowns made up of small plywood shacks climbing the vegetation-less, dusty brown hills surrounding Lima. There was no electricity, and water was brought in weekly via trucks and stored in barrels. People coming in from the countryside to find work and a better way of life would set up and live in these shantytowns. I went to Lima several times and visited some of the same communities numerous times while also going to new *pueblos jóvenes*.

After Peru, I translated in mission clinics in Ecuador and the Dominican Republic, then returned several more times to Peru. Each trip was different—the people we served, the doctors I worked with, and the words I had to learn to support different medical scenarios.

During a trip in Ecuador, after I had been doing medical missions for several years, the Nurse Practitioner I was translating for made it her personal mission to find words I didn't know. "Clot?" she asked. When was I supposed to have learned clot? *That was a good one!*

Of all the missions I traveled with and translated for, two stand out because of their remoteness and because they challenged me the most as a translator. Both were in Peru, but they were so different they could have been in different universes.

Peru has ninety different microclimates, which make it one of the most environmentally diverse countries in the world. It has the Altiplano—the high plains above the tree line that are barren and windswept. It has mountains like Machu Picchu, which are lush and vegetated. Peru is also home to Cerro Blanco, the second-highest sand dune in the world. It's near Nazca but looks like it should be in the Sahara. The Nazca lines, which you can fly over from Ica, were drawn on the ground more than 2,000 years ago and have endured because of the dry conditions. Then there is the jungle—deep, Amazonian jungle.

My favorite missions were in the Altiplano and the Amazonian jungle.

When I heard we were going to the Altiplano of Peru, I had envisioned serving people in mountain villages, like ones you might find in Switzerland or Nepal. Cute villages with wooden homes. I knew we would be sleeping in schools, and this would be one of the most remote trips I'd ever been on. There were only a handful of us on the trip: two American doctors, a nurse, myself as a translator, and then the trip organizer, the driver, and the cook. There were no more than eight of us total.

We met up in Arequipa and packed a minibus with medical and hygiene supplies and food. We drove several hours to Chivay, Peru, the gateway to the Colca Canyon at almost 12,000 feet. From there, we drove another six to eight hours on roads that changed from pavement to gravel to dirt and then continued over what was barely a rutted track.

We stopped in front of the first school we would be staying at. It was in a valley tucked between treeless mountains, somewhere around 15,000 feet, far above the tree line. This was no "mountain village." It was literally a school in the middle of nowhere, surrounded by nothing. The school also served as a community center for the people who lived as llama and alpaca herders somewhere in the mountains.

Of course, there was no electricity. Don't even ask about Wi-Fi or cell phone coverage. There was a line of outhouses behind the school building. We brought sleeping bags and layers for warmth, but I couldn't get warm. That first night, we all huddled around the kitchen area and waited for dinner. Our cook, Domi, was incredible. I don't know how she did it. Of the eight of us, two were vegetarians, and one was celiac gluten-free. For every meal she made, Domi had to calculate for each of our needs. If she made noodles for the other vegetarian and me, she made eggs for the celiac. Since were over the tree line, there was no wood, and there was no natural gas or electricity for a stove. Domi cooked over a fire literally made with big tufts of moss the size of a cowboy hat. She cooked multiple versions of meals with the food we had brought on the bus over a moss-fire, using a flashlight to see into the pot since there were no lights. It all tasted incredible, and none of us got sick. Well, except one night when she put crushed-up crackers in the cream sauce and forgot the celiac doctor couldn't eat it. He spent the night visiting the row of outhouses.

After a night shivering in my sleeping bag—I don't know why I couldn't get warm (oh, right, no heat either!)—we woke up, ate Domi's incredible breakfast of coffee, bread, and eggs, and got ready for the day's clinic.

At 9 a.m., the kids whose school we were inhabiting showed up, walking over the hills in ones and twos. The parents came too, but most of them showed up later in the morning, bringing babies and small children. Most of the families raised llamas or alpacas and lived up in the hills. They made money by selling the wool. The mothers and older girls were usually dressed in the traditional style, with full skirts and their hair in two long braids, similar to the style Tera and I had seen in Bolivia.

I knew Quechua was spoken in the high hills of Peru. I had a thin little Quechua–English dictionary from Lonely Planet that I had bought when Tera and I traveled, which I managed to find. It could help me with words like *hello, house,* and *family*, but it wasn't any good with medical discussions. I assumed that most people spoke Spanish. I was wrong.

The children who had been attending school spoke Spanish, but the majority of adults and all of the older generation only spoke Quechua. The local pastor was helping with the clinic and translated from Spanish to Quechua, or sometimes the older kids in the family would translate. This created a chain of translations. The doctor would ask a question such as, "Where does it hurt?" I would translate that to Spanish, and the next person would translate to Quechua.

There is little crossover between Spanish and Quechua, except maybe for modern words, like "airplane," that Quechua has adopted from Spanish. Quechua was the language of the Incas and is unique.

The other thing that is interesting about Quechua is that it was not a written language. There were a few school workbooks written in Quechua, and I asked the school director about them. He said writing in Quechua is a modern adaptation. Even my Quechua–English dictionary is based on the modern attempt to write down the Quechua words phonetically and standardize them.

I later asked a friend in Lima who spoke Quechua and Spanish if he could read the written form of Quechua. My friend was educated and could read and write in Spanish, but he couldn't read Quechua. He said whenever he tried, the words would get all scrambled and he couldn't make sense of them. At first, I didn't understand; you'd think if you could read the sounds, you could understand the words.

But then we played the game Mad Gab. In Mad Gab, there are cards with words and phrases in English, but the spelling and spacing are all wacky. If you try to read them, they just don't make any sense. The goal of the game is to figure out what the cards are saying. For example, *"Led Skit Auto Fear"* is "Let's get out of here," and *"Ache Loot Toothy Pus Hull"* is "A clue to the puzzle."

My sister-in-law and I figured out the best technique when we played together (usually against our husbands). One of us would read the card phonetically aloud while the other kept her eyes shut and listened. We found it was much easier to make sense of the words by listening, since seeing the nonsensical spellings interfered with our ability to understand. It scrambled the words, just like my Quechua-speaking friend said. He never learned to read in Quechua.

So, while it might have been easier to write down a few questions for our Quechua patients instead of relying on a triple-translation, that wasn't going to work.

One of the problems the doctor kept seeing was that all the patients were dehydrated. He kept telling them to make sure they boil their water and drink two liters of water each day. I learned that phrase in Quechua (sort of) because we repeated it so often. *Iskay litros sapa punchay.*

The Quechua translator always said it again in Quechua because no one ever seemed to acknowledge that they understood me when I used that phase. *Was I pronouncing it wrong? Did they not understand me? Or, were they just shy in front of strangers?*

We kept telling them to drink more water, but to make sure they boil it first. In the back of my mind, I kept thinking, *Who are we kidding? There are no trees. They have to cook their dinner using moss tufts like Domi did. Are they going to boil their water over moss tufts too? What do they even eat for dinner?* Their lives were so different—they were so remote—the situation was difficult to comprehend.

The next morning, one of the doctors decided he would walk to the next school. He said it was only a mile or two over the hill and it would take the bus longer on the road because it would have to go around. The drive to the first school had been so long, I wasn't eager for another bus ride. And I thought a hike sounded fun.

The doctor was a marathon runner—I should have known better. We were at about 15,000 feet, so oxygen was more of a nice memory than a reality.

There were a few of us who decided to do the trek. The doctor took off and went up and over the hill and was gone.

I walked about ten feet and had to stop and breathe. I hadn't wanted to sit down and stay there that badly since Jon and I hiked Thorong La in Nepal.

One of the nurses on the trip stayed back with me. "Walk at whatever pace you can keep going. Slow and steady," he said.

I slowed down so much that some of the moss tufts passed me by. However, it was good advice, and I started to make progress. Very, very slowly.

The second school was about 1,000 feet higher, so the path was entirely uphill. It was a mile or two, all up. Finally, I made it. I was no longer cold, but I wanted to do nothing but lie down when I got to the next school. *Wow, that kicked my butt!*

We had five days of holding clinics, each in a different school—each trip bringing us closer to our starting points of Chivay and Arequipa. I learned a few more words of Quechua that proved useless, since no one acknowledged my attempts at speaking, except the translator, who humored me. I also gained a better appreciation for the beauty of this uber-remote place—plain old *remote* just won't cut it.

At one point on the trip, both of our doctors decided it was okay to drink water from one of the rivers. They thought it would be all right because we were "above where the animals graze." I'm no doctor, but *nope!* I did not join them in drinking it. They both got giardia.

Once we got back to Chivay, we went to a pizzeria in town to celebrate completing the clinics. The doctor with celiac ordered a pizza. I couldn't believe it. "How are you going to eat pizza?" I asked, remembering everything Domi had to do to make special meals every day.

He swallowed a handful of enzymes, and said, "I can't do it every day, but for pizza after that trip, it's worth it!"

Then there was the mission to the Amazon jungle.

We took a bus from Lima, traveling up over the mountains from sea level, where Lima sits, up to about 10,000 feet, and then back down to the jungle. It was brutal. It was hours and hours of torture winding up and over the mountains and then back down. I got motion sickness in a way I've never experienced before. I've felt nauseous before, but I don't think I ever actually hurled on a bus or car ride until then.

We transferred from the tour bus to a small school bus that would take us to our destination. I'd never been so glad to get off a tour bus. It was actually no better on the school bus. It seemed to magnify every bump and rock in the road, and by then we had left paved roads far behind.

Our destination was so remote we had to put the bus on a ferry to cross a river. The ferry was essentially a raft—one step above logs tied together with string. We all got down and watched the vehicle cross. I wasn't sure the bus would make it. But it did. We followed on a second trip. Then we got back on the bus and finally rumbled into the village.

It was an actual village this time, not just a school or community center. There were a few buildings, including a log cabin elevated on stilts, where we slept. The main clinic where we worked was a turquoise-blue concrete structure that clashed with the natural greens and browns of the surrounding jungle.

This time, the local people spoke Ashánika—a language I'd never heard of and certainly had no Lonely Planet dictionary for. Even fewer people spoke Spanish, so I buckled in for the slower pace of triple translations and tried to learn a few words of Ashánika along the way. Unlike the Quechua speakers, who wore full skirts, alpaca sweaters, and long braids, the Ashánika people wore long, straight, tunic-like dresses that ended just above the ankles. Their hair was long and unbound. They looked like a tribe of people whom you might see in a documentary about the rainforests of the Amazon. It was the Amazon, so, yes, it was exactly like that, but not what I had expected, since I'd traveled to Peru multiple times by then and had seen nothing like this community.

When I was there, I kept seeing mugs with the names of one of the presidential candidates. It was an election year. I asked one of the organizers why there was election paraphernalia out in the jungle.

He told me that Peru has mandatory universal elections, which means that every adult must vote or will be fined. The people in that village had the same rights and obligations to vote as people in Lima, which I thought was great. Still, they had no access to radio, TV, newspapers, or internet. How would they be informed enough to know who they were voting for?

The Quechua speakers in the high Altiplano, whom I'd visited on my previous trip, would have to vote then, too. I couldn't imagine how they would know which candidate would best support their needs.

Then again, I realized that even with the internet and all the cable news channels, we still only know what we're told. How sure is anyone that they're voting for the best candidate?

I went on one or two mission trips every year for about ten years, covering multiple countries. Now, twenty years later, a trip like that might get labeled voluntourism, but at the time, the trips felt vital and necessary. We were serving people's needs in ways their countries could not. I was invited into communities and met people I never would have met otherwise.

I was on trips where we provided wheelchairs to children, reading glasses to elders, dental care, and minor surgeries, in addition to the standard clinics. We genuinely cared, and the doctors, physical therapists, dentists, and others gave up their free time to care for others.

In Peru in particular, the economy improved over the years that I traveled there on medical missions. At the beginning, patients came to us with no other options. In the later years, after the economy improved, the basic services provided by Peru became more available, and our clinics became less necessary.

At about the same time as Peru's economy improved, several of the mission groups I'd been traveling with closed up shop. There was also a movement for communities to serve themselves, so those kinds of missions fell out of favor. My working life was also ramping up, so I had less time for mission work. Because of all those factors, I stopped going on mission trips but always valued the time I spent on them—serving, translating, improving my Spanish, and even learning some words from indigenous languages.

Those trips re-opened my eyes to the world as an adult, similar to how traveling to Spain as a fourteen-year-old had. I met people whose lives were so very different from my own but who were still the same in many ways. The women who brought their children to the doctors had the same fears and hopes for their children as I had for my son. The elderly had the same aches and pains as many of my elderly relatives had.

I always had a hard time re-adjusting to "normal" life back home after those trips. Going back to work, emails, and time reports just didn't have the same interest or urgency afterward. Knowing that even within just the country of Peru that such vastly different worlds could exist was awe-inspiring and humbling and truly put life in perspective for me.

CHAPTER 13

U.S.:
THE 50 STATES

Whenever I told people I liked to travel internationally, I often heard protests like, "But there is so much to see in this country." I don't get why people do that. If you like to travel internationally, cool. If you like to travel domestically, great. Yes, the U.S. is a beautiful country, but that doesn't mean I shouldn't go anywhere else. Going to other places doesn't mean I love my country any less.

Also, for the record, many people assume that international travel always costs more than domestic travel, but that's not true. Some places overseas are quite economical, especially compared to the U.S., so even factoring in flights, trips can be cheaper abroad.

To be able to respond to the "But the U.S. . . ." people, I took stock of how many states I'd been to. I had grown up in the Midwest—North and South Dakota—and then went to college in Colorado. *Check.* I had traveled quite a lot with the Air Force, including competing in gymnastics in Alaska for the Air Force Academy and doing a two-week military program in Hawaii. I'd been stationed in Texas and lived in Washington State. *Check. Check.* Then, while living in New Jersey and working as a technology consultant, I had traveled to most of the Northeast and the East Coast, including Maine, Georgia, and Florida. *Check. Check. Check.*

By the time I took stock of my state count, I'd been to forty-six organically. The only four I hadn't yet visited were Alabama, Arkansas, Mississippi, and Louisiana, which are conveniently clumped together. I decided I needed to hit all fifty states, but those states were too far from New Jersey, and my husband had already been to several of them, so they didn't make it to the top of our travel list.

Then, my company sent me to a two-week women's leadership program at Smith College in Massachusetts. The intervening weekend was free, and my family was in Haiti for a mission trip, so there was no point in going home.

It had been a crazy period at work. I was pushing for a promotion to the executive level, working remotely in Philadelphia, which meant being on the road constantly. Weekends were for seeing my family, doing chores, and catching up on work. I had no "self."

In order to do the two-week course, I transitioned my role at work to junior members of my team. I'd be moving into a new position when I got back, so there wasn't even any work I needed to do.

For one weekend, I had absolute freedom. I barely even knew what that meant anymore.

The other women in the course were going to Boston

or Vermont, but I'd been to both places before, so I wasn't that interested. I'm also an introvert, and after having spent the whole week in a classroom filled with over a hundred women, I needed to be by myself.

I considered my options:

1. I could read in my hotel room, never leaving except to eat. I'd done that once over Thanksgiving at the Academy and loved it, but I thought I'd go stir crazy if I did that this time.
2. I could go driving. I used to do that back when I was a young lieutenant in the military. I'd just drive and not even have a destination, and then, when it was time to return, I'd figure out where I was and map a route back. However, I'd spent a lot of time in the Northeast, and I wasn't excited by that.
3. I thought of those four remaining states, and thought, *That's it!*

I checked flights and found one to New Orleans that didn't cost too much and fit in my schedule.

Friday night after class, I drove three hours to Stewart airport in New York and flew to New Orleans. (Louisiana—forty-seven— *check*!) I rented a car and got to my hotel around midnight. Since I only had the weekend and had to be back for class on Monday morning, I had my work cut out for me to go to all four states.

I got up early on Saturday around 6:00 a.m. and drove my rental car through Louisiana to Arkansas, a journey of about five hours. The states seem close, but there is a lot of territory there! I enjoyed the road trip, connecting my iPhone to the car stereo and blaring Muse, Awolnation, White Rabbits, and Depeche Mode.

I drove past bayous and stilted homes that looked nothing like what I had seen growing up in the Midwest, or in any of the other forty-six states I'd visited. The sky was expansive and spread out in front of me, and I felt myself breathing for the first time in what felt like several years. In New Jersey and the Northeast, there are so many trees, you never get the wide-open sky feeling like you do in the West and Midwest.

I crossed the border to Arkansas, taking a selfie with the "Welcome to Arkansas" sign (forty-eight, *check*). I drove until I got to the first town, which was Grand Lake. I drove around and looked for a place to stop for lunch.

A lot of storefronts were boarded up, and frankly, the town was a little depressing. I found a Mexican restaurant and relaxed a bit before getting back on the road. I know it's not much of Arkansas, but I ended up going to Little Rock for work to meet with a client a few years later, so I can count Arkansas in the list of places I went to "organically," as well.

After lunch, I headed back to New Orleans. I had a lot of ground to cover to get back to my hotel by nightfall, and I don't like to travel unfamiliar roads at night if I don't have to.

On Sunday, I let myself sleep in (until 7:00 a.m.!) because it was just over two hours to Mobile, Alabama. It was a beautiful day, and there was gorgeous light filtering through the clouds along the Gulf. I had to cross Mississippi to get to Alabama, so I stopped at the state border of Mississippi (requisite selfie—forty-nine, *check*) and to walk along the beach at Gulfport, Mississippi.

Once I finally crossed into Alabama, I took a selfie with the final state of the trip—my fiftieth state— *check!* I drove through Mobile and found a Starbucks. Unfortunately, there was no "Alabama" mug at the time. I bought coffee and a snack and headed back to New Orleans.

My weekend was almost over. My flight was later that evening, and I wanted to see more of New Orleans than the hotel on the edge of town I'd stayed in. I drove straight to the

French Quarter, just as it started raining cats and dogs.

Since everyone said the food was amazing in New Orleans, I'd planned to do a late lunch there. But as a vegetarian, I had a hard time finding anything that didn't contain sausage, bacon, shrimp, or all three. I hopped from restaurant to restaurant, looking at the menus, trying to stay under the cover of the awnings to keep myself from getting drenched.

Finally, I found a diner where they had all-day breakfast, and I got pancakes and eggs. If I had more time, I might have found a place with better vegetarian options, but with my crazy four-state weekend and a super rainy day, pancakes and coffee sounded just about perfect.

While running back to my car—ducking under eaves and balconies—a leather store caught my eye. I popped in and bought a western-style leather laptop bag with silver studs to replace the standard-issue black nylon laptop case I'd been given as a new joiner in my company twelve years earlier. I also found a Starbucks, and they had a New Orleans cup!

I flew back to New York that evening before driving the three hours back to Smith College to be ready for classes on Monday morning. I didn't get to my dorm room until after midnight, but it was the perfect weekend for me. It was more than just completing all fifty states; that mini solo trip helped me feel like I was reclaiming control of myself and doing what I needed for me.

The next morning, one of the friends I'd made in class asked me what I'd done over the weekend. I said, "I flew to New Orleans and road-tripped to Mississippi, Alabama, and Arkansas."

"You what?" She shook her head in disbelief.

As the class started, the instructor asked how everyone's weekend was, and a few people got up and talked about their road trips to Boston, Vermont, or elsewhere in the Northeast. I stayed silent; standing up in the room of one hundred women really wasn't my thing.

"Tauni had an interesting weekend," my friend volunteered.

Rolling my eyes, I stood up and gave everyone a quick summary of my weekend and achieving my goal of hitting all fifty states, then sat back down. I didn't do the trip to impress anyone. I did it for me, to choose something for myself that had nothing to do with work or family.

I carried that New Orleans laptop case for the next ten years, rebranding my personal style. It served as a constant reminder of taking back a tiny bit of control in my life.

CHAPTER 14

BELGIUM & THE NETHERLANDS:
THERE MAY NOT BE A LATER

Traveling for work may sound fun—maybe even glamorous. You get to dine out on the company dollar, stay in fabulous hotels, jet around the country. Amazing, right? Well, maybe.

As a consultant, I spent four days a week in Philadelphia, Hartford, Reston, Virginia, Dallas, or similarly exotic locations every week. There were a lot of late nights at the office, followed by crashing in the hotel for a few hours. I ate hotel breakfasts of mass-produced scrambled eggs and spent countless hours on the road, plane, or train. And of course, all those days and nights were spent away from family.

After regretting not exploring Asia when Jon and I got married in Korea, I made it a point to take better advantage of my work travels whenever I went somewhere interesting. Of course, I still had to balance family and home, but sometimes I could add a day or two of travel at the end of the trip to see something outside of the conference room. Or, on the rare occasion that I had to be gone for two weeks, I could see something on the weekend in the middle.

When Jono was a teenager, I was assigned to an international client with several office locations—New Jersey, Dallas, Antwerp, and Paris. I spent most of my time locally in New Jersey but occasionally traveled to Dallas. Every couple of months, I'd go to Antwerp and Paris.

Everyone can agree that traveling to Connecticut isn't glamourous. But traveling to Paris . . . that has to be amazing, right? Not exactly. My client's main work location was outside of Paris. As in: land in Paris, get a rental car, and drive and drive and drive until you hit cows. We stayed in a hotel that looked like a storage unit with garage-style doors. I didn't love traveling to "Paris."

The first time I flew to Belgium, I landed in Brussels and followed the signs to the trains, which are a few levels below the airport. I went to the train station counter to buy a ticket to Antwerp from an actual person—sometimes it's easier than trying to figure out a self-service kiosk the first time in a new country. For about ten dollars, there was a train leaving for Antwerp in a few minutes. I bought the ticket and ran to the escalator to get to the right platform.

A few minutes later, I was on a train to Antwerp. It was so easy, so logical. It was one of the first times I realized how challenging the transportation system in the U.S. is. A person arriving in the U.S. from Europe couldn't do the same thing—not by a long shot. Not even in the Northeast, where there are comparatively lots of mass transit options.

The train arrived in Antwerp, and I walked out into what has to be one of the most beautiful train stations in the world. (Architectural Digest *only* rates it as #8). The train arrived multiple levels below the street level, so I had to take several escalators up, and then there were vaulted ceilings, arched windows, and a huge clock on the wall. It was like walking through Big Ben.

I arrived at one end of the station, and the office was just a block away from the other end, so I walked through the station, stopping at a shop to get coffee and a pastry along the way. It was so civilized—so much nicer than most, if not all, of the places I'd traveled to for work.

Antwerp itself was beautiful too. There were hotels near the train station, which meant I could easily walk to work, going through the train station if it was cold or rainy. I could also walk to Antwerp's old town, which was filled with shops, a gorgeous cathedral, merchant houses with the triangle-shaped façades similar to those in Amsterdam or Brussels, and even a castle! There were cobblestone streets and wide-open plazas. Antwerp was small enough that I felt like I got to know it, but large enough that it had everything anyone could want.

Whenever I was in Antwerp, I would take my main client, Randy, out for dinner. I almost always ended up eating pizza or pasta—available as options in most restaurants and suitable for vegetarians, though not exactly "local" cuisine.

One evening, we were having dinner on a nice night, eating outside on the restaurant's patio. I was starving. I had just flown in that day, and my body clock hadn't adjusted yet. I ordered an appetizer for us to share. I ate a piece or two but didn't want more or I wouldn't be able to eat my dinner, but I kept picking at the appetizer because I was so hungry. The food didn't come.

Finally, Randy talked to the waiter and then asked if I was done. I said I was. The restaurant had been waiting for me to "finish" the appetizer before they brought out my main meal. I kept picking because they didn't bring the meal. We were in a vicious cycle of waiting. I knew there were cultural differences in Europe. For example, you have to ask for your bill—they won't just bring it. But I'd never heard the "stop-eating-your-appetizer-if-you-want-your-main-course" rule. That was a new one to me.

At the end of the meal, Randy asked for the *rekening*.

"The 'reckoning' is the bill? Like the 'final reckoning' from *Highlander*," I said, using the accent from the movie.

Randy laughed. As a native speaker of Flemish (a dialect of Dutch), he had always just understood it to mean "the bill." He'd never thought of it that way

The other major cultural difference—especially when we worked out of the "not-Paris" office—was that eating at your desk was definitely not done. My "normal" lunches back in the U.S. consisted of heating up a microwave meal I brought from home and eating at my desk. I rarely went to the cafeteria because who has time to walk all the way to the cafeteria, especially when the food wasn't that great anyway. As a vegetarian, my options were usually salad, salad, or salad. I've eaten so many salads in my life I'm surprised that my eyes haven't turned green.

In France, I didn't have frozen microwave meals with me, so I was happy to walk to the cafeteria with my clients and the team. When I asked for a box or a disposable tray to bring my food back to my desk, you'd have thought I asked if it was okay to pick my nose. They were so disgusted by my question. How uncouth!

I had to get my food (which was all remarkably good) and sit at my table and eat like a civilized person. I had to build that hour into my schedule when I was in France. If I were absolutely desperate to get back to my work, there was a little shop where I could get a baguette sandwich, but they would look down their noses at me if I did it.

The first time I had an extra day to visit Belgium, I asked Randy where to go. He told me to go to Durbuy, which is one of the smallest towns in Belgium. Durbuy is in the Ardennes—the closest thing Belgium has to mountains—where the Battle of the Bulge was fought during World War II.

On the way there, I stopped at Dinant, a cool town with a citadel perched high on a hill and the home of the inventor of the saxophone. Yep, Adolphe Sax. There were statues of saxophones along one of the bridges across the river.

Durbuy was exactly what I like in a town—beautiful and surrounded by hills. It was small enough that I could walk from one end to the other from my hotel, and it had a lot of nice cafés where I could eat, read my book, and relax. It couldn't have been a more perfect town for me.

Each time I went to Belgium for work, I took an extra day or two to travel. I visited Leuven, a university town like the Cambridge, Massachusetts of Belgium. I went to Bruges, the tourist town everyone flocks to. It's quaint and surrounded by canals, but it was too touristy for me. I preferred Ghent, which is still filled with canals and pointy-roofed, merchant guild-style houses, but feels like real people live there.

I loved Belgium so much that Jon, Jono, and I spent Thanksgiving in Belgium that year. Jon and Jono flew to Belgium and met me in Antwerp. We went out to dinner with my client Randy and my Belgian team. It was so nice to connect my family with my work life and to have everyone meet each other.

I took my family to the places I liked the most—I showed them my favorite places in Antwerp, took them to Ghent, and then to Durbuy in the Ardennes, a place I absolutely loved.

While we were in the Ardennes, we also went to the World War II Museum in Bastogne (which had been recommended by Randy). That museum was a true multi-media experience. Through headphones, you could hear the perspectives of the war from three characters, depending on where you were standing in the museum. They included a Belgian schoolteacher, a German solider, and an American soldier.

There were huge dioramas of battlefields and villages in the area, each brought to life through both video and the characters' voices in our ears. At one point, chairs and tables came down from the ceiling and landed in formation around us making us feel like we were in someone's home—huddling together in their kitchen against the gunfire and blasts outside.

I was in tears almost immediately and felt like I was living through the war with all of them.

Afterward, we walked outside the museum and were blown away to see an almost 40-foot-tall monument to the United States, shaped like a five-pointed star with all fifty states engraved on it. Wyoming and South Dakota and New Jersey, all of them! It's enormous and overwhelming—and it's in Belgium!

Randy had said something like, "It's a nice little museum," when he recommended it to me. He had a dry sense of humor and was often ironic . . . but I hadn't picked up on it that time. I had no idea what a massive museum it was. I was overwhelmed by his "nice little museum."

After the museum, we went to a local pub in Bastogne to get a snack and a drink. We were playing gin rummy, which we often did when we traveled.

A couple of local men asked us if we were American.

"Yes," we said. "We just went to your amazing WWII museum."

They bought us a round of drinks and said, "We haven't forgotten what America did for us. Cheers!"

After visiting so many places where the U.S. isn't very popular—Guatemala comes to mind!—we were taken aback by how much Belgium still appreciated the role the U.S. played in liberating Belgium (and Europe) during World War II.

After Thanksgiving weekend, we all flew home together. Of course, I had to head back to Belgium again shortly thereafter to spend time with my clients and my team.

After I'd spent several weekends on my own in Belgium, I wanted to spend some time in the Netherlands. I considered going to Amsterdam, which would have been an easy trip from the Antwerp train station, but for some reason I wasn't very excited about it. I also assumed I could go anytime. So, I rented a car and charted a course through some of the smaller towns instead.

I stopped at Gouda—like the cheese but pronounced "Houda." It was a cute town surrounded by canals, with a town square full of cheese shops and kiosks, like a farmers' market devoted entirely to cheese. Of course, I bought cheese. My favorite was a gouda speckled with mustard seeds.

Then I went to Delft, famous for its white-and-blue porcelain tiles and dishes that I think everyone's grandmother has. In fact, my mother-in-law has plates in that style decorating her dining room. The town itself was filled with porcelain shops, and there were porcelain tiles decorating walls and alleyways.

It was a rainy day, and I was wearing my favorite pair of red cowboy boots. I'd been wearing them almost nonstop since I'd bought them. I spent the day wandering through the plazas, going back and forth over the canal on various bridges, and window shopping. Then, as I turned a corner, the leather on my sole literally tore through, and water started seeping into my sock.

I was on my way back to my hotel to get my other pair of boots, but then I saw a cobbler's shop and went in.

I took my boot off and asked, "Can you repair these?"

"Yes, of course," the cobbler said, as if I'd asked Monet if he could handle a paint-by-numbers kit. "Would you like to leave them here?"

"How long will it take?"

"We could have them back to you Monday morning. We are closed on Sunday." It was about 4:00 p.m. on a Saturday. I had to be back in the office in Antwerp on Monday morning, so that wasn't going to work.

"No, I leave tomorrow," I said, thinking I'd just have to slog back to the hotel and wear my other boots for the rest of the trip until I could get home and take them to my usual shoe repair shop.

"We can do them right now. We can be done before we close tonight," he said, helpfully.

I let him have the boots, and I sat on the floor of the store for an hour in my socks. It made me think of the wooden clogs that are so iconic in the Netherlands. The cobbler repaired my boots with amazing workmanship, and those soles are still on the boots today.

I stayed the night in a little family-run place with stairs so steep that carrying my suitcase up to my room was a little precarious. Still, it was cozy, and I felt like family as much as a guest. I asked the hotel owner where I should go the next day. He said I should either see the iconic windmills of the Netherlands or the coastline, but there wouldn't be time to do both. I chose the coastline, thinking it was likely to be less touristy.

The coastline, starting just south of The Hague, isn't a long, straight stretch of beaches—there are massive inlets jutting in. To cross them, three enormous bridges span the waterways. I wished I had a GoPro or something to record the bridges while I drove; they were mostly empty stretches of road seemingly floating over the water.

There were also offshore windmills out in the ocean, not the iconic ones—but the energy-producing type. I also passed over industrial facilities and ports. This route was the modern Netherlands, not the tulips, wooden clogs, and classic windmills that I would have seen if I'd taken the windmill route. I liked it because it was quiet and windswept, with endless stretches of road over the inlets.

Several months later I had a Saturday to travel, and I had planned to go to Amsterdam, but I was tired from working all week. Keeping up with both European hours and U.S. colleagues meant I was usually in the office early and stayed through the majority of the U.S. workday, until 8:00 or 9:00 p.m. in Antwerp.

During the week, the shops in Antwerp closed at 5:00 p.m., so even though there were beautiful shops right near my hotel, I could never go after work. So, on Saturday morning, instead of taking the train to Amsterdam, I stayed in Antwerp and went to the stores and wandered through the old town. It made me so happy to stay someplace familiar and explore more of the town I loved. And I was just too tired from work to go anywhere.

There was a clothing store that looked so hip, with blue and white glass bottles hanging from the ceiling, and all of the clothing was bright and fun and fantastic. I'd never heard of Desigual (a brand from Spain) before Antwerp, but since that trip, it has become my favorite brand. Desigual helped me rebrand myself at work, moving from suits to something a little more modern and off-kilter. I also went to an Esprit store and bought a bright green raincoat. I used to love Esprit as a teenager, but if any Esprit stores remain in the U.S., they're few and far between.

Shortly after that Saturday in Antwerp, the project ended, and I was never able to return to Belgium. Despite thinking that I could go to Amsterdam whenever I wanted, it never happened. I was onto the next assignment and the next round of work travel.

I was so glad I'd taken the opportunity to travel when I had and had been able to see so much of Belgium. I felt like I got to know the country more like a local and less like a tourist.

I only wished I had found a way to fit Amsterdam into my schedule. Not seeing it felt like a major oversight and was a good reminder that there isn't always a "later."

CHAPTER 15

DENMARK / SWEDEN:
BETWEEN THE CITIES

About a year after I'd stopped traveling to Antwerp, I received a seemingly impossible deadline: five months to build a whole new website from scratch. My team and I worked from one of our offices in New York City, so I was leaving home at 6:00 a.m. every day to beat the traffic and getting home around 8 p.m. After the site went live on time and I made sure things were stable, I needed to get away. It was October, and I'd worked straight through the summer with no break. I was fried.

I asked my husband if he was up for a trip. He said, "You go." He knew I needed the time to regroup and recharge. Our son was in college by then, so he couldn't go either.

While I had done several solo weekends (or Saturdays) as add-ons to work, especially in Belgium, I hadn't planned a whole trip by myself since before I was married.

I usually do most of the travel planning for the family, but this time I didn't have to take anyone else's preferences into account. I could literally go anywhere I wanted. It was so freeing, so rejuvenating, and that was before I even stepped on the plane.

The thing about Europe is that it's easy to hit the capitals or big cities and miss everything else in between. I suppose that's true anywhere, but it seems especially so in Europe, where so many great cities are close together and easy to reach by train or on cheap flights (Ryanair is shockingly inexpensive once you're in Europe). However, my favorite places to travel are usually the smaller towns and the countryside. Even though I regret not going to Amsterdam when I worked in Antwerp, I would go to Delft and Gouda again if I had the chance.

When I was planning the trip, I opted for Denmark and Sweden—honestly only because the flights were cheap and I hadn't been there before. I booked my flights into Copenhagen and out of Stockholm, but I didn't want to just spend my time in the cities. I wanted to see as much as possible in between.

I had a Skagen watch at the time, and a friend from Denmark commented on it. She taught me how to pronounce *Skagen* (no "g" sound—it's more like *Skein*) and, most importantly, that it's an actual place in Denmark.

Skagen is at the very northern tip of Denmark, and it sounded absolutely beautiful, remote, and unique, and there were also car ferries to Sweden from there. It sounded like the perfect way to get to my next destination without missing all of the places in between.

Next, I needed to figure out the logistics, one of my

favorite parts of traveling. It's problem solving and puzzles on a much larger scale. I found out that if I rented a car in Denmark, I couldn't drop it off in Sweden. Since my flight home was from Stockholm, that wouldn't work. If I rented a car in Sweden, I could drop it off in a different city in Sweden, but I could still drive it in Denmark. The last puzzle piece dropped into place when I realized that Malmo, Sweden was just across a bridge from Copenhagen. I could rent the car there, drive it back through Denmark, then ferry to Sweden and drop the car back off in Stockholm. *Perfect.*

I flew into Copenhagen. It was fall, the leaves were changing, and it was so peaceful and beautiful. I thought fall should be high tourist season, but of course it wasn't. The weather called for a hoodie and a jacket, but I didn't mind. And yes, I took the obligatory selfies in front of the picturesque Nyhavn, with its slender, steep-roofed, multicolored houses squeezed together on both sides of a narrow canal. The boardwalk in front of the houses was filled with tourists, cafes, and food carts. Tourist boats and fishing vessels lined the canal. Every picture you've ever seen of Copenhagen has probably been taken there.

But Nyhavn wasn't my favorite part of Copenhagen. I wandered the winding streets, losing myself and dodging cyclists whenever I drifted onto a bike path, which seemed to happen about every third step I took. I crossed bridges over canals, walked back between apartment buildings, and wondered what it would be like to live there. I didn't go into any of the museums or shops. I just wanted to wander, so I did.

On my last day in Copenhagen, I went to an amusement park called Tivoli because there were advertisements for it everywhere, and it had been decorated with a Halloween theme. It was actually more fall-themed than Halloween—more pumpkins, fewer witches. Pumpkins lined walkways and were piled decoratively. There were pumpkin-shaped lanterns hanging from arches that guided visitors into the park. The leaves ranged from crimson to gold, as if I'd been dropped into Vermont at the height of leaf-peeping season.

It's not like amusement parks in the U.S. Yes, there were rides, but it felt more like a park, with trees and open spaces, where some rides just happened to be tucked in the corner. There were also nice shops and restaurants.

I wasn't interested in the rides, so I went into a few of the shops, looking for presents to bring home for Jon and Jono. The shops were more like farmers markets, garden centers, and high-end boutiques rather than the plastic souvenir and T-shirt stands of U.S. amusement parks. Still, nothing struck me as a must-have or as something they would love.

I stuck my head in a few cafés, looking for a place with the right vibe to get a cup of coffee. I brought my iPad with me so I could read my book whenever I was in a café or at lunch.

I stopped in my tracks when I saw a campfire set up outside a cafe, and a few people were drinking wine and roasting marshmallows. That's just what I wanted! I sat in front of the fire with a glass of wine and a marshmallow, and I read. It was just cool enough to make the fire feel magical, but not so chilly that I got cold. I ordered a second glass of wine and another set of marshmallows. It was one of the best moments of the whole trip.

After Copenhagen, I took a train to Malmo. Europe is so well-connected that it was easy to do. I walked a few blocks from the train station to the car rental agency in Malmo. The car rental agency was a counter inside a convenience store—like an Avis tucked into a 7-Eleven. I stocked up on sodas and snacks while I was there and set out for Denmark right after I got my keys.

Another thing about Europe—driving is expensive, which is another reason it's so easy to focus only on the main cities.

The bridge between Malmo and Copenhagen is no simple bridge. It's called the Oresund Bridge, and it soars about five miles over the Oresund Strait before dropping down into the Drogden tunnel for another couple of miles. I knew it was a toll bridge, but I didn't realize it would cost THAT much—it was about fifty dollars! I thought the New York–Hudson River crossings were bad, paying thirteen dollars every time I went through the Lincoln Tunnel to get to work for my project in NYC. *But fifty dollars?!* Still it wasn't like I was going to turn back, since I had the whole journey through Denmark planned. I coughed up the money and kept going.

Google gave me two options to get to Skagen—the long way over several more bridges or the short way with a ferry, both of which were supposed to take the exact same amount of time. Having just crossed a five-mile bridge, I was wary of bridge tolls. And since there weren't many car ferries where I lived, I opted for the ferry crossing.

The thing about estimated times for driving versus ferries is that you have much more control when driving. If you arrive at the ferry station even a minute after the last boat has left, you have to wait. No one cares if you're in a hurry. The ferry station runs on its own time and waits for no man (or woman).

Because I had just missed the last one when I arrived and because I had driven up without any understanding of the schedule, I was the first car to line up for the next ferry. It was confusing, but it was one more puzzle to solve. I successfully paid and got in line, then pulled out my iPad to read. What else was I going to do? It's freeing in a way, because there's nothing you can do but relax and wait.

Although the only reason I went to Skagen was because of my watch, it was so worth it. Not the town itself, though it was cute, with a ton of shops and cafés. The real draw was the Skagen peninsula— called Skagen Odde—which juts out to the north.

First, I don't know what it was about the light, but it was soft, warm, and welcoming. I got out of my car several times, hiking across dunes on the approach to the peninsula, trying to capture the perfect picture—the perfect view of the ocean and the sunlight. I've heard that Skagen attracts artists who can make a whole career out of trying to capture the light, like an addict always chasing that perfect high.

Second, at the tip of the peninsula, the Baltic Sea and the North Sea meet. They're different colors, and you can see where the blue and the gray touch but stay separate, no matter how many waves roll them together, like oil and balsamic. I don't know how long I stared at the waves, willing them to fuse, knowing they'd separate back to their original sides. I took a few pictures, trying to capture the blues and grays, but just as I had failed to capture the light on the dunes, I couldn't capture the two seas meeting.

Third, there were seals. Real seals, just hanging out enjoying the day, trying to get some sunshine to warm their bellies. They were just lying there flopped on the sand, completely unaffected by the people milling around them.

I was surprised by how many people were out on this tiny spit of land at the end of Denmark. I'll give everyone props for not bothering the seals, though. Everyone was taking pictures, but no one was touching or teasing them.

After the peninsula, I made my way to the dock for the ferry to Sweden. The ferry I'd taken to get to Skagen had been a small, flat boat with only about twenty cars (though certainly bigger and sturdier than the ferry our bus crossed on in the Amazon region of Peru). This one was enormous. There were semi-trucks and cars all lined up to get on, and we were all being loaded into the belly of the beast. But it was an international ferry, so what did I expect? Honestly,

I had no idea what it would be like.

After the 3-hour-plus journey across the sea, which I'd spent in a lounge reading on my iPad, I returned to my little red car, parked in the hold, squeezed between semis. After the ferry docked, I zipped down the ramp which wound around several times to get to street level. I felt like a race car driver. I loved it and would almost go back to Denmark just to drive off the ferry again.

Sweden was also at peak fall foliage, but the air was brisk, so I was forced to wear my puffy jacket. I stayed in Gothenburg that night, then took another ferry—just a small passenger ferry, no zipping around in my car this time!—out to some of the islands in the archipelago around Gothenburg.

I had heard the word archipelago in geography class, but I don't think I'd ever really understood what it meant. I'd certainly never been to one. An archipelago is a string of islands, and there were islands scattered all around Gothenburg. Some were so small there was only one house on them. The idea of your own private island might be nice in that beautiful fall weather . . . but in the winter? Does anyone live there then?

I hopped off the ferry on one of the larger islands. And by "hopped" I mean I carefully studied the ferry schedule so I would know exactly when the next ferry was returning, making sure I wouldn't be stranded on the beautiful island forever. According to the schedule, I had a few hours before the ferry came back—like a city bus on its rounds, but with islands and water and no other way to escape.

The island was several miles across, with a café near the ferry stop and some roads leading into a residential district. I hiked the opposite way of the residential district, looking for the path to a hill that I'd read about in my guidebook. That hike was my reason for picking that island.

I hiked to the top of the hill which allowed me to see

across the whole island, with its rocky shorelines and lots more little islands scattered out in the ocean. It was so beautiful, quiet, and peaceful. I was the only one on top of the hill, and I was glad to be traveling in the off season to have it all to myself.

After visiting Gothenburg and the archipelago, I drove across Sweden toward Stockholm. The road was lined with aspens, their yellow leaves glittering and winking, welcoming me, and whisking away the remains of my work stress.

It was only about four hours to Stockholm, so I planned to drive there directly, stopping only for necessities. I stopped at a gas station and tried to pay at the pump. Everything was in Swedish, and there was no button to change languages on the pump. I thought I could figure it out. *How hard could it be?*

I put in my card and followed a series of prompts, but then I got hung up on a question, and the pump wouldn't activate. I tried again and got hung up at the same place.

Finally, I went inside the gas station and asked if anyone spoke English. After having traveled for over a week, it felt like a silly question because everyone seemed to speak English in both Denmark and Sweden. I couldn't say more than one word before everyone would switch to English. The clerk in the gas station shook his head at me but then called out to someone else. *Ooh boy.* I pointed to the pump and my car outside, and finally a young man followed me out. He spoke English but was definitely not comfortable with it. I walked to my car and the pump, and I restarted the process with the young man watching me. When I got to the unknown prompt, he said, "Number."

"What number?"

He pointed to the number on top of the pump. I was at pump number five.

Seriously? Stupid computer on the stupid pump didn't

know what number pump it was on? I designed and built computer systems for a living at work . . . computers should be smart enough not to force users to answer stupid questions. I shook my head, hit number five, and the pump was activated. *Errrgh!* I thanked the young man, and he retreated back into the gas station.

The hotel I reserved in Stockholm turned out to be more like a retreat center than a hotel. It felt like the facility in Chicago where I was sent by my company for training every couple of years. It sat right on the riverbank, with a long walking and biking path alongside. It was peaceful—the perfect spot for a retreat center. The cost was reasonable too.

There was a retreat in session, so I felt like the odd man out. Everyone gathered in the dining room for breakfast and dinner together. Instead of trying to fight for a table, I escaped and went into town.

I didn't have that much time in Stockholm having spent so much time driving through Denmark and Sweden to get there, so I skipped the ABBA Museum—surely to the everlasting disappointment of one of my best friends who is a die-hard ABBA superfan. I went to the old town historical district and wandered the winding cobblestone lanes, old cathedrals, and cafés.

Let me just say . . . Sweden had the most amazing cinnamon bun in the world. Sorry, Grandma—and the family cinnamon roll recipe, which has been fiercely guarded and made with religious fervor every holiday. The cinnamon is so strong in these buns it's almost spicy, with big chunks of sugar on top that add a crunch. The cinnamon buns aren't rolled but braided or twisted. Honestly, it makes me want to take flights connecting through the Stockholm airport just to have a cinnamon bun en route to wherever. Flying from New Jersey to California . . . is there a way to go through Stockholm?

I went to Denmark and Sweden to take a much-needed rest from work, and when I think back on that trip, I am filled with the same sense of calm and peace that I found at the campfire in Tivoli gardens with my marshmallows and wine, driving through the twinkling aspens on the lonely highway between Gothenburg and Stockholm, and walking along the river walkway at the retreat center in Stockholm. Remembering hiking on the quiet hill overlooking the archipelago near Gothenburg and Skagen's effusive light will always bring me back to those moments of peace and renewal.

CHAPTER 16

INDIA:
IT WASN'T THE FOOD

In 2012, I was going to India for work for the first time to meet my India-based team members and to introduce them to my clients who were also making the trip. I was really excited to go—I'd always wanted to travel to India, ever since I was a cadet.

But I was afraid of not being able to eat there and wondered if I would find anything I'd like. I had avoided Indian food since I was in Nepal. After all of our food was doused with curry powder for three weeks straight, I just couldn't face it.

Also, everyone told me that traveling to India was no joke

health-wise and that I needed to go to a doctor for immunizations and malaria pills. I made an appointment with the same doctor my clients were seeing.

The doctor gave me a hard time because I'd been so busy with work that I hadn't had a check-up—or any of the normal preventative screenings—in a while. I also found out I had rosacea, which made my face red and breakout. I knew my face was a mess, but I didn't know what it was and hadn't had time to get it checked. I figured it was stress-related acne or something. *Who knew?*

He handed over a handful of prescriptions for the screenings and malaria pills and gave me the recommended vaccines. "What kind of a doctor would I be if I only wrote you a prescription for malaria pills and didn't take care of your overall health?" he asked. He wasn't wrong. Thoroughly chastised, I went back to work and started taking my malaria pills.

My colleagues and clients warned me that they had always gotten sick in India and told me not to drink the water and to eat only in the nicer hotels. One of my bosses had recently been to India and told me he brought packages of Oreos and granola bars and ate those almost exclusively. That sounded terrible to me. He admitted that even with all the precautions, he'd still gotten sick as a dog the last time—after ordering a hamburger at his super-luxury hotel. I raised my eyebrows at him. I hadn't been to India yet, but I knew better than that. How could he have possibly thought a hamburger would be a good idea? Cows are sacred in India, so beef isn't really eaten there.

I was picked up at the airport in Bangalore by one of my team members who took me to the hotel our clients selected. The ITC Gardenia in Bangalore was the most gorgeous hotel I'd ever been to. In the middle of the hotel was a reflection pool with a gazebo bar at its center, connected by walkways. The courtyard around it was open to the sky, and the most amazing breeze greeted me as I walked out to the gazebo. There were also scents wafting through the hotel—floral, with an undertone of spice—creating a vibe of relaxation and peace. To this day, I have never stayed in a hotel quite as enchanting.

Driving in from the airport, India reminded me a lot of Peru, where I'd been over a dozen times during various mission trips. The streets were lined with squat concrete storefronts with corrugated tin roofing, and the traffic was overwhelming. The only real differences were the writing on the signs (since India uses its own unique script), the women's traditional outfits, the thousands of motorcycles, and a few wandering cows on the roads. Otherwise, India felt very familiar and less foreign than my colleagues led me to expect. I figured if I lived by the same hygiene rules I used on all of my missions to Peru, I'd be fine.

I arrived late Friday night and had Saturday to get acclimated to the time zone (10½ hours ahead of the East Coast). On Sunday, there was an excursion to a temple with the client.

The hotel, like most hotels in India, had a full restaurant. The breakfast buffet was expansive, offering an array of Indian breakfast foods—savory soups, curries, and rice. It reminded me of going to the Korean side of the hotel for breakfast on our three-day honeymoon and deciding fish soup wasn't for us. I wasn't ready to have curry for breakfast.

They also offered all the Western options: omelets, baked beans (unusual for breakfast in the U.S. but very common in the UK and Europe), sausages, and tons of pastries. There was also a whole section of sliced meats and cheese, sliced vegetables, and piles on piles of glistening fruit.

I've heard some people say that in luxury hotels in India with fancy chefs, the fruit is safe to eat. Maybe, maybe not.

I followed the rule I learned in Peru: if it's raw, I don't touch it. The only fruit I would ever touch there is a banana I peeled myself.

I've seen the consequences when people aren't cautious, like on our second trip to Nepal when Jono bragged about his iron stomach, ate a sliced cucumber, and ended up sick for two days while we trekked.

I skipped all the fruit and stuck with an omelet, baked beans, and a croissant.

I didn't touch the water, either. I made sure there was no ice in my Diet Coke and I didn't brush my teeth with the water. And, there's no way would I ever drink juice which is a combo of raw fruit and questionable water. On our first trip to Peru, when Jono was about ten, he drank some juice he was offered and spent two days sick in bed.

On one mission trip, some people bought popsicles from a street-side vendor—basically bacteria on a stick. No way I'd eat one of those! In Peru, I visited a patient's house in a shantytown, and she had rented a refrigerator to make popsicles and sell on the street. Her house had dirt floors, and the water she used was trucked in weekly and stored in a barrel. *Um, no thank you!*

Later that afternoon, a friend and colleague of mine—Srinivas, who also happened to be in Bangalore for work—texted to see if I wanted to meet up with him. It sounded more fun than hanging out in my hotel room. The ironic part is that Srinivas is also from New Jersey and only lives an hour away from me, but with work and family, we'd been too busy to see each other in years.

I met Srinivas at his hotel, and then we hopped a taxi to a shopping district. Srinivas was originally from India, but he and his parents had immigrated to the U.S. when he was a child. His wife Myrna had a similar story. Jon and I were lucky enough to be invited to their wedding—a lavish affair by U.S. standards. Their celebration started at 10 a.m. on Easter Sunday (they'd booked the date and got a discount, not knowing Easter was such a big thing) with the groom riding in on a white horse, surrounded by his family and friends, in a hotel parking lot. The wedding featured multiple ceremonies, two meals, Bollywood-style dancing, and lasted well into the night. By Indian standards, a multi-day wedding with hundreds of guests is normal, so it was probably pretty conservative by comparison.

Srinivas and I went into a store lined with shelves of brightly colored fabrics, with a large glass counter and chairs sat neatly in front of it. We sat and were served tea. Srinivas was in his element, and he started pointing at various fabrics. The staff would bring over a stack of fabric which turned out to be women's *kurtis*—tunic-style dresses paired with slacks. Srinivas glanced at a few, then casually pointed to a different stack.

Once he found a few that he liked, he took pictures and sent them to Myrna to see if she was interested. She was originally from Bangalore, so shopping for her felt like a way of supporting her even though she wasn't with us. I marveled at the way Srinivas sat calmly and pointed. The shop attendants brought each new stack of *kurtis* over to Srinivas. Soon piles of *kurtis* covered the counter in front of us.

If I were there on my own, I couldn't have done that. I would have walked the store myself and pulled out individual items I liked, and I'd put them back where I found them. I'm much more of a self-service gal, and this full-service shop (and full-service culture) would have given me anxiety.

As it was, I wasn't the one shopping, so I could sit back, relax, drink my tea, and watch the process.

Eventually, he bought a few items for Myrna (with her approval), and we headed back to our respective hotels. We promised to get together back in NJ soon.

On Sunday, I drove with the client to Mysore Palace. When I say "drove," I mean I sat in the back seat of my client's rental car, which came with a driver. There was no way any of us were going to try to drive in India. The driver and the client were in the front seat. One of my competitors (from a competing consulting company) sat in the back seat with me.

I had done no research on Mysore Palace, so I didn't know what to expect from the journey. I jumped at the chance to go anyway, partly because I was not letting my competitor get an advantage by spending the day with the client alone, and also because I was happy to get out of Bangalore and see the countryside.

India is a special kind of chaos. As I said, cows are sacred, so they will often wander the streets. And these are not Bessie-the-cow kinds of cows. These are enormous beasts with humps on their necks and big horns. I called them "Brahma bulls," and I might or might not have been accurate. They walked alongside the road, laid on sidewalks, and ate trash. They seemed docile, but I never tried to pet one to test my theory.

There were so many motorcycles! Some had whole families stacked on them—dad driving, mom in the rear, and one or two kids tucked in the middle. Some had multiple men or women heading to work together. The women's saris and sashes trailed behind them, flying like sails in the wind. Men carried bushels of wares to and from the market, the basket perched on the seat behind them or on a wide footstep of the motorcycle.

There were almost as many moto-rickshaws—three-wheel motorcycles with a frame built over them to seat passengers behind the driver.

There were also huge, colorful trucks; people walking on the side of the road; taxis and cars; and everything in between. Lanes on the road seemed more like suggestions, as vehicles weaved in and out of traffic as fluidly as a river. It was chaos. It proved impossible to see everything and even more impossible to capture, even on video. The drive to Mysore was two to three hours, so there was a lot to take in.

Mysore Palace itself looked iconically Indian, similar in style to pictures I'd seen of the Taj Mahal: rounded cupolas atop towers and turrets, arched windows and doors, and arches leading into courtyards, all surrounded by vast gardens. The tallest tower had a golden dome.

Though the location had served as a palace for royals of the Kingdom of Mysore since the 14th century, previous palaces burned down. The current palace was completed in 1912 under the direction of a British architect who incorporated elements from Rajasthani, Islamic, and Gothic styles.

It looked distinctly Indian, but it was a reminder to me of the British influence (colonialism) which ended in 1947. . . not all that long ago.

Afterward, we went to a restaurant near the Palace for lunch. There was another huge buffet laid out, which seemed to be the thing to do in India. They only served Indian food—no Western-style foods.

The default in India is vegetarian. Not only are there a ton of vegetarian options at every meal, but everything is also clearly labeled: a green square for vegetarian and a red square for non-vegetarian. Even cans of Diet Coke had a green square.

In the cafeteria at work later that week, I saw that even the microwaves were labeled "Veg" and "Non-Veg," so that meat-eaters don't contaminate the Veg-only microwaves! *I loved that!*

I had no idea what any of the food was, and the labels meant nothing to me, so I took a tiny spoonful of each green-squared item and arranged them on my plate like paint on a palette.

There were a few "Nope's!" that I tried but didn't like. I don't know what they were. There were also a few things I did like, and I went back for a second scoop of the good ones.

I did that the whole time I was in India because we almost always ate at a buffet, and there was always a huge array of dishes, which seemed different every time, though I finally started finding some foods that I liked which were common enough that they were usually included in the buffet. After lunch, we rode back to Bangalore. The competitor and I argued in the back seat, reminding me of family road trips with my brother. We compared our consulting companies and careers, then swapped military stories, each trying to one-up the other. He'd been in the Army. My client looked back and said, "There sure is a lot of testosterone back there."

The next morning—and for the whole week I was in India—I had a rental car and driver dedicated to take me wherever I wanted to go. It was too far for one of my team members to escort me, since the drive could take up to two hours each way, depending on traffic.

The driver took me to the office complex where my team worked. It was enormous! It had four buildings, each with six to eight floors, and this was just one of nine office complexes.

One of my team leads came to get me from the lobby and brought me up to where the team worked. There were people streaming everywhere, heading to their offices or meetings. After nearly colliding into someone in the hallways or on the sidewalks for the third or fourth time, I realized that since Indians drive on the left (another legacy of the British), they also walk on the left.

Where my instinct is to always move to the right—"guide right," as my father taught me—the cultural norm of people in left-side-driving countries is to move to the left. When we both do what is customary for us, we walk into each other. I had to keep reminding myself, "Guide left," whenever I went up stairs or down a hallway.

I spent some time with my team leaders first. I spent a lot of time on the phone with them, but you never truly know someone until you can look them in the eye and shake their hand.

Then, they took me to meet the team. You can picture how people are working and imagine the office environment, but you don't really know until you see it. Despite being on the other side of the world and seeming like it would be so different, my team was spread out in a huge room full of cubes. The same kind of "cube farms" that my teams worked in back in the U.S. The client's logo and the same goals, objectives, and timelines were on the wall—just like the other office. It was *my* team! It filled me with such joy to see everyone and understand where they worked.

Every night, I went to dinner with a different part of the team so that by the end of the week, I had spent time with everyone. I tried to meet each person individually, asking them about their role and fun facts about themselves and continually shifting my seat so I could connect with everyone. Outside of work, some people were musicians, cartoonists, writers, played sports, and spent time with their families. I was energized by their enthusiasm, by how much they liked the work they were doing and how creative they were at solving problems.

One morning at breakfast, my hotel gave me a little card that said, "Happy International Women's Day" (IWD). I was shocked—I'd never seen anything like that in the U.S., where IWD has mostly become a day for corporate events and is not generally celebrated. In India, it was definitely a day to celebrate!

At the office, on IWD, all the women wore the most gorgeous saris versus the more pragmatic *kurtis* they wore other days. I wore a navy-blue suit and felt like a shadow among all of the women in their beautiful, vibrant colors.

I met with the women on the team, and we talked about life and leadership. I was so happy to be a part of their women's day.

On my last night in Bangalore, as I was ferried back to my gorgeous hotel after dinner, I laughed at the malaria pills I was taking. I don't think I ever saw a mosquito, so I figured my risk level for malaria was about zero. After that first trip, I never went back to the infectious-disease doctor, especially if he was going to lecture me, and I never took malaria pills again.

As I headed toward the airport on the morning of my departure back to the U.S., I told my driver that I wanted to stop at Starbucks. There was a new one that just opened, and it didn't look too far out of the way. Of course, this was Bangalore where traffic was horrific, so I should have known it wouldn't be that easy. The Starbucks website gave only the street name—Mahatma Ghandi Road—no numbers. My driver did an Indian head bob, a simultaneous vertical and side-to-side motion that can mean many things. This time, I think it meant, "Okay, crazy lady. I'll try."

When we got to the road, I knew we were in the right area because I started seeing shops like Nike and Levi's. Starbucks would fit right in there. It was about 9:30 a.m., and we drove slowly up the street. The driver had no idea what Starbucks was, so he didn't know what to look for. I tried to describe their green logo. We didn't see anything.

Finally, after doing a U-turn to go down the other side of the road, the driver saw a coffee shop and stopped. It wasn't Starbucks, but he said he'd go ask the owner if they knew where Starbucks was.

It wasn't about the coffee, though I do enjoy the coffee at Starbucks. I was still collecting Starbucks location mugs, and who knew if I'd ever make it back to India again? I had to try to get a mug.

The driver came back out of the coffee shop and pointed directly across the street. It was tucked back a little from the road, so we hadn't seen it when we cruised by on that side of the street earlier.

There were three lanes with five rows of cars, motorcycles, moto-taxis, and everything else zipping by on each side of a boulevard. It was not easy to drive through or to turn around. We couldn't just drive across the street.

"Wait here," I said, and started across the street Frogger-style. I made it across, only to discover it didn't open until 10 a.m. What kind of coffee shop opens at ten?

I made my way back across the street. My driver was probably frantic—what would happen to him if his passenger was hit by a car?

We decided to wait for it to open. There was another Starbucks, but it was well out of the way and would probably make me miss my flight. The driver said no to that one.

When 10 a.m. rolled around, I ran across again. This time, the driver came with me, leaving his car parked in the driveway of the other coffee shop. He was smart and figured some of the other tourists he'd drive would want to go to Starbucks. It was exactly what you'd expect, with the usual Starbucks vibes—except they had India mugs!

There are many more Starbucks locations in India now, and I've gotten mugs from a few cities since then. That first India mug is still one of my favorites, mostly because I had to Frogger across the road four times to get it.

I went to India for work several times after that first trip, visiting Mumbai, Pune, and Hyderabad, in addition to returning to Bangalore. I learned to enjoy the Indian food while I was there, but I don't seek it out when I'm in the U.S. I consider it a victory that after all my times in India, I've never gotten sick.

I had worried about hygiene and what I'd be able to eat, but the reality was that it wasn't the food that mattered. For me, India was about getting to spend time with my friend Srinivas and see a country I had wanted to visit ever since I was a cadet at the Academy. I also spent time with my client and kept my competitor from getting a foothold.

What really made the trip worthwhile was meeting my team and getting to understand them better. I was a better leader after that visit—learning how to build relationships with my India-based teams and realizing that they were just as much a part of my team as anyone else, no matter which slice of the earth they lived on.

CHAPTER 17

SINGAPORE:
WEEKEND VACATION

On one of my work trips to India, I had to be there for two weeks, which meant I had a free weekend in the middle. I didn't feel like spending it in Hyderabad because it was about 1,000 degrees there at the time. Even though I hadn't done much sightseeing in India—besides Mysore Palace—and still hadn't seen the Taj Mahal, I just wasn't excited to do it on that trip.

I had plane tickets to Sri Lanka which was only a two-hour flight away. However, when I arrived in India, there had just been a bombing in the capital of Sri Lanka, the Easter bombing. Colombo was in chaos. I still thought about going, but it just didn't feel safe. *Sorry Sri Lanka, not this time.*

After work, I pulled up Google maps and the Kayak app to look for some other nearby places to visit. I'd already been to Nepal. Pakistan was not an option. I needed time to prepare for Bhutan, and it deserved more than a weekend.

Considering I only had a weekend, Singapore seemed to be the only reasonable option. It was a longer flight—four hours—but tickets were cheap, and Singapore is small enough that I would be able to see quite a bit in two days.

Friday night after work, I stepped onto a red-eye and landed in Singapore on Saturday morning at 6:00 a.m. local time. Singapore was a full 12-hour time zone shift from the East Coast and another hour and a half ahead of India, so my body wasn't ready for it to be morning. I was also exhausted, which didn't help.

The previous week, I flew into Mumbai and spent a few days there with my team, then drove three hours to Pune to see another part of my team before flying to Hyderabad. I would fly to Bangalore on Monday. I was also working triple duty: the shift with my team in India, taking the team to dinner, and then working an evening shift with multiple meetings with my team back in the U.S.

I still had another week left in India, which would be filled with the same triple-shift work, plus a client visit. Having a weekend in Singapore without any meetings or obligations was going to feel like a vacation.

Arriving in Singapore felt like stepping through a portal into an emerald oasis, a welcome respite for an India-weary traveler. I took a taxi to the hotel, and it was the most peaceful ride ever. Where traffic in India was overwhelming—drivers with one hand on the wheel and one on the horn, and roads a scene of insane chaos—Singapore was orderly and calm. No horns, no cows, no trash. Sheer serenity! Some might say Singapore takes orderliness and cleanliness to an extreme—they have a nationwide ban against chewing gum in order to keep the sidewalks clean.

I stayed at the Westin. Since I had a Titanium Marriott status from traveling so much for work, they let me check in at 7:00 a.m. and go to the breakfast buffet that morning! It was heaven. During the last week in India, because I had to be so careful with food and hygiene, I hadn't had any fruit. In Singapore, I went straight to the mounds of fresh fruit at the breakfast buffet. They had mango, dragon fruit, and pineapple, and I ate as much as I wanted.

In India, I couldn't just wander around on foot—partly because the roads are so hazardous, and partly because I was working all the time. My team escorted me from the hotel to the office, to dinner, and back, so I never had a chance to explore on my own. In Singapore, I set out on foot right after breakfast. It felt so good to just walk and see what I wanted without having to be driven by my team or worry about crazy traffic.

I had pictured Singapore as a city of wall-to-wall white skyscrapers filling every square inch of the island. The image was wrong, of course. While there were skyscrapers, Singapore is so much more interesting and unique than I imagined.

From my hotel, I could see the Gardens by the Bay, which are structures that look like towering tropical trees that light up at night. I had seen images of them on the internet and was so excited to see them, I beelined straight for them and wandered through the park to where they stood. Honestly, they were less exciting to walk by during the day than I'd hoped. It was like standing at the base of a telephone pole and looking up to see the "flower" at the top, which looked like a tree in the winter with bare branches and no leaves. I think they're better viewed from afar or at night when they're lit up.

I wandered across the Helix bridge, with its spiraling, braided metal structure, and saw the ArtScience Museum, shaped like a lotus flower. It felt like I was walking through a sci-fi movie set. In the distance, I saw the Marina Sands Hotel—the iconic hotel with three towers topped by a platform with a swimming pool and probably some amazing rooftop bars, but I had too many other things to see, so I didn't make it there.

I left the ultra-modern zone and wandered into a multistory greenhouse pavilion filled with orchids. It was like a zoo for flowers. A path wound through the pavilion, starting on the lower level and spiraling up to the top stories. A waterfall cascaded 50 to 80 feet.

There were orchids everywhere, of every variety—white with pink, pink with white, red, orange, yellow speckled with purple, yellow with purple stripes, and deep purple. They ranged from the size of my pinkie to bigger than my fist. I had no idea there were so many kinds of orchids.

After wandering through the park, I walked through the heart of the city, aiming for the older, historical neighborhoods. I passed a few open areas that looked like mall food courts. I went through them but didn't get anything to eat. I was still full from the breakfast buffet, and as a vegetarian, I always find it hard to know what's okay to eat. I'm also not the most adventurous eater. After I watched *Crazy Rich Asians*—and spent the whole movie saying, "I was there!"—I realized I'd probably missed out, since food stalls in Singapore are definitely a must-do.

I knew I had made it to the older areas when I passed by a huge old banyan tree that made me want to sit down, lean against it, and read, except I didn't have a book or my iPad with me. While I loved the modern area, I felt myself relax once I reached the older neighborhoods. The streets were tiny and charming, lined with beautifully maintained traditional homes painted in bright blues and oranges, with intricate wooden shutters and ornate façades.

I wandered around, choosing the narrowest streets and alleys to walk through, winding through the different neighborhoods until I ran out of steam.

I ducked into a small grocery store and bought some Coke Zero and a few snacks—I passed on the "salt and seaweed" flavored Pringles. It was late afternoon by then, and I was on the opposite side of the city, so I took a taxi back to the hotel.

Since I only had one night in Singapore, I had to decide if I wanted to see the Gardens by the Bay at night when they were all lit up or go to the Night Safari, which I'd found online. I picked the latter because it seemed so unusual.

The Night Safari is a zoo that you go to at night to see nocturnal animals like bats and Tasmanian Devils. It sounded so cool! A ton of people were there, waiting in long lines just after dark. I waited for the time on my timed-entry ticket and then jumped onto a bus filled with other tourists.

As the bus wound through the park, it was hard to see much at first in the dark. Gradually, my eyes adjusted, and I was able to see the animals the bus driver pointed out as we drove past fences housing larger animals like hippos, lions, and deer.

After twenty or thirty minutes on the bus, we were allowed to get off and walk by ourselves. The trail wound past exhibits of smaller creatures like wallabies and leopards, and, just like any other zoo, you could move at your own pace.

My favorite was the bat house, like a birdhouse but filled with bats—some as big as dogs with wings (flying foxes). I loved watching them swoop through the air and crawl upside down on the roof of the cage. I could have stayed there the whole night watching them, but my weekend vacation was passing quickly, and I had to get back to the hotel. I hadn't slept much on the red-eye flight from India the previous night, and after walking all day, I was worn ragged.

The next morning, I was walking back to the hotel from a nearby Starbucks, where I had dashed over to get coffee and a mug! Two middle-aged men approached me, one wearing a Boston Celtics T-shirt. The T-shirt had caught my eye, but there are so many tourists in Singapore, I didn't think anything of it. One of them asked, "You're Tauni, right?"

I was so shocked I don't think I said anything. Maybe I nodded. Maybe not. Maybe I blinked like a deer in headlights.

They followed up with, "Do you know us?"

What a diabolical question! Clearly, I had no idea who they were. No one but my husband even knew I was in Singapore. I had no idea who they were.

It turned out they were clients from my current project, which was at a global firm. They had met with people on my team to provide requirements for the system we were building. They knew me since I was the lead of my consulting team, even though I had never met with them personally. Once they introduced themselves, I said, "Oh, what are you doing here?"

"Working," they said, as if I'd asked the dumbest question ever. Indeed—their global business took them everywhere, so it made sense.

"What are YOU doing here?" they asked, as if they thought I was playing hooky.

"I am in India for two weeks and just came down for the weekend."

We all laughed about the small world and went our separate ways.

It's really, really, frightening how small the world is. You think, *I'm halfway across the world, no one will know me.* If I was talking on my cell phone about work or home or anything else, no one could possibly know or care. But you just don't know in today's global world. You could run into someone you know anywhere.

I had seen so much of Singapore on the first day that I took a much slower pace on Sunday.

I went to Chinatown, which is just like it sounds, with its temples, restaurants, and shops featuring Chinese products, culture, and food. I've also heard there is a "Little India" in Singapore that is so much like India you feel like you're actually there. I skipped it since I would be back on the plane to Hyderabad in a few hours.

By early afternoon, it was time to head to the airport for my flight back to India.

I had a multiple-entry visa for India, otherwise I would have had to stay in the country for the weekend. Even so, when I landed back in India, I had to show my visa papers several times and point out the multiple-entry part. I was sweating pretty badly—and not because of the 1,000-degree heat—when they finally let me through.

How terrible would it have been if I hadn't been let back into India for my client meetings? Especially when I'd already been caught "playing hooky" on the weekend in Singapore.

Some people have told me that the thought of a whirlwind trip like that would exhaust them. But for me, exploring a new part of the world is like a buffet for my brain. Getting to explore a new country—figuring out where to go, what to see, and being inspired by marvels like the orchid pavilion and the Night Zoo—fills me up and renews me in a way nothing else can.

Getting to explore allowed me to focus on something other than work. It let me to breathe in a way that only travel allows. I had a productive second week in India, refreshed after my weekend "vacation" to Singapore.

CHAPTER 18

WALES:
BUT IT SHOULD BE

I was in London for the week for client work, and since this was only going to be a one-time trip, I wasn't going to waste an opportunity to explore.

I only had Saturday free—my flight home was early Sunday morning.

I considered my options:

1. I had enjoyed working in London—I especially loved Pret's "Posh Cheddar and Pickle" sandwiches—but I'd been to London a couple of times before, both for work and solo, so didn't feel the need to spend more time there.

2. Scotland and Ireland were too far for one day.
3. I could take a train to Northern England... Liverpool? Manchester? Both were possible.

Then I thought of Wales. I had never been to Wales, and apparently, I'm a quarter Welsh on my father's side, so—Wales it is!

On Friday night at the pub with my coworkers, I told them I was going to Wales the next day. Just to see how they would respond, I threw out the question, "Would visiting Wales count as having been to a new country?" There was a wide range of people at the table: someone from the U.S., a New Zealander living in London, a person from London, and another from Scotland. It was like dropping chunks of meat into a shark tank—everyone attacked the question.

The colleague from London, of course, said Wales is not a country, just a part of the UK.

The people from Scotland and New Zealand were advocating for Wales to be seen as separate.

The other U.S. person said, logically, if I counted Puerto Rico as a separate country, then I could count Wales separately as well. If not, I couldn't. I agreed with his logic. On that basis, Wales was not a country.

Someone raised the question, "Do they compete in the Olympics separately?" The U.S. coworker added that Puerto Rico competes separately from the U.S.

I'd never considered that question before. Puerto Rico competing under their own flag blew my mind and made me reconsider my position.

My stance on country-counting had always been that a place only counts as a country if it's on the United Nation's (UN) list of sovereign states, which currently includes 195 countries. Wales is not on it. According to the UN, Wales is part of the UK.

Regardless of the outcome of the hearty debate, I still wanted to see Wales. I keep a list of territories I've visited too—someday they may gain independence; you never know.

The next morning, after nearly a two-hour train ride, I stepped onto the platform in Cardiff and almost changed my mind about whether to consider Wales a separate country or not.

All the signs were written in both Welsh and English. Welsh is entirely different and looked non-sensical to me. The letters were Latin, but the words were all different. Cardiff was "Caerdydd."

As I walked out of the train station, there were Welsh flags blowing in the breeze everywhere. The flag is super cool—it's a huge red dragon on a green and white background.

I stopped in a shop to buy chocolate, and I wished I had subtitles. The clerk was speaking English, but I had a very hard time understanding his accent. It was as difficult for me to follow as a heavy Scottish accent, though the sounds were different.

I spent the day wandering through little shops and the market. All the products in the market were labeled in both Welsh and English, and I loved trying— and failing!—to make sense of the Welsh writing.

I found a gourmet shop that offered tastings of Welsh whiskey. I'm not a whiskey drinker, so I declined to taste any—it would have been wasted on me. However, I bought a bottle of Penderyn Welsh whiskey for Jon, partly because the person who was offering tastings recommended it so highly (they were not at all biased, I'm sure) and also because there was a dragon on the bottle. It turned out to be a huge score because it became Jon's favorite whiskey, and it's hard to find in the U.S.

For lunch, I found a cozy little restaurant tucked into a tiny alleyway lined with shops, and I ate Welsh rarebit (not rabbit!)—just toasted cheese and mustard on bread but done so well that I'd happily eat it for lunch every day.

There was an enormous castle in Cardiff that made me feel like I was no longer in the UK (yes, I know the UK has castles, but this one dated back to the 11th century and felt distinctly medieval).

I was only able to spend a few hours in Wales before I had to hop on the train back to London. Even if Cardiff hadn't been such a fun place to explore, the two-hour train ride from London was worth the trip. The land outside London was green, rolling, and peaceful, and I was so glad I'd taken the extra day to explore after my week of work.

Wales wasn't a new country (at least according to the UN), but it felt new to me, and I was so glad I got to see a tiny part of it.

CHAPTER 19

MILAN:
THE APOCALYPSE

I flew into Milan for a work trip on Sunday, March 1, 2020. I knew things were "off" when a man in a hazmat suit shot me with a temperature gauge as I walked off the airplane.

My boss called me right after I got to my hotel. He said, "Don't come. The city is shutting down because of Covid."

"I'm already here," I said.

This was the very start of the pandemic. Northern Italy was the second place in the world to be affected after China. But none of us knew what was coming, not really.

Because I arrived on the red-eye, it was still early Sunday morning. I had the day to myself, so I walked through Milan.

Even though I'd been there before, what's not to love about Milan? I walked almost two miles from my hotel to the square in front of the gorgeous Duomo Cathedral because I always prefer to walk as much as I can rather than just taking an Uber straight to the sights.

When I got there, Duomo square was almost empty. A few tourists like me who weren't sure what else to do wandered around, but everyone else was at home.

I spent some time in the shopping zone near the Duomo, hitting the new Starbucks Reserve Roastery that had opened only a few years earlier. *Italy finally had Starbucks cups!* Afterward, since it was a beautiful spring day, I walked back to the hotel along a different route, stopping at a few stores—including Desigual, which had been my favorite since my project in Belgium—plazas, and other interesting spots along the way.

Later in the evening, I looked for a place for dinner and saw Eataly. The Eataly in NYC is one of my favorite places to go. It's a huge marketplace of Italian food, and it also has gelato, a bakery, and several Italian restaurants. It was always elbow-to-elbow and push-your-way-past-people full. Always.

I had never been to the one in Milan, but I assumed that it would be similar. Even if it wasn't quite as full as the NYC store normally, walking into the Milan Eataly on March 1, 2020, was positively post-apocalyptic. There was *no one* there except me and a few workers. It was three floors of restaurants and markets, all empty. I rode the escalators to the top and then back down. And then I left. It was just too weird to be in there, and it didn't feel right to get dinner there.

I found a little restaurant that was still open and where there were other people eating, so I went in. In retrospect, maybe it would have been smarter to eat in Eataly where there were no other customers, but it felt more comfortable to huddle together with a few other souls brave enough to go out in the city.

After dinner, I went back to the hotel, but it was still too early for bed. I wanted to keep myself awake until 10 p.m. to get adjusted to the time zone.

I went down to the hotel bar to have a glass of wine. I chatted with the bartender; I was literally the only person there. I asked the bartender if they had Nero d'Avola, and he opened a whole bottle for me. That was one of the few times I've ever asked for something that wasn't on the menu.

It was so quiet in the bar. The bartender said the hotel had already dropped to 30 percent occupancy. The response was that fast.

I had two days of meetings planned in our offices in Milan with team members from across Europe—Germany, the UK, and Italy, along with myself and my boss from the U.S. We had been struggling to reserve a conference room because Milan is one of my company's busiest offices, and I had to provide one of our internal charge codes to reserve a premium office.

The company had no decision on COVID; they just said to do what our clients did. For an internal meeting like this, where there were no clients, we didn't know what else to do, so we decided to meet.

On Monday morning we met in the "premium" conference room, which was now the ONLY conference room in use. The rest of the office was a ghost town.

After two days of meetings, my boss and I decided to change our flights and get back to the U.S. a few days early. We weren't necessarily afraid for our safety in Milan, but we were definitely afraid that the U.S. might shut down the border or turn back flights, especially from hot zones like Milan.

My European co-workers who'd been at the meeting were put on a strict two-week quarantine and weren't allowed to go back to their offices. They didn't say it, but I think they were angry that I'd called the meeting, thereby forcing them to stay out of the office.

I worked from home for a few days to "quarantine," but it felt ridiculous; I didn't think there was any way that I was exposed in my short time in Milan. *I'd seen so few people!* And also . . . I didn't like working from home. I felt isolated, alone. No one in my company worked from home. I felt like I was going to go crazy after about four days.

I went back to work in my New York City office, visited a client site in Connecticut, and attended an International Women's Day event in Philadelphia.

I realize now that if I had been exposed to COVID in Milan, I would have been a super-spreader. The last week before the U.S. shut down for COVID, I went back to both Connecticut and Philadelphia, and was supposed to head to Austin as well, but the Austin portion of the trip got canceled.

If I had to do that Milan trip over again knowing what I know now, I still would have explored the city, but I would have stayed outdoors, seeing sites like the Duomo. I would have skipped Eataly and grabbed wine, bread, and cheese from a grocery store for dinner and eaten it in my hotel room instead.

No one knew what was coming, and I "got" to see the pandemic before it hit the U.S.

TRAVEL BUDDY

CHAPTER 20

MONACO, LIECHTENSTEIN AND...
HOW ABOUT TIMIOSORA?

We were celebrating our nephew's birthday at Outback Steakhouse one October when I said to Jon, "I want to go to Greece for Christmas."

Michele, my sister-in-law, was sitting across from me and said, "Ooh, I want to go to Greece too."

There were about ten of us from our extended family at dinner, so the topic quickly shifted, and we didn't have a chance to talk much further about Greece.

Jon, Jono, and I had been traveling over Christmas as a

family for the last few years, so I filed Michele's comments under "fun dinner conversation" and didn't take them seriously.

But in November, when I was trying to plan our family trip and asked Jon for input, he said, "You should go with Michele."

I was shocked. "Really? But we always travel at Christmas."

"You should cultivate your friendship. Have another travel buddy. Someday Jono is going to be grown up and gone."

I texted Michele: "Do you really want to travel?"

"Yes!" was the immediate reply.

Michele's husband, Pete, was supportive, except he wanted to go to Greece someday too—and didn't want us to go without him. He urged us to pick someplace else.

Were we really going to do this? What had started as a comment tossed out at dinner was turning into reality.

We set the dates first. We'd only have about five days together, plus travel time. Michele couldn't be gone long since she's a teacher and had to be back for the next semester in January. She also didn't want to be gone from her sons for too long—one was a tween and the other a teenager. My son was an older teenager and was used to my traveling for work, so I had a bit more flexibility.

While I would have loved to travel for a week or two, part of me was happy that it was only five days. Five days seemed like long enough to determine if we would get along well as I thought we would—but not so long that it would be miserable if we didn't.

Rooming with the girl from my Spanish class trip to Mexico—who I thought was fun but turned out to be lazy and sloppy—made me wary of travel partners. You either travel well together . . . or you don't.

I was pretty sure Michele and I would get along well. We had been sisters-in-law for over twenty years by that point and lived just ten minutes apart, but we had never traveled together or really spent time together outside of family events.

We decided to fly in and out of Milan because it was the cheapest flight to Europe we could find. We could go anywhere from there.

After I hit all fifty states a few years earlier, I decided to try to visit fifty countries by the time I turned fifty, so my only request for the trip was that we go to a new country. Liechtenstein and Monaco were both "next door" to Italy, so we thought we could hit both of those countries while we were there.

Over the next week, Michele kept texting me with other ideas. "There is a Ryanair flight to Timisoara from Milan for thirty-seven dollars." While I was looking up where Timisoara was (Romania!), she proposed an alternate. "How about Krakow?"

It's amazing how little flights on some of the budget carriers cost in Europe—far less than anything in the U.S. domestically. Michele was like a kid in a candy store.

I finally said, "Pick wherever you want and buy us the tickets."

She booked two round-trip tickets from Milan to Warsaw for about forty dollars each.

We flew out Christmas night after I hosted our families for Christmas dinner.

We felt like we were playing hooky. Getting to travel and leaving the family behind over Christmas?! It felt positively decadent.

We landed in Milan and found the car rental agency. Michele had reserved the car, so she walked up to the counter and started speaking in Italian. I knew she was good with languages—she taught middle school and high school and was dual-certified in Spanish and French—but I didn't know she knew any Italian. I could mostly follow, since Italian is close to Spanish, but I was impressed.

We planned to drive over the Italian Dolomite Mountains into Switzerland and then into Liechtenstein. We were told it was mandatory to bring snow chains. I wasn't sure how to put them on, but I had grown up driving in North Dakota, so I wasn't going to let a little snow stop me.

The roads weren't icy or covered in snow, so I just took it slow. It was a three-hour drive up through the Dolomites. The whole way, we wound through snow-covered mountains. Every turn revealed a new angle and fresh view of the mountains, as if the world was unfolding in front of us.

I was more comfortable driving on the twisty roads, so I did most of the driving that trip. Michele was an expert at navigating us on her Google phone, which seemed to get better data coverage everywhere.

Liechtenstein looked and felt very much like Switzerland. The homes and buildings were Germanic and Tudor-style, the town was ringed by mountains, and everything was as expensive as in Switzerland. But it's not Switzerland.

I knew Liechtenstein was small, but I looked it up while we were there and learned that it covers only about 62 square miles, tucked between Austria and Switzerland, with a total population of around 40,000. The whole country had only 40,000 people? That was smaller than my hometown, Minot, North Dakota, which is no booming metropolis. That's bonkers.

We explored Vaduz, the capital of Liechtenstein. The Vaduz Castle stands above the town, high on a hill, but it is still the home of the royal family and is not open for touring. The whole town is surrounded by snow-capped mountains.

The main square was set up for winter with an ice-skating rink and filled with people enjoying the ice. Michele and I went in some of the souvenir shops around the square. She looked for patches of the country's flag to add to her collection. There was no Starbucks in Liechtenstein, so I couldn't add to mine.

We found an Italian place for dinner, fortified ourselves with pasta, and then drove to the hotel. By the time we got there, we were both ready to pass out. After Christmas, the red-eye flight, exploring Liechtenstein, and staying awake the whole day, by 10 p.m. it felt like we had been awake for three days.

I woke up to Michele saying, "Get up, it's noon!"

I sat up. "What? It's still dark."

"It's just the blackout curtains," she said. She got up and pulled open the curtains, and it was full daylight.

We slept from 10 p.m. the night before until noon. That wasn't just jet lag; it was . . . year lag.

We both worked, had families, and dealt with the chaos of getting ready for Christmas. We were exhausted. Since we didn't have to be anywhere until the evening, we hadn't set an alarm.

We got up and started talking about options for the rest of the day. Neither one of us stressed about the fact that we'd just "lost" those hours. Things always go wrong in travel. You oversleep, flights get delayed, reservations get messed up, museums close—but traveling with someone that focuses on problem-solving and next steps, versus getting upset, is my number one test for a travel partner.

In order to get back to Milan to catch our flight to Warsaw that night, we calculated a 3-hour drive plus two hours to check in before the flight. We figured we'd have a few hours in the afternoon to go see something.

We decided to drive to Lake Como, which was en route to Milan.

I drove again, and Michele navigated.

Lake Como had their winter market set up near the lake, so we walked past all the booths, checked out the souvenirs, and got some mulled wine. We ordered slices from a small pizzeria and ate real Italian pizza while perched on stools, watching crowds walk by outside.

Then it was time to head to the airport.

We landed in Warsaw at the Modlin airport around 10 p.m. Michele had made reservations for the Modlin bus, which would take us into Warsaw's city center. Finding the best way to get into the city from the airport is another of Michele's superpowers. I don't usually think about that until we land, and then I either follow signs or ask an info center. If it's really late, I just take a taxi.

The Modlin bus arrived almost immediately and dropped us off in a parking lot in the middle of Warsaw.

It was freezing and dark, but we were only a few blocks from our hotel, so we walked. Big snowflakes fell, sparkling under the light of the streetlights. It felt like we were walking through a snow globe.

As we checked in, Michele asked, "What time does the bar close?"

I looked at her, shocked. We both like a glass of wine or two, but that question seemed so out of character for her.

"The bar closes in five minutes," the hotel clerk answered.

We got our keys and dragged our suitcases straight over to the bar. "We're in Poland," she explained. "We have to get vodka in Poland."

We got two vodkas, neither of which we finished. But it wasn't about the vodka—it was about taking it all in. We did a "cheers," and then after a few sips, went up to our room.

We set an alarm this time so we wouldn't "waste" any of our precious 24 hours in Warsaw before we flew back to Milan.

In Warsaw, we walked through the old town. The Christmas trees were still up, and the ice-skating rink was still open, but they had broken down the Holiday market.

We walked through the old town, found the old Jewish Ghetto, and dodged into cafés or stores occasionally to warm up. It was no longer snowing on us, but it was freezing. It was a bright sunny day, but the sun's warmth didn't reach us.

We went to the recently opened Museum of the History of Polish Jews. On the plus side, it was a warm, inside activity, and it seemed mandatory to understand a piece of Warsaw's history. On the downside, it was just as impactful and gut-wrenching as you might expect. It started out in the Middle Ages, giving the context of the Jewish people in Poland. And then, of course, it progressed to the horrors of World War II.

Afterward, we made our way back to the airport.

In Milan the next morning, we took the metro to the Duomo Cathedral. We didn't have much time in Milan since we planned to drive to Monaco for the last leg of our trip. But, I'd seen the Duomo with my family years earlier and didn't want Michele to miss it.

The Duomo is gorgeous—made of brick and white marble, covered in gothic spires, and one of the largest cathedrals in the world. Years earlier with my family, we'd climbed to the top and walked on the roof, but this time it was too cold to do that.

A Christmas Tree stood in the plaza in front of the Duomo, surrounded by the still-open holiday market, which made the whole area more festive and fun.

After the Duomo, we drove to Monaco. This was one of those "it looks close on the map" moments; it took us over five hours to drive. While I generally enjoyed driving in Europe—the curvier the roads the better—the five-hour haul started to feel too long for a five-day trip.

Maybe it would have been better if we'd taken a train or stayed in Milan or Warsaw for longer.

We made the best of it though. We had snacks and drinks in the car and enjoyed seeing the Italian countryside, with rolling hills, occasional Italian villas, and castles perched on hilltops.

As we got closer to Monaco, we drove near cliffs overlooking the Ligurian Sea. I wanted to pull over and check out the views, but I also wanted to push on to get to Monaco.

Monaco is only 2 square kilometers. It's the second smallest-country in the world, second only to the Vatican. Monaco made Liechtenstein seem positively gargantuan! Monaco was so small that as we drove on the road from Italy to France, we actually missed the exit the first time. It's literally a "blink and you miss it" exit. Once we got turned around and took the exit, it was thrilling to zip from the highway on the cliffs down into the streets of Monaco like a Formula 1 driver.

To take full advantage of the limited real estate, Monaco was built vertically into the hillsides. There wasn't a shred of land left undeveloped. After we dropped off the car at the hotel, we discovered pedestrian elevators that took us from the lower levels (where our hotel was) up to higher streets, where restaurants and some shops were located.

We walked straight to the Winter market, which was set up by the ocean. It was the best winter market we'd been to yet and still fully operational. They had a ton of food stalls selling everything from waffles to mulled wine, with cartoony blow-up decorations including Christmas trees, festive cupcakes, and gingerbread houses.

The swimming pool had been turned into an ice rink, and there was a Ferris wheel along with other rides. Monaco was warmer than Warsaw and Milan by far, so we could walk through the market and not feel like we had to run into a shop to warm up. We kept our coats on, but we weren't cold at all and stayed outside all afternoon.

At night, the whole city was lit up, and we could see all the ships and yachts anchored along the piers in the ocean. There were so many boats that it was almost like another kilometer of real estate spreading out into the sea.

We passed by multiple casinos, but neither of us were interested in gambling.

Michele, of course, was in her element, speaking French to everyone. I was limited to *merci* and *oui*, but I mostly understood when she spoke.

The next morning, before our return to Milan, we went to the most beautiful Starbucks ever. It was on a rooftop, with the Starbucks counter housed essentially in a gazebo, and the seats spread out across the rooftop under green umbrellas. From that spectacular vantage point, we could see the ocean, the cliffs and mountains into which Monaco is built, and the city. Even though we had to keep our coats on, it was very pleasant on the roof—we could have spent the whole day there.

Then it was the time for our long drive back to Milan to catch our flight home. We could have easily spent another week exploring the area, especially given as much as we'd packed into our itinerary.

It had only been five days, but for us, it felt like the best Christmas present ever. We not only got to experience new places, but we also got a new travel buddy that we could go explore the world with.

After we got home, Michele got an extra "present." We found out that in Lake Como, although I thought I was just following the flow of traffic, I might've enjoyed driving too much, since we were caught by more than one traffic cam for speeding. The car was in Michele's name, so the tickets were sent to her. Whoopsie!

CHAPTER 21

THE BALTICS:
MOTHER RUSSIA

"Are you trying to enter my country without a visa?" the woman asked in a heavy Russian accent. She was dressed in a brown military uniform with a fitted jacket and skirt. Her hair was pulled back in a tight bun, and she wore masculine-looking black leather shoes.

"No, no, no," I said. "We are trying to get a visa."

Moments before, my sister-in-law Michele and I knocked on a very large, very dark wooden door that looked more like the entrance to a vault or dungeon than to an office in an airport, hoping to find someone who could help us get a visa to enter Belarus.

We found someone all right. She came out of the door,

closed it behind her, and was now confronting us about our lack of visa in the middle of a hallway in the airport in Minsk, Belarus.

How did we end up here, a rational person might wonder. Michele and I were on our second trip together.

Estonia had been in the news for focusing on education, digital literacy, and bringing the country into the global economy, which sounded interesting and not what I would have expected from a so-called Eastern European nation.

When I looked up where Estonia was, I saw that it was tucked in tightly with Lithuania and Latvia. We thought it would be fun to go to all three at once, and it would bring me closer to my goal of fifty countries by fifty.

As we were researching the trip, Michele noticed that there was a small Russian enclave of Kaliningrad, located right next door to Lithuania. *How fun would it be to go there?* And since we were in the area, we planned to hit Belarus, too. *Why not?* It all made sense at the time.

We were only going to spend a day in Kaliningrad, but it's Russia, so of course it required a visa. Even getting the visa for Russia was nerve-wracking. We had an appointment at the Embassy of Russia in New York City, and we went to the address, which was several floors up in Midtown Manhattan. When we got there, the office looked like it had been ransacked—garbage was on the floor and chairs and tables were turned over.

After Googling and double-checking our address, we discovered that the embassy had moved. We walked a few blocks to the new address and were still able to make it in time for our appointment. The actual Russian embassy looked like a bank office, with nice carpeting, a check-in desk, a waiting area, and a long counter sectioned off with privacy screens for meetings with embassy staff. Definitely not a scary-looking place.

When it was our turn, we handed all the paperwork we had filled out ahead of time to the agent. He read through it while we waited nervously. The Russian agent handed mine back to me. "This one is not correct."

"Can you just fix the information?" I asked.

"You would like me to do the form for you?" he asked.

Maybe it was just the way he said it with his Russian accent, but there was no way I was going to answer yes.

"Can it just be corrected?" I asked.

"It will cost you." *Was he trying to sound threatening?*

"How much will it cost?"

The fee to have him change the one piece of data I'd gotten wrong was something like thirty dollars. It was better than having to leave, make the change, make a new appointment, and get back to the embassy. It was a bit ridiculous though, given that we were already paying over a hundred dollars in visa fees just to stay one night in Russia. He made the change. Anything for the almighty ruble.

He then put our passports in his desk, gave us receipts, and said they'd be ready in two days. We had gone into New York City specifically because we hoped they could process the visas quickly. By quickly, we hoped for "while we watched." But no.

Leaving our passports at the Russian embassy felt like walking out naked. Our flights were less than a week away—since Russia was a last-minute add-on—and it was the Russian embassy. We felt so exposed.

Despite our misgivings, we got our passports back and made it to Tallinn, Estonia—the first stop on our Baltic expedition.

Estonia was nothing like I expected Eastern Europe to look like. I envisioned Soviet-era gray, square buildings. But Tallinn was adorable—like something out of a fairy tale. Tallinn's Old Town is filled with shops and restaurants crowded together on tiny, cobbled streets. There were stone buildings with round turrets, capped with red roofs. Church spires poked up everywhere, and the entire area was enclosed by a stone wall topped with a wooden walkway.

As we walked through the town, we saw a sign dedicated to Estonia's independence, on August 20, 1991. Michele and I were struck by that date because we had both graduated from college that year. It seemed so recent and so at odds with the magical beauty of the town. *People our age had grown up in Tallinn as part of the USSR, learning Russian, living under Communism? How is that possible?* We also saw a KGB museum but decided not to go. It was too hard to reconcile the KGB and the USSR with the beauty of the town.

At our next stop, Riga, Latvia, we found another charming old town, but this one was filled with triangle-roofed merchant houses that reminded me of Antwerp or Ghent in Belgium. There was also an enormous cathedral . . . and another KGB museum. It felt like we were being followed by the KGB. We decided to face the music and go in.

Unsurprisingly, it was not a nice museum showing all the crimes that the KGB solved and brought to justice. It was essentially a museum of torture. There were small prison cells for solitary confinement, along with signs commemorating the terror inflicted on the local population during the period when Latvia was a part of the USSR. Latvia also gained its independence in 1991—which felt way too recent.

The day we were headed to Kaliningrad, we were perhaps a little extra on edge about Russia after visiting the KGB torture museum, so we double- and triple-checked our visas and passports. *What's the worst that could happen?*

The bus took us from Klaipeda through the Curonian Spit—a narrow strip of land between a quarter of a mile and two and a half miles wide—stretching 61 miles between the Baltic Sea and the Curonian Lagoon. The land is divided in ownership between Lithuania on the northern side and Russia on the southern side. It is essentially a long sand dune covered with tall, thin pine trees, which gave the whole spit a dark, brooding look.

We passed through Nida, a beautiful little seaside town in Lithuania—the last stop before Russia. The last chance to change our minds.

At the border, our bus stopped. An agent came down the aisle and collected everyone's passports. We handed ours over reluctantly and had to keep ourselves from following the agent. Losing sight of them made me feel so powerless. The guard came back shortly and handed back all the passports. We let out a sigh of relief—until we realized that was only the exit process. We were *out* of Lithuania, but we hadn't gone *into* Russia yet.

The bus rolled forward a hundred feet or so, and everyone had to file out and go into the Russian border checkpoint. *Were we supposed to bring our stuff or not?* There were no instructions, but no one else seemed confused. We watched what everyone else was doing, but it really wasn't clear. We brought our backpack and purses and left our suitcases on the bus.

We got into the building and stood in line. I debated whether I should have brought the boxed lunch our hotel had given us that morning because it had an apple in it. U.S. customs are so forceful about produce, I always assume every border will be as strict about fresh foods. Maybe it was a ridiculous thing to worry about, but I was on edge. I tried to go back to the bus for the boxed lunch, but there was a gate blocking us. We were locked in, and the only way to go out was through the guard and into Russia.

It's worth noting that this was before the war in Ukraine.

We never would have gone into Kaliningrad in the current political climate.

Michele and I walked up to a female agent together, and she looked at us and said, "One at a time!" She sounded like a drill sergeant from my military days—and with that Russian accent, needless to say, we did exactly what she said. I stepped up, and Michele stepped back.

"Why are you coming to Kaliningrad?"

"To see it?" I said, though the answer sounded questionable even to me. She glared at me but my visa was in order, and she must have decided I wasn't a threat. She stamped my passport.

Michele stepped forward.

"Remove your glasses. Why do you go to Kaliningrad? How long you stay?" the woman semi-shouted at Michele.

Thankfully, Michele's visa was deemed acceptable as well. So, after she finished yelling at Michele, we proceeded back to the bus.

Despite the terror of getting into Russia, Kaliningrad was nice. There isn't that much to do there—it's like the Ohio of Russia (*sorry, Ohioans!*). There was an amber museum, some nice parks, and a castle. We also went to the mall and took pictures in front of McDonald's, because seeing the name written in Cyrillic (Макдоналдс) was cool.

While we ate lunch at a little café near our hotel, a man seated at a table near ours leaned over and asked, "Are you from America?"

"Yes," Michele answered.

"Why are you here?" he asked. Unlike the border guard, he didn't sound threatening—he sounded genuinely curious. How did we end up in his corner of the world?

We told him the same thing: "Just to see it." And it was still true.

The next morning, we ate breakfast at the hotel and

reviewed our travel plans for the day. We were flying into Belarus that afternoon and both felt a little nervous about it. We'd read online that Belarus was the last dictatorship in Europe.

After we reviewed our flights and researched what to do in Minsk, Michele went back to the official website and reviewed the visa information.

When we had researched for the trip, the website said there was a visa-on-arrival process. You could get a visa for three days if you arrived at the airport in Minsk. So we planned the itinerary to fly into Minsk versus taking an overland route. We had no intention of staying more than a day or two, so a three-day visa would be great.

But the visa process had changed.

The official website now said, effective a few days earlier while we were traveling, "Belarus would now offer 30-day visas upon arrival for passengers arriving in Minsk by air." *Okay, that's good!* We didn't need 30 days, but that was fine. However, they had also added a clause: *Except for passengers coming from the Russian Republic.*

Except we were in Kaliningrad, Russia. *Except* we wouldn't be able to get a visa.

We had about fourteen hours remaining on our one-day Russian visa—until midnight, and we wouldn't be able to get a visa for Belarus. We couldn't stay where we were, and we couldn't go where we'd planned. Travel always, always throws curveballs, no matter how well you plan. But this one was a doozie!

We started using Google and Kayak to determine other flights out of Kaliningrad. We also went to the local office of the airline we'd booked with to see if they had some more up-to-date information. It was Belavia, which sounds like a friendly, pleasant airline, when really, it's just Air Belarus.

The Belavia office was of limited help—absolutely none,

actually. They spoke almost no English, and though Michele had studied one year of Russian back in high school, we were barely able to communicate. And there was certainly no miraculous loophole or solution offered to us.

But on the upside, we did pick up a new Russian word—заѳтра, pronounced *zaftra*—which we learned means "tomorrow," because the unhelpful airline rep kept talking about *tomorrow*, even though our visa expired that night.

As for other flight options, it's Kaliningrad, not JFK. Most of the flights that afternoon went to other cities in Russia. Not surprising, but not helpful. We started looking for flights out of Minsk, and there were a few more options there.

We decided to get out of Russia. We couldn't stay without a visa, so we just had to get out. We thought maybe, just *maybe* we'd be able to get a visa in Minsk.

We decided to get on our scheduled flight to Minsk and bought tickets from Minsk to Kyiv as a backup option, each flight only about a hundred dollars. We bought the tickets on the tarmac as we rode the airport bus from the terminal to the airplane in Kaliningrad.

When we landed in Minsk, there was no security, no customs, no anything. It was like a domestic U.S. flight from Ohio to Michigan or something. Russia and Belarus are so close they were treating flights from Russia like domestic flights, with no need for customs.

Except now we were in the Minsk airport—with no visa.

Earlier at breakfast, we researched what would happen if we just waltzed out into the country without a visa. The scenario that most resembled our situation was what would happen if we overstayed our visa, which was chillingly described as: "The police would happily detain you for three days, just for the privilege of paying a fine." Yiksey-yikes!

We were in the airport in Minsk with backup flights to

Ukraine in a few hours, and we thought we'd just *ask* if we could get a visa. Let's just see. *What could go wrong?*

"You are trying to come to my country without a visa," said the scary woman from earlier. This time it was a statement, not a question. Clearly, stammering "No, no, no" didn't help.

"We flew in from Kaliningrad. We didn't know that you couldn't get a visa upon arrival from Kaliningrad."

She continued to look at us. "You have Russian visa?"

"Yes, yes, Russian visa." We handed her our passports with the Russian visa.

"It is only for today," she said. "You need a visa."

"Yes! Can we get a visa?"

"I can take you upstairs to the police. You can talk to them. Maybe they will give you a visa," she said. She shrugged one shoulder. Maybe, maybe not.

Oh crap! Or they will happily detain us for three days.

"What if we leave the country?" I asked.

"You leave the country? Today?"

"Yes, what if we fly today to Ukraine. We have tickets."

"You have tickets?" We showed her the tickets we'd bought on Ukraine International Airlines (UIA)—pronounced "meow" for some reason.

And suddenly, it was like we were talking to a different person. She smiled and her voice softened. "I will show you where to go. Come with me."

She escorted us to the UIA counter, all chatty and smiling, like we were her favorite tourists ever. She pointed to the counter, said goodbye, and walked briskly away back to her dungeon.

UIA checked us in and gave us an upgrade to business class. I had no idea why. Clearly, we had no status on UIA. Maybe they just saw how freaked out we were and decided to be nice to us.

Before we bought the tickets to Kyiv, we had double-checked we didn't need a visa. But Ukraine still felt risky to us. This was in 2018, after the Russian annexation of Crimea. Ukraine didn't feel entirely safe since Russia still occupied territory. However, we had little choice. It was the least bad of all the options, since we couldn't stay in either Russia or Belarus.

I booked a hotel in Kyiv while riding the airport bus from the Minsk terminal to the airplane.

We landed in Ukraine, got through security and customs with no problems, and arrived at our hotel. We had 24 hours in Ukraine before our flight back to Lithuania, since our flight home was out of Vilnius.

As it turned out, there was no need to be nervous about Ukraine—everyone was so nice and friendly. We had obviously done no research on Ukraine or Kyiv, since we hadn't planned to be there. We looked up the top attractions, and Michele texted a Ukrainian colleague of hers back home for her counsel. We wandered the city on foot and saw the beautiful Saint Sophia Cathedral, and it was like we were meant to be in Ukraine all along.

Ukraine ended up being my 50th country, and we toasted the accomplishment with a honey-chili vodka, selected from a whole menu of different vodkas—it seemed like the thing to do in Ukraine. Like in Poland, we didn't finish that vodka either.

Michele and I had only planned to spend one day in Russia on that trip. We visited the little bitty corner of Kaliningrad—an enclave cut off from Mother Russia—not any of the big cities like Moscow or St. Petersburg. And yet... it felt like the entire trip was overshadowed by Russia.

Each of the countries we'd traveled through had only recently gained their independence and were still healing from the scars of occupation and Communism. Belarus was so closely tied to Russia it was almost like being in Russia.

And Ukraine... Russia wants us all to believe that Ukraine is part of Russia and that it is somehow justified in taking Ukraine's territory. Traveling through the Baltics and feeling the specter of Russia the whole time gave us a small taste of what it must be like living in those countries—knowing Russia is out there, always threatening, or in Ukraine's case, outright invading.

And yet, the places we visited were so vibrant, so charming. We were enamored with the region because it was so beautiful, and the places we actually visited (even Kaliningrad, not Belarus) were all so friendly.

CHAPTER 22

BALKANS:
REEMERGE AND RESTORE

Michele and I had planned to take our third girls' adventure in the summer of 2020—but, of course, that didn't happen. Like the rest of the world, we were locked down, isolating to avoid COVID.

As a foreign language teacher, Michele spent the year trying to teach middle and high school students French and Spanish remotely, while also trying to keep her own teenagers focused on school. Challenging at best, a fool's errand at worst.

After my escape from Milan at the start of the pandemic, the project I had been on the cusp of starting was canceled. There was so much uncertainty that my client didn't want to invest in a new project. So, I was out of a project and in very real danger of being laid off because anyone who was "on the bench" (between consulting roles) was easy pickings.

I took a role in an industry I didn't know, working for a leader I'd never met, on a massive project that was starting from scratch entirely remotely with everyone behind the screens of their laptops. I know I was lucky to have landed a role, and very lucky to still have a job, but it was a horrible project.

I was in a leadership role without the authority to do it properly. A woman bullied my team and I—outright bullying like I hadn't experienced since junior high. Conference calls were nonstop from morning until night because the only way to talk to anyone was through a screen. I remember having an almost out-of-body experience one morning. I was talking to a client one-on-one, and suddenly it was like I could see myself sitting at my desk in my little basement office. And all I could think was . . . *What am I doing? What is going on?*

The only things that kept me sane were being home with my husband and son and having dinner together every night—something that had almost never happened since I had traveled so much for work. We also adopted our first pet: a 9-year-old orange cat named Finny, who instantly became the boss of the house.

As 2020 transitioned into 2021, the vaccines came out, COVID rates started to fall, and Michele and I were both itching to get away; we were prepared to go anywhere. We scanned the internet daily to see what countries were allowing travel and what their requirements were. We were like Finny pawing under a closed door, desperate to go through, regardless of what was on the other side.

We found a few countries that would let us in as long as we were vaccinated, including Romania, Bulgaria, and

Moldova. Nearby North Macedonia didn't have any restrictions in place. Maybe no one was clamoring to go there in the first place? We added it to the itinerary.

We flew into Athens so we could use British Airlines points, but we didn't plan to spend much time in Greece. Both of our husbands still wanted to go to Greece someday, and while they weren't jealous of us going to Romania or Bulgaria, Greece was another story.

As we landed and made our way to the hotel, I saw the Acropolis lit up on a hill. I remembered that one of my friends, a colleague who had recently retired, had just posted almost that same image of the Acropolis on Facebook. I messaged him: "Are you still in Athens?"

"No," he responded. "We're on our way to Thessaloniki."

What? We were going to Thessaloniki the next day. Who goes to Thessaloniki? Especially in August of 2021.

The whole reason we were going to Thessaloniki was that it was the only way to make our itinerary work. Because of the pandemic, many of the bus routes weren't running, and there weren't trains going between the countries we wanted to visit. We couldn't rent a car one-way and cross that many borders—we tried! We considered changing our plans and reducing what we would be able to see when I found a service called Daytrip. It was a service that would take us from point A to point B, even across borders, *and* let us stop at a few tourist sites along the way. We wouldn't have to worry about directions, parking, or tickets. *Perfect!*

We couldn't get a driver from Athens though, so we flew to Thessaloniki, and a driver would meet us there. After we mapped out the route, we would take four cars, crossing borders almost every time. At first, it seemed perfect, but it also made us nervous how much we would have to rely on unknown drivers.

When I was packing for the trip, Jon said, "You should

take my emergency satellite device."

"Why?" I asked. He had it for when he climbed in the mountains, in case he ever needed a rescue or if there was an emergency when there was no cell service. "We're going to be in Europe. Cell service should be fine."

"You're going to be crossing borders in those car services. You never know. It's small," he said, handing me the device. I tucked it into my pack.

"You should bring thermal underwear too, just in case," he added.

"Honey, it's going to be pushing 100 the whole time we're there. The last time we traveled, I roasted. I don't think I'm going to need thermals."

"They pack up small," he said. "And you'll be in mountains, right?"

I think he was just nervous. Traveling during the pandemic, especially where we were going—Moldova is the least-traveled country in Europe—made all of us a little nervous.

I tucked them into my suitcase.

By the time we got to Thessaloniki, after having spent the day in Athens, it was late, dark, and there didn't seem to be anything open near the hotel. As we checked in, we asked where we should go for a late dinner.

"Ladadika," she said, and pointed "that way" a few blocks. *Okay, hotel lady, sure!*

Despite the fact that it was dark, there was no one on the streets, and we didn't have any better directions than "that way," we found Ladadika. It was paradise! It was as if all the light had been sucked from the darks streets we'd just walked through and poured into that neighborhood. Several blocks were filled with cafés adorned with string lights; the streets teemed with people and buzzed with music.

There was an open area where a few streets came together

that was filled with tables. It was almost impossible to tell which table belonged to which café because there was no space between them. We found one of the few open tables and grabbed it.

In front of "our" café was a small acoustic band—a singer and a couple of guitarists—and a few other cafés had similar musicians scattered across the courtyard. We hadn't seen that many people gathered in one place for at least a year and a half. It was outdoors, otherwise, we might not have felt comfortable enough to stay. But outside, with the music and the lights, it felt like life itself.

We spent half of our time watching all the people, most of whom looked like they were locals, some of whom were young and likely on dates. We spent the other half of our time watching all of the stray kittens wandering between the tables, looking for scraps. We ordered fried zucchini—not really kitty-friendly, so they didn't stay near our table long.

Each time a cat wandered by, I tried to snap a picture but, of course, never quite captured their adorableness. After attempting to take the umpteenth picture, Michele said, "Who are you?" Not that she wasn't trying to get her own pics. She was always a cat person, but not me. We never had any pets, and I would never have considered myself an animal person. Not until Finny sauntered into our house. Then, every little kitty caught my eye.

The next day, we met my friend Mike and his wife for lunch. They were staying in the swank tourist district, and it felt beautiful but sterile compared to the Ladadika district we'd hung out in, though much nicer than where we stayed. I'll admit it; we were staying at a Holiday Inn because I'd found a final cache of IHG points—it was definitely not in the swank zone.

But I was happy we stayed there because the route

between our hotel and theirs passed by so many ruins interspersed among the rest of the city. There were hospitals built on top of old Roman walls, subways that were started and not completed because they'd run into Roman ruins. Old temples and churches—and very little of it seemed restored or preserved. It was just there, which I loved, actually. I loved thinking of the layers of life and history living in that single place since the Roman era. That's not something you can see in the U.S.

We led Mike and his wife to Ladadika because it was so much fun the night before, we thought it had to be much more fun than the tourist zone.

However, Ladadika was apparently still sleeping off its hangover and had turned back into a quiet, old neighborhood. We found a café that would serve us drinks until the kitchen opened.

We caught up on where Mike and his wife were traveling. They were following a slow travel plan, taking six months at a time and visiting only a few countries.

I asked Mike, "How do you like being retired? I'm considering it . . . but how do you know it's the right time?"

Michele looked at me, eyebrows raised but didn't say anything.

Mike, like me, had been a technology executive, working twelve- or eighteen-hours every day. "Have an off-ramp," Mike said. "Have something to do after you stop working that still engages you and makes you feel like you're relevant." He was working on the board of various charities, so those made his transition feel less like a cliff.

I started getting pings from the driver who was coming to get us, saying he was late due to a backup at the border because it was a national holiday in North Macedonia. So, we kept talking. The kitchen opened, and we ordered lunch.

After we left Mike and his wife, we found the driver and

settled in for the ride. It was early afternoon and over 100 degrees outside. Inside the car was comfortable enough with the air-conditioning on full-blast. It was about three hours to Skopje, North Macedonia.

Michele said, "I can't believe you asked about retirement. I never thought you'd retire." The subtext was another *Who are you?*

"Me neither," I said. But the horrible job where I was being bullied took a toll on me. And being home every day with my family helped me start separating myself from my professional identity. Before, I was almost afraid of working from home because I'd feel like I was being left out, left behind, or irrelevant. But during the pandemic, I enjoyed being home with my family. I looked forward to the end of the weekend when all of the chores were done, when I knew I could shut the door and not have to leave the house again for the week. I didn't know how to explain all that to Michele, though. I just said, "I'm tired of projects that sap my soul." She'd heard about some other projects on our trips in the past, so she understood.

There were two planned stops on the drive. The first was an architectural dig, which sounded interesting when we booked it. When we pulled up to it, there was an open field of dirt, with no shade. It was 107 degrees outside. We walked past the old Roman theater, several standing columns, and what might have been a bathhouse, just long enough to be polite, but then we scurried back in the car, which the driver had kept running with the AC blasting. Of course, there was no one else at the dig; it was scorching out there. Good thing I had my thermal underwear packed!

After we started driving again, I asked our driver, "Why is your country called 'North' Macedonia? What happened to East, West, and South?"

"Macedonia is trying to join the EU," he said, "and Greece has a lot of conditions before we can join." He explained,

"Greece has a region called Macedonia in the north, and they don't want us to use that name. We think that region of Greece should really be the southern part of North Macedonia."

He added that part of Bulgaria should be East Macedonia, as North Macedonia's borders used to extend into Bulgaria. *Of course it should be!*

Our next stop was Matka Canyon. I thought, how does a 30-minute stop for an entire canyon make any sense? Would we pull up to it, look over the edge and nod our heads, like the Griswolds at the Grand Canyon in *National Lampoon's Vacation*? We offered to skip it, not eager to leave the AC again, but our driver pulled up to the canyon and pointed to the walking path.

It was a lovely, shaded path, with a cool breeze coming off the river raging alongside the canyon. We joined a ton of other people who decided to enjoy their National Holiday and escape the heat by enjoying the canyon.

After we got back to the car, it was a quick drive to Skopje.

Our hotel was right on the edge of Macedonia Square, which was a big, open space filled with families and tourists. There were white marble façades on many of the buildings, which gleamed in the late afternoon sun. In the middle of the plaza was a statue of Alexander the Great. At a distance, the statue looked normal, but as we approached, we realized it was enormous—way out of proportion, as if the Statue of Liberty had been plopped in a plaza (okay, not quite that big, but still weirdly huge). There was also a Times Square-like electronic display blaring Chinese propaganda above a café.

At first glance, the square was gorgeous and shiny, but after we soaked it all in, it felt . . . off. Then I remembered reading about the city's facelift—done to improve the Communist-era vibe of the city and attract tourists through an effort called Skopje Project 2014. Critics said the results were garish, almost Las Vegas-style, and that the enormous amount of capital could have been better spent on schools, roads, and hospitals.

Parts of the city retained its original styles, which felt much more authentic. The post office was a brutalist concrete bunker, but kind of cool in a funky, retro, midcentury modern way. There was a castle on the hill overlooking the city, which had thankfully not been redone either.

We walked to the old town, and it felt like it belonged to a different city entirely. There was a row of small cafés, each with an awning overhead. We stopped and got coffee at one because it was just so inviting. The old town was also filled with tons of shops featuring expensive gold jewelry, traditional clothing, and some souvenirs.

The bridges were lined with statues, and there were more oversized statues in the museum district. I don't know what Skopje looked like originally, and I don't know if I actually liked the way the city looked with its garish beauty, but I'll grant them that it's memorable, especially because of the architectural contrast between ancient buildings, over-the-top modernizations, and the brutalist concrete.

Skopje was so interesting and unique, it made us wonder, *"Who goes to Skopje?"* It made us want to tell people about it. There were so many other interesting places we'd seen that no one else we knew had ever visited. *We should start a travel blog!*

After Skopje, we had three more drives. While we had reserved the drives as a means of getting to the cities on our itinerary, the drives themselves became what we looked forward to most. Each new drive brought us a new driver, new conversations, often a new country, new scenery, and new sites to explore.

On our second road trip, we stopped at two monasteries in Bulgaria. One of them—Rila Monastery—was tucked into the mountains: peaceful, holy, and ancient, dating back to the 700s. Saint Joachim Osogovski Monastery was perched on the side of a hill—colorful, small, and covered with frescoes.

We told the second driver, who was Bulgarian, that the North Macedonian driver had said Bulgaria should really be East Macedonia. The Bulgarian driver said, "No, actually Macedonia used to be part of Bulgaria." *Of course!*

Our third trip wound through Transylvania in Romania, and we stopped at two castles. One was the inspiration for Dracula's Castle, and our driver called it "too touristy." It was guarded by a gauntlet of vendors selling T-shirts with vampire fangs dripping blood instead of a moat. The second castle was like a Tudor-style mansion on steroids—stately, serene, filled with dark carved wood, and surrounded by vast green lawns perfect for strolling.

We talked to our third driver about how challenging the pandemic had been for him and his family since he worked in the tourism industry. We were some of the first international tourists he'd seen traveling since the pandemic.

On our fourth and final trip, en route to Moldova, our only stop was a salt mine. We imagined we'd see machinery and conveyor belts with little saltshakers coming out at the end. We took a bus packed with people—no one was masked but us—down into a huge, cavernous chamber.

Down in the mine, not only was there no machinery like we expected, there were basketball courts, soccer pitches, playgrounds, and picnic tables. There was a food stand, a store, and a chapel. The families on the bus with us brought picnic lunches, books, and games, and everyone started just hanging out. *What in the world?*

We found out later that defunct salt mines are believed to

be restorative, and people spend hours there hoping to soak up the purported health benefits.

Coming out of the mine felt a little like emerging from the pandemic. When the COVID shutdown happened, no one knew what to expect or how long it would last. I'd been working in my basement all year for my supposed health—like those families spending time in the restorative air of the mine. We came out from the shutdown blinking at the sun, finding that the world had changed—and so had we.

For me, that trip was about seeing the world with four different drivers who took us on a journey across four countries. It was seeing vast landscapes and unique cities, experiencing everything from monasteries and castles to salt mines.

It was connecting with other people who were emerging from the pandemic and charting their own path to retirement. Where I used to identify as a consultant and never saw myself retiring, I began to look ahead to a world where I could step away from work—maybe even start that blog.

It was leaving the dark streets of Thessaloniki or the dark tunnels of the salt mine, reentering the world, and finding life again.

CHAPTER 23

CAUCASUS:
HIDDEN GEMS

As Michele and I considered options for our next annual-ish girls' trip, Georgia kept popping up to the top of the list. Georgia is in the Caucasus mountains, and I kept seeing images of an isolated orthodox-style church pictured against the backdrop of an enormous green mountain. It all looked so remote, peaceful, and frankly lonely. Even though I was starting to see more articles about Georgia, that one image made it seem so beautiful and off the beaten path! It was calling to me.

Of course, Georgia is also known for its wine, which is always a bonus for me!

The clincher was an article about a diamond-shaped café

that had just been built, *hanging over* a massive canyon in Georgia. *What? How cool is that?* The article was frustrating, though, because there was no information about how to get there or even where it was. The subtext of the article was "It's cool, but no one will ever go there." *We were going!*

We also decided to go to neighboring Azerbaijan and Armenia, the other two countries that share the Caucasus region. Even though I was no longer pushing for a country count after hitting fifty, I'm always up for seeing more, doing more—and if we were going all the way there, why wouldn't we want to see all three?

Georgia, Azerbaijan, and Armenia had been part of the USSR and huddled just south of Russia. The Russia–Ukraine war was ongoing, but we figured Russia was so focused on Ukraine that we'd be safe in the Caucasus.

As we planned the trip, we came across multiple warnings to avoid the region of Nagorno-Karabakh, which had been fought over by Azerbaijan and Armenia and was still contested. The rest of both countries was apparently safe to travel. We had no desire to go to Nagorno-Karabakh—having never heard of it before we started planning—so we didn't think it would be much of an issue.

There were a few other rules we had to consider, which reminded me of one of those logic puzzles—the kind that go, "If four people have to cross a river in a boat, but only two can cross at a time . . ." For our itinerary, we had to travel to Azerbaijan before Armenia, since the Azerbaijani officials might have given us a hard time—or even deny entry—if we had an Armenian passport stamp. We could not cross directly from Armenia to Azerbaijan or vice versa. Plus, the land border into Azerbaijan, even from Georgia, was still closed post-COVID.

In order to accommodate all of the rules, we planned to use Tbilisi, Georgia as our home base. We would start in Tbilisi, fly to Azerbaijan for a few days, then fly back to Tbilisi. From there, we would drive into Armenia for an overnight trip before returning to Tbilisi to fly home.

A few days before our departure, my godmother Beverly sent me an email asking, "Isn't there a war going on? Am I the only one speaking out?"

She followed it up a day later with, "Canada is an interesting place." *Good one, Bev!*

I studied Russian on Duolingo for a few months prior to leaving. My primary goal was to be able to read Cyrillic letters and not feel blind if I was confronted with Russian—after having been frustrated that I couldn't read it during our previous visits to Bulgaria and Kaliningrad. Michele was also using Duolingo to refresh her high-school Russian.

We assumed that in all three countries, three languages would be in use: the local language, Russian, and English. In Georgia, that might have been true before the Russian invasion of Ukraine. What we found was that the older generation spoke Russian, since they had grown up in the Soviet Union and never learned English. We found our limited Russian helpful when interacting with taxi drivers (who all seemed to be older men). Once, when one of the taxi drivers was pestering us for a ride, I managed to say, "*У меня экскурсия*"—*I have a tour*. He nodded and left us alone, and our tour guide came to pick us up a few minutes later.

The younger generation primarily spoke English, in addition to their native Georgian, and actively rejected Russian. We made a mistake when checking into our hotel in Tbilisi. We stayed at The Moxy, a hip hotel chain where the lobby is a huge hangout area, and the registration desk doubles as a bar. Actually, the bar doubles as a registration desk.

The young woman who checked us in was in her twenties. We dropped a word or two of Russian in front of her, simply because we love languages and get excited when we know a word. But even saying an innocuous word like "five" in Russian didn't sit well with the hotel clerk. She looked up at us and said in perfect English, "Do you know what the Russians did in 2008?"

She told us that Russians took the regions of South Ossetia and parts of Abkhazia and destroyed Georgian villages there. "My family was from South Ossetia. Russia killed some of my family and displaced the rest," the hotel clerk explained. We could see the anger and hurt in her eyes.

After that, we were very careful when using Russian—only to read signs ("Fish!" I yelled once, sounding like a little kid, proud of myself for recognizing the word) and to speak with the older generation. Never with the younger generation.

The Moxy wasn't in Tbilisi's old town or a touristy area; it felt more like a business district where real people lived and worked, which I loved. We left our hotel and immediately walked through a flea market laid out along a bridge. Michele found a pin of Georgia she wanted to buy, but we hadn't changed currency yet.

We wanted to see as much of the city as possible on foot, so we walked to the funicular that would take us to Mtatsminda Park. On the way, we walked through parks and plazas, past old wooden homes with balconies overhanging the road. Street art ranged from intricate murals to sprayed graffiti with anti-Putin and anti-Russian sentiments. One read, "Russians go home."

At the top of the funicular in Mtatsminda park, we could see all of Tbilisi nestled in a valley. A huge Georgian Church with a gold dome on top stood as the centerpiece of the city, while a fortress perched high on a hill overlooked Tbilisi.

After riding the funicular back down, we walked through town toward the fortress. As we walked, the buildings looked older, with more color and graffiti. Everything felt funky and had almost a hippie vibe. Looking down over us was a "Mother Georgia" statue. She held a sword in one hand and a goblet of wine in the other. *I loved her!* She was happy to host and serve wine to all her guests—unless and until they messed with her. Then, she would be ready with the sword. *Watch out, Russia!*

We had managed to walk *up* to the top of the hill with Mother Georgia and the Narikala Fortress—*of course!*—so we took a cable car down. We landed right near the Bridge of Peace, which was ironically one of the least peaceful points of the city. People with peacocks and monkeys were available for pictures and selfies (for a fee), hawkers offered boat rides on the river or other tours, and tourists serpentined their way between the vendors. We dodged people, crossed the bridge, and walked alongside the green Kura River back to our hotel.

As much as we loved Tbilisi, we had to go to the Kazbegi region. We hoped to see the iconic Gergeti Trinity Church against the backdrop of that beautifully looming green mountain, Mt. Kazbegi. The tour we chose was titled "Hidden Gems," and our guide prided himself on taking us to unique spots that other guides supposedly wouldn't—along with all the top spots.

We stopped at a few churches on that trip, all of which had been defaced during the Soviet era. All of the frescoes inside had been destroyed, and the walls were now whitewashed, which was an incredible shame.

We had an amazing lunch at the home of a local bed-and-breakfast. Our lunch included many small, *tapas*-like plates—and Georgian wine. Our guide taught us about Georgian wine culture, where wine is for drinking with family and celebrating. He said, "Toasts should first be made to God, then to country, then to family." The wine was so good, with a spicy edge to it—like a Rioja, but spicier, edgier?

There were definitely some unusual stops—possibly the hidden gems—where there weren't any other tourists. We hiked to a waterfall and visited an ancient fire tower once used to signal an invasion. We could see other towers on the horizon. There were huge faces carved into boulders, including Jesus. It was like a Georgian Mount Rushmore, but smaller and weirder.

We stopped at a relatively new church built on a hill for our last stop. The guide pointed out the Georgian border with Russia. From where we stood—about one kilometer away from the border—we could see a lineup of trucks waiting to enter Russia, and the Georgian flag flying on our side of the border. We pulled up Google maps to see just how close we really were.

I took a screenshot to send our location to my godmother, so she could keep entertaining me with her hilarious emails. Maybe next time she'll tell me New Jersey is interesting.

In order to complete the next piece of the Caucasus puzzle, we flew to Azerbaijan.

Baku, Azerbaijan felt entirely different from Tbilisi, Georgia. The languages, currencies, and religions were all different. Georgia is a predominately Christian nation, where Azerbaijan is mostly Muslim.

Even the tourists in Azerbaijan were different. In Georgia, there was a heavy concentration of Russian and European visitors, but in Azerbaijan, most visitors came from Muslim countries. We met people from Saudi Arabia, Libya, Malaysia, Algeria, Pakistan, and Turkey.

My friend who lives in Qatar said that travel to Azerbaijan is heavily marketed there, so I assume the same is true in the other Muslim-majority countries.

In our hotel restaurant, a woman wearing a *niqab*—a

veil covering everything but her eyes—was eating breakfast. I watched as she ate, lifting her *niqab* with one hand just enough to get her fork underneath and take a bite. Did I stare? Probably. Should I have? Definitely not.

The other major difference is that Azerbaijan has money! Azerbaijan is an oil country, and its capital, Baku, is modeling itself after some of the other major cities in oil-rich nations with huge glass skyscrapers, like Dubai. There are three iconic Flame Towers, shaped like flames that dominate the skyline. At night, they light up with alternating flames and flags of Azerbaijan in LED lights. There was also a striking horseshoe-shaped building with an open center. Even the mall was shaped like a glass lotus flower.

Perhaps most surprisingly, there were European-style buildings inspired by Venice and Paris, which were funded by the first wave of oil wealth in the late 1800s and early 1900s. Some of the buildings weren't just *inspired by* Europe, they were actually replicas of specific structures that were rebuilt in Azerbaijan.

Still, not all of Baku has been modernized. There is a Persian-style old town, like you might find in Morocco, with low walls made of sand-colored brick and clay with wooden windows and accents, squeezed in tightly along cobblestone streets.

We began our walk through Baku with a stroll along the boardwalk which fronts the Caspian Sea. We dipped into the lotus flower-shaped mall just to get a breath of air conditioning. The McDonald's caught our eye because the menu was written in Azerbaijani (similar to Turkish). Michele tried to snap a picture of the menu board, but the manager came over and started telling her off for taking pictures of the people working the counter. While he was distracted, I got a shot of the menu, trying not to get the workers. *What can I say, we both love languages!*

We took a tour up to the mountains to a town called Sheki. The tour was led by a young guide in his twenties who had fought against Armenia in 2020. It was about a four-hour drive to Sheki. As the guide gave an overview of the countryside, he told us, "Armenia is our enemy country." The statement was so blunt, it felt at odds with his otherwise lighthearted, friendly manner. Not just "we're in a conflict"—it was "enemy country," period. He explained the conflict using words like *genocide*, as if reciting from a script.

That took us completely by surprise. We knew there was a contested region, but that statement was so black and white, so unexpected. When we asked the guide about their position on Russia, he shrugged his shoulders and said, "We have to be friends with them. We are so little compared to Russia, and we have oil that Russia wants, so we must have good relations with Russia." He wasn't concerned about Russia.

Sheki was up in the mountains and cooler than Baku. It was old and historical, without the infusion of oil money that Baku had. Where Baku felt like a different world from Tbilisi, Sheki felt familiar again. Sheki was less than two hours from the Georgian border—if we were allowed to cross.

We saw the Palace of Shaki Kahns (go ahead and sing it, I know you want to!), visited a caravanserai—an old inn where traders carrying goods on the Silk Road would stay—and wandered down a street filled with candy and souvenir shops.

The oldest and best candy shop on the block, according to the guide, had the most amazing baklava ever. I've never been a huge fan of baklava; it's usually too sweet for me. But this baklava was infused with saffron, and its savoriness offset the sweetness of the honey and made it irresistible. We bought two boxes of it.

After flying back to Georgia, we did a two-day trip to Armenia. On the way to the capital of Yerevan, we stopped at several churches. Unlike the churches in Georgia, the ones in Armenia hadn't been defaced and retained their ancient frescoes. It made the churches look older, darker, and more sacred.

We also stopped at a defunct cable car tower overlooking a valley. It was easy to see why the cable car had been built there, with its expansive view over the valley, a river snaking through it, and surrounded by several layers of treeless mountains. But now the cable car platform was graffiti-covered and had not run for years. The cable car tower was in a residential neighborhood with houses sheltered behind fences made of old car parts, and there were concrete apartment buildings that didn't look like they'd been touched since the Soviet era. The whole area looked like it could be still in the USSR circa 1950, and it was disconcerting.

We wondered if the rest of Armenia would feel like it was stuck in the Soviet-era, until we arrived in Yerevan. We stayed in a hotel right on the Republic Square, the city's main plaza. The whole square was teeming with people, like Times Square in New York, and everyone seemed to be dressed up. We had been traveling all day and felt dusty and bedraggled by comparison.

Our guide recommended several restaurants, and every one of them was booked solid. One after the other turned us away. It was a Monday night! I kept thinking . . . Yerevan? A city I'd never even heard of. It was so alive and vibrant.

There was a singing fountain dancing to music, with hundreds of people crowding around. Vendors sold balloons and trinkets to the tourists milling around the plaza.

The next morning, the guide took us to a few must-sees in Yerevan. I was blown away by the Cafesjian Art Center—an entire hillside that been turned into a sculpture garden and art museum. Yerevan was a truly unique and gorgeous city.

On our way back to Georgia, despite not intending to go anywhere near the contested region between Azerbaijan and Armenia, we nervously watched the GPS dot on Google Maps bob and weave between Armenian and Azerbaijani territory.

There are numerous enclaves of Azerbaijani territory throughout Armenia, and the reverse is also true—pockets of Armenia surrounded by Azerbaijani land. It's like whoever was drawing the border lines splattered ink and never went back to clean up the blotches.

The road didn't exactly follow the borders, but as we progressed, the roads were empty. Even though we crossed in and out of the two "enemy" countries, there was no issue for us.

I thought about sending my godmother a picture of that map too, but I didn't think she'd understand it.

Our last day in the region began back in our home base of Tbilisi, which by that point felt like home. The same guide who had taken us on the Hidden Gems tour to the Kazbegi mountains drove us to Tsalka Canyon. He hadn't been there since the hanging diamond-shaped café was built, so he was interested to see it too.

It was honestly pretty magical. A glass bridge led to the diamond café, so even walking out to the cafe you could see through the bridge to the canyon below. The café itself was two stories tall, with glass floors, suspended 400 feet above the river. The café part wasn't open yet, and there were hardly any people there. We were able to take pictures in it and look out over the canyon as long as we wanted.

It was so cool! Some people might get a tad freaked out—or super freaked out—but I loved it!

We were so excited to see the hanging diamond, we could

have left and been entirely satisfied, but our guide wanted us to see the canyon itself, which he had been to many times. A beautifully groomed path led all the way down into the canyon, at the bottom of which was a waterfall. Benches had been placed on a platform in front of the waterfall, giving us a perfect place to watch the waterfall cascade—and to look up at the diamond café hanging above us. Honestly, it was an amazing spot, and it would've been a shame to miss it.

Figuring out how to navigate the logistical puzzle to see all three countries was absolutely worth it. Georgia was every bit as amazing as we'd hoped—with its comfortable, beautiful old city and remote mountains. I'm sure Jon and I will be back to hike and climb there someday.

We were surprised by how much we liked both Armenia and Azerbaijan. Yerevan on a Monday was hopping! And in Azerbaijan, we loved the contrast between the ancient old city, the European-style buildings, and the ultra-modern glass architecture.

That diamond café, the gorgeous canyon it was suspended over, and—perhaps especially—the fact that it was still relatively unknown, made it a true hidden gem.

CHAPTER 24

ALBANIA:
WHAT HAPPENS IN ALBANIA . . .

We decided to visit Albania and Montenegro because we'd been to the Balkans a few years earlier, and there were a few countries, including Albania, that we weren't able to visit. Michele taught several Albanian students, so she was also interested in seeing where they were from.

As we were planning the trip and discussing transportation options, Michele said, "Let's get a car so we can explore on our own. But this time, *you* rent it."

We hadn't had a car since we rented in Milan on our first trip. In the Baltics, we took busses or flew, and in the Balkans, we had those amazing Daytrip rides. In Georgia, Azerbaijan, and Armenia we used a series of TripAdvisor tours. I agreed with her that while there were a lot of benefits to tours and drivers, there was so much freedom in being able to drive ourselves.

And Michele was right. I definitely needed to rent the car, since "she'd" gotten all of those tickets on our first trip together—which were my fault since I had been driving. "You know I love driving!" I said.

However, there were no options to pick up a rental in Albania and leave it in another country. I know each country has its own rules, and different car rental companies have different policies, but we found absolutely no options to pick up a car in Albania and drop it off elsewhere.

The best we could do was pick up a car in Montenegro. We also decided not to drive in Albania, having heard that the roads were terrible and that the country had one of the highest rates of vehicular deaths in Europe—yikes!—so we opted for drivers there again.

When we landed in Tirana, the first thing we did after checking in was to take a taxi out to Bunk'Art 1, one of the North Korean-style bunkers built into the hills.

Albania had been a communist country and part of the Eastern Bloc, but it was neither in the USSR nor in Yugoslavia. It was its own isolated communist dictatorship. Its leader, Enver Hoxha, actually met the leader of North Korea and was inspired to dig bunkers. Any time you can say "inspired by North Korea," you know it was a true dictatorship.

Bunk'Art 1 was like an underground city, with more than 100 rooms and five floors of tunnels dug into the hills, where the Communist government could hide and continue to rule if necessary. I had déjà vu walking into the bunker. It reminded me of some of the fortified bunkers that were on my Air Force Base when I was stationed in South Korea.

Those bunkers were much smaller, though, meant purely as defensive positions for personnel and munitions.

Bunk'Art 1—and the smaller Bunk'Art 2 in the heart of Tirana—had been converted into museums with detailed historical narratives of the era. Some rooms were preserved as they might have been during that era. There were maps, phones, and desks, as well as a large room with a theater for mass assemblies.

Other rooms featured displays showing the abuses of the regime. One room had a barber chair used to cut the hair of anyone entering Albania who didn't meet the regime's idea of a "proper" haircut in keeping with communist ideals. The sign said, "No hippies," so surely it would've been a short cut for men. I'm not sure about women's styles.

We went to another museum and learned that Mother Teresa, though having been born in Skopje, North Macedonia, was raised in an Albanian Catholic household. Her mother and sister lived in Albania during the communist era. When her mother fell ill, Mother Teresa requested permission to visit but was denied entry by the anti-religious communist state. She only returned to Albania in 1993, after the fall of communism four years after her mother had died.

Denying Mother Teresa the ability to visit her dying mother? *Seriously?* That one fact put the dictatorship in perspective for me, and frankly, gave me chills. Of course, there are now statues of Mother Teresa in Albania, but—wow—talk about too little, too late!

After the bunker, we took a cable car up to the top of Dajti Mountain, sharing the car with two guys from the Netherlands who had come to Albania for a long weekend. They told us that Albania was going to be the "next Croatia." Albania was extremely cost-effective—cheap! —making it a great getaway for weekenders or anyone looking to travel without breaking the bank.

Albania was still developing its tourist infrastructure. It wasn't yet a top tourist destination, so it wasn't overcrowded. I hoped that "the next Croatia" didn't mean that Albania would soon be overrun, but it probably did.

The cable car itself was amazing, traversing a significant horizontal distance across Dajti park before ascending vertically up the mountain. On top, there was a gorgeous overlook of all of Tirana and Dajti National Park below.

After Tirana, we rode with a Daytrip driver over Llogara Pass to Dhermi. We chose to go to Dhermi literally only because it's at the base of Llogara Pass. I had been so excited about the Pass—numerous travel blogs said it was one of the "must-see" things in Albania. It was a high mountain pass, and even on Google Maps, I could see all of the switchbacks of the highway winding over the mountains.

I have to admit—I was disappointed. Only a month earlier, I had driven over Independence Pass in Colorado, between Aspen and Colorado Springs, while visiting family. Independence Pass is an extremely narrow, winding pass through the Rocky Mountains, and even in June, it was still covered in snow. In my opinion, Independence Pass is absolutely gorgeous, and you feel like you're right in the middle of the mountains.

The only thing that made Llogara Pass stand out was that you could see the ocean on one side and the mountains on the other. You could definitely not do that in Colorado. Maybe if I'd been able to drive it myself, I would have loved it more. From the back seat of the car, it had nothing on Colorado, though I might be biased.

After Llogara Pass, we arrived in Dhermi, where our driver dropped us off at a small four-room guesthouse on a back street.

Dhermi is a beach town. Michele isn't really a beach

person either, despite having grown up near the Jersey Shore. We had never gone to the beach on any of our previous trips. Still, we thought, why not enjoy the beach since we were there? We checked in, put on our swimsuits, and walked down toward the shoreline, following Google Maps.

Dhermi is definitely still under development. Google navigated us straight down to the shoreline, but we were on back roads that were still half under construction. Google said the route was "mostly flat," even though we were on a steep decline.

It wasn't the first time that trip that I wondered how solid Google's mapping was in Albania, but it was the first time it was completely wrong. *Mostly flat, ha!* At the bottom of the hill, we stood in a parking lot, looking at the shore and trying to figure out where to go. Apparently, we were in the parking lot of a police station, and we were told we needed to move along. *Whoops!*

We walked to the right from the police station and found a section of the shoreline that was less a "public beach" than a rocky stretch of land that didn't appear to be owned by anyone. We ditched our shorts and waded out in the water in our swimsuits, sunning ourselves on giant boulders in the surf like mermaids.

We finally found the beachfront hotels. The beach itself was dotted with cabanas and lined with beach chairs and umbrellas. Every square foot of the beach looked like it was either part of a hotel package or for rent. I was happy we'd found the little bit of undeveloped shoreline back by the police station. And as packed as it already was, it also made me wonder what it would look like if it became "the next Croatia."

After three days of traveling in Albania, we had one day left in the country. Michele needed to get some money from the ATM, since most places outside of Tirana only took cash.

Albania is not in the EU, so it has its own currency, the lek—which is apparently named after Alexander the Great, as in "A-LEK-xander." Instead of withdrawing 7,000 lek (seventy dollars), Michele accidentally pulled 70,000. One extra zero and she had $700 worth of lek. We were both shocked the bank let her take that much out—there were no warnings or "Are you sure?" messages. We were heading to Montenegro the next day, so we figured we could simply convert the lek to euros in Montenegro, since Montenegro uses the euro.

We took a bus from Albania to Kotor, which took about three hours—much longer than you'd think it should take for under 70 miles. As soon as we got off the bus, we picked up our rental car. The man at the agency berated us for being "late" for our reservation and rolled his eyes when I said the bus had taken longer than expected. He said, "The bus is always late."

He "did us a favor" and still let us have the car, but he charged a higher rate. We considered walking away, but all of our plans hinged on the car.

I questioned the wisdom of getting a rental car again while driving to the small guesthouse near the walled city Michele had reserved. As we followed Google Maps, the roads got progressively narrower. All of them seemed to be one-way in the wrong direction, and it felt like we were going straight up the hillsides at such an angle that I could barely see the road.

The guesthouse wasn't marked from the outside, or at least not well-marked. After driving in circles, I started to get frustrated and afraid I'd run into something. When it looked like the guesthouse was down a too-narrow dead end, Michele got out and walked a half block to the address.

She found the owner, and he came with her back to the car. He shooed me out of the driver's seat—I was all too happy to comply—and I climbed into the back seat. He zipped through the one-way, narrow, almost-vertical roads like they were nothing to him, — or like he had been driving them all his life. He parked the car in front of his guesthouse. *Whew!*

After checking in, we walked straight to a bank. The bank teller told us that not only could they not exchange Michele's lek, but also that no bank in Montenegro would. That seemed like a bold statement, so we tried two other banks—and he was not wrong. *Uh oh!*

I called ahead to our next hotel and asked if they could exchange Albanian leks. They said, "Yes, ma'am, we have a full-service exchange counter . . . wait, what currency did you say you wanted to exchange?"

"Albanian lek."

"Oh, no. No, we don't exchange leks. Sorry."

We started looking online and found out that the Albanian lek is a closed currency. You can only change leks inside Albania, and any lek you have outside Albania is less valuable than Monopoly money. At least you can buy Boardwalk with Monopoly money.

The next day, we had a cooking class in Kotor, Montenegro. It was something we'd never done before, and it sounded interesting.

It was so much better than we'd hoped. The best part was being in the home of a local woman and learning about her life while chopping vegetables. Let's be honest: she did all the real cooking; we were just choppers.

Our hostess was a home cook and told us all about her life growing up in Yugoslavia. She was proud of being Yugoslavian and felt that life had been easier in those days. For working eight hours a day as a nurse, the government provided her with an apartment—the same apartment she still lived in and where we were cooking with her.

"Yugoslavia used to have the strongest passport in the world," she said. It was the second time we had heard that that day. Yugoslavians could travel to any of the Eastern Bloc countries, but they also maintained relations with the West, allowing travel to the U.S. and Europe as well.

I asked her about Albania, and her answer was quick. "They are not like us," she said. "My cousin, she went to Albania to shop one weekend. That's when the dictatorship took over. We didn't hear from her for 25 years."

After the cooking class, we had a free afternoon which we'd planned to use to explore Montenegro, but we decided to make the trek back to Albania to exchange Michele's $700. $700 is a lot of money for it to be completely worthless, and when would we ever make it back to Albania?

Kotor is only 100 kilometers away from Shkoder, Albania, the first real city across the border—and probably only 80 kilometers from the border itself. That's only 60 miles; how long could it take? Google said over two and a half hours. But . . . 60 miles? There was no way it could take that long. Maybe Google just didn't know what it was talking about again. The bus had taken that long on the way to Kotor, but that was a bus. Surely it was just traveling slow.

Montenegrin driving is insane. Montenegro is mountainous, and there is one long road snaking between the ocean and the mountains. We stayed on that for quite a while, and it was like a video game with hazards popping up randomly—cars stopping to let people take pictures, pedestrians emerging from the beaches—and it seemed as if every car had to immediately pass the one in front of it, despite oncoming traffic.

Google said we had to take a left, and I said, "No way that is the road." *Google must not have all the roads mapped in Montenegro!* There were cars coming out of the road, and there was no room for me to turn into. It was only one lane wide.

I kept driving straight, thinking that Google would find me a better road. It kept telling me to turn left at every possible road. Finally, we realized that if we didn't go left, we were going to be completely off course, and I doubled back to one of the turns.

The road I picked was also one lane wide with two-way traffic—so narrow that whenever I saw an oncoming car, one of us had to find space to pull over to let the other pass. It was so curvy that it was like a continuous blind corner; I never knew when the next car would come at us. On the smaller lanes, there were fewer pedestrians, but cows and sheep were added to the menu of pop-up road hazards.

We were in residential neighborhoods behind agricultural fields, and I kept thinking, as one hour stretched into two . . . *how is this the best road? Is Google just dumb here and leading us down the wrong roads?*

Finally, after two and a half hours of white-knuckled driving, we pulled up to the border of Albania. The border guards barely glanced at our passports and waved us through. Rolling forward, we thought we were done, but then we were waved over to another set of guards—the Albanian guards. They also glanced at our passports and gave them back. No questions, no stamps. Just boredom. We drove into Albania.

Shkoder was another twenty or so kilometers away and we were racing against the clock because it was almost 6 p.m. and some of the exchange offices would be closing soon. Our backup plan was to return to the hotel where we'd stayed the night before, which had a sign saying they exchanged currency. I noticed it at the time but never thought we had to change money before leaving Albania.

About five minutes after passing the Albanian border, I saw a small convenience store, and it had a sign showing Albanian leks, dollar signs, and euros. I pulled in, thinking we just might get them to do the conversion. I pointed at the store. "Try there. Maybe they'll change your money." Michele ran in.

I stayed in the car to let the adrenaline drain and my nerves settle. I was spent after having done two and a half hours of black belt driving and didn't want to drive another 20 km to Skhoder if I didn't have to. Finally, I felt bad about sending Michele in on her own, so I pulled into a proper parking spot, locked the car, and joined her inside the store.

She was standing in line with about twenty Russians buying cheap Albanian liquor. The store clerk was a young woman, and she had no help. Since we had an unusual request, Michele waited patiently. I roamed the convenience store to see if there was anything interesting. I grabbed a few Coke Zeros for the return trip.

Once the line died down, Michele asked if she could convert her money. A man in line behind us spoke excellent English and helped us with translations. The young clerk called her boss and asked if it was okay to exchange, and if so, what rate to use. She counted out the money and gave Michele euros at the current exchange rate. I thought for sure they'd give us a worse exchange rate because it wasn't an official money-exchanging place. But nope! *Hallelujah!*

Driving back to Kotor took another two and a half hours, and it was just as winding and crazy as before. Apparently, that was the only road to take, or at least the only one Google knew about. Once we had changed the money and knew what to expect, I found the drive enjoyable. I felt like Mario Andretti zipping along, facing the obstacles of the racetrack. I love a challenge, and that drive definitely pushed me. It was also beautiful. I thought again that if I'd been able to drive Llogara Pass myself, my opinion about it might have been different.

It wasn't quite what I'd envisioned our afternoon of "exploring Montenegro" to be, but we certainly saw a lot of the country. Michele took videos of the racetrack route, and we laughed about the drive. There is a reason that people kept stopping to take pictures on the main road that wound between the ocean and the mountains—it was gorgeous!

On a quiet-ish stretch of road, a thought struck me. I asked Michele, "Is Albania a permissible country on our rental agreement?" We had gotten cross-border permission so we could enter some of the other countries in the Balkans.

She read the list of countries and said, "No! We were not allowed to drive in Albania."

We hadn't even asked when we got the car because we never thought we'd drive back into Albania. Why in the world would we?

If we had run into any trouble in Albania, or if the border guards hadn't allowed us back *into* Montenegro . . . what a disaster it could have been! But on the Albania–Montenegro border, they didn't give us a second glance, either inbound or outbound. *Thank goodness.*

Our problems with money, rental cars, and the attitude of our cooking-class hostess in Montenegro were eye-openers for us. Albania is still an outlier in the region. (There are also allegations of rampant corruption in Albania, which could also play a part in the rules.) We learned about "closed currencies" and resolved to be much more careful about always exchanging currency before leaving a country. And, we got to "explore" Montenegro like a race car driver.

We enjoyed our time in Albania, but we were also glad to move on.

THE LATER YEARS

CHAPTER 25

SAUDI ARABIA:
WHEN IN ROME, BUT NOT AT HOME

Having been in the 11th class of women to graduate from the U.S. Air Force Academy and having served as a Security Police officer in the Air Force, I faced a great deal of discrimination. Some of it was subtle—like radio dispatchers not responding to my call during training because "we didn't think there were any women lieutenants, so we thought it was a prank." Some of it was more overt, like when my commanders called me in for a "father-daughter" talk whenever I was assigned to a new post, to ask if I was "strong enough to carry my weapon." *Seriously?*

Technology consulting is another male-dominated field, and during my 25-year career, I was rarely in a room or meeting when women represented more than 20% of the attendees. Bias was still a problem, though it was much less in-your-face than in the military.

Then I went to Saudi Arabia and found out I didn't know anything about discrimination or what it felt like to truly be treated like a second-class citizen.

One of my Air Force Academy buddies, Dave, served at the Embassy in Saudi Arabia. *Of course we had to go!* We planned to go for Christmas and coordinated with Dave and the embassy to get "family-invite" visas, since no tourist visas to Saudi Arabia were available in 2016. When the visas came, we only got two of them. One for Jon, one for me, but not one for Jono. The explanation was all in Arabic, of course. Google Translate wasn't where it is today, so we didn't know why we only received two. We assumed it was because Jon and Jono have the same legal name, except for a suffix—Jono is the 2nd.

We called Dave and the Embassy, but there wasn't anything we could do. We replanned our holiday trip with Jono to go elsewhere, and then Jon and I went to Saudi Arabia on our own in the spring.

It was the first trip Jon and I had taken together without Jono since he was born. We always planned our trips around Jono's school breaks, even when he was in college. But that time, we had to purposely plan for when he would be at college, since we never could get that third visa. Going without him felt strange, but he was in college and growing up, and he wouldn't be able to travel with us all the time anymore.

Dave picked Jon and I up from the airport and brought one of his wife's *abayas* for me. At that time, women—including foreigners—had to wear an *abaya* (a long black robe) and a *hijab* (a headscarf). The only thing I didn't have to wear was the *niqab*, (the face covering that leaves only the eyes exposed).

I was already wearing a *hijab* I bought on the internet, which I put on in the airport bathroom. A woman saw me struggling with it, took pity on me, and helped me wind it around my hair, showing me how to wear it properly. Of course, it never looked as good the rest of the trip when I did it myself. She made it look drapey and lovely; when I put it on, it looked like I had a black bandage wrapped around my head.

Dave studied Arabic through the Defense Language Institute in the Air Force and had served at the embassy for the previous few years. He understood the language, the culture, and the rules as well as anyone could who wasn't from there.

I kept running into "rules" I didn't even know existed.

After touring us around Riyadh, we went to a Dairy Queen, which is incidentally the biggest Dairy Queen in the world. There were two doors on the Dairy Queen: one for men, and one for women and families. If Jon and Dave had gone there alone, they would go to the regular door. Since they were with me, they had to go to the family door. Women are not permitted in the "normal" section of the restaurant. That was true for every restaurant we went to, including Starbucks.

At Dairy Queen, when we sat down, Jon sat on the inside of the booth, and I sat down next to him. Dave was up at the register handling the order. He came back to the booth and shook his head.

"Tauni, you have to sit on the inside."

"What?"

"Switch. Women on the inside. What if some man walked past the table and touched you?"

I shook my head, and we switched.

While I don't doubt that was custom, was it a rule, or just a custom? Could I have gotten away with staying on the outside? Probably. Was he partly messing with me by making me switch versus letting it go? Probably. But as I looked around, all the women were sitting on the inside, and the men on the outside.

The same rule applied when we walked on the street. I always like to walk with my husband on my right because I hang my purse on my left shoulder. However, in Saudi Arabia, Dave made sure that when we walked along the street on the way to the National History Museum, Jon had to be on the outside, closest to the street, and I had to be on the inside.

The other thing I noticed as we walked — I was absolutely melting. Wearing an *abaya* is fricking hot. It's black and it's hot and it's Saudi Arabia. Jon, as a man, got to wear whatever he wanted. A T-shirt and jeans or slacks. I was too hot to think or breathe. Of course, the women of Saudi Arabia are probably much smarter than I am about what to wear underneath, something light and airy, maybe. I was wearing jeans, a T-shirt, and boots; and I was on fire.

As a foreigner, I willingly followed the rules, however much I hated them. It was not my country, not my culture, not my place to fight them. But it goes beyond "when in Rome." At the time, there were still morality police who would stop women if the *hijab* wasn't worn properly—or for other offenses. Dave's wife had been stopped several times for improper head cover.

After 2016, many of those rules were relaxed. I heard from a friend who went to Saudi Arabia for work that she was able to wear normal office clothing for her client meetings. Women can now drive cars, tourist visas are being issued, and reforms have reduced the authority of the religious police. Perhaps I just got "lucky" enough to see the country when rules were still strictly enforced.

As we drove back to the embassy compound where Dave lived, I looked out the window at the streets of downtown

Riyadh. There were mostly men. Men walking to work, men working, men walking with friends, men driving. The few women we saw would hop out of cars, always in groups of three of four, and rush into whatever store they were going to, as if they were playing "the floor is lava"—except the entire city was "lava" for women.

Riyadh was oppressive. And frankly, it made me angry. I had never experienced anything like that before.

One night, Dave invited us to go to an embassy party with him. I hadn't brought a dress or anything besides jeans, so I had to wear an *abaya*. Since it was in the embassy compound, I didn't have to wear a *hijab*, which was a relief.

The embassy party was large, maybe 200 people, and of course, Jon and I didn't know anyone. While Jon was entirely entertained by the gathering, I am an introvert, and those kinds of parties make me extremely uncomfortable.

He met someone from the Mexican embassy and said, "So I hear you're going to pay for a wall?" It could have been a completely cringe moment, but it was taken for the joke it was and everyone laughed. At one point, Jon went to find us drinks, and I stayed put, doing my best impersonation of a wall.

When Jon came back, he said, "I found some people from your company." He brought me over to them.

There were five or six men, (all men, of course) all expats from the UK or Australia—none from Saudi Arabia. Alcohol was served at embassy parties because it's on the embassy compound, whereas alcohol isn't allowed in Saudi Arabia proper. This made the parties major draws for anyone who could get an invitation.

I had been at my consulting company almost 20 years at that point, and it didn't matter that we were in Saudi Arabia. We had a common language and an instant connection. I asked what projects they worked on and how long they'd been there. Most of them were working on oil and gas projects—duh, I should have guessed that—and had been there for several years.

I also asked if there were any women on their projects. They said yes, but the women had a separate side of the office, walled off the same way as the two sides of the Dairy Queen. They could talk to the women through phones, which made me think of the phone booths in prisons in movies—except in prison it's better, because you can see through the glass.

I wondered if it was even worth being in the office as a woman if you could only talk to the rest of the team through the phone on the wall. But of course, they could talk to the other women in the office. I can't imagine how frustrating that would be.

After Riyadh, we went to a Bedouin village museum, like the Colonial Williamsburg of Saudi Arabia. It had adobe-type walls, and all the houses were connected, with small lanes winding through the village. I got out of the car and took a few steps toward the village. Dave and Jon were right behind me.

"Tauni, what are you doing?" Dave asked.

I stopped. "What? I'm just checking it out."

He said, "You have to get 10 feet behind us."

"You're kidding me, right?"

"Look around at the other families."

There weren't a lot of people in the village. Since tourists weren't allowed in Saudi Arabia yet, there were only a few Saudi families. Dave was right, of course. Of the three or four family groups, the men were in front, and the women were several feet behind. Hating, hating, hating it, I hung back until Jon and Dave passed me, then fell in step right behind them. I stayed close on their heels—no way was I walking ten feet back. That's ridiculous.

We went through the village and saw various houses that had been turned into museums. They were interesting, but by then I was so conscious of stepping out of line that I barely noticed the museum itself. In one house-museum, the owner asked Jon if he was American, and he said yes. He and Jon talked about America for a while, and I felt like I was invisible.

At another house, Dave sat on a little couch, and I sat down next to him because we'd been on our feet for a while. I realized that people must think that Dave and I were married, and Jon was our American friend. No way should I have been sitting next to Dave if he weren't my husband. I felt simultaneously super self-conscious and conspicuous as a "female" getting the rules wrong, but also invisible as an individual. I was no longer Tauni. It was so disconcerting.

When we got to the airport to return home, I gave Dave back the *abaya* I had borrowed and took off the *hijab*, which was no longer required in the international airport. Oddly, it felt weird to be out of that garb. As disconcerting as it felt to wear it, there was something freeing about the invisibility of being under an *abaya* and *hijab*. I was wearing red cowgirl boots and jeans and felt like everyone was staring at me, like I was on display.

When I was back in the U.S., you would think I'd have been so excited to be back home where I could be myself and not feel like I was treated like a second-class citizen. I'll be honest: I became utterly intolerant of any discrimination or sexism that I might once have overlooked or put up with. Walking ten feet behind might be required in Saudi Arabia, but it doesn't fly at home.

Shortly after our return, I went to a company office-wide event where they gave out T-shirts to everyone. I asked for a women's T-shirt and was told they only had unisex—which really just means men's. "Unisex" is clever branding to make men's shirts seem more acceptable to everyone. But they're men's shirts. Period.

The office lead at the time was a mentor and friend of mine, and I asked her why we only gave out men's T-shirts. She said, "You know, I never thought about it. I always give company T-shirts to my son."

In my twenty years at the company, I'd never once been given a women's T-shirt. She could say the same for her thirty plus years. After that, my company started providing both men's and women's shirts at events in New York. It's a small thing, but I was no longer willing to tolerate small things in the USA in this day and age, not after what I'd seen in Saudi Arabia.

CHAPTER 26

JAMAICA:
WEEKEND ADVENTURE

A friend at work told me about his favorite resort in Jamaica. I like resorts about as much as I like beaches, but . . . I needed a break from work, and taking a four-day weekend trip and adding another country to my list sounded great, especially if I could take his recommendation and not have to spend time researching places to go. I just wanted a break. Work had been exhausting, which seemed to be the case more and more often.

After our success at traveling on our own to Saudi Arabia, Jon and I decided to take the trip to Jamaica on our own. And, Jon and is always up for "waterfront ops."

As I was going to book the resort, a couple of other resorts popped up on the website. They were part of the same family of resorts. One was on the beach—just what you'd expect for Jamaica—while the other was in the mountains, tucked in lush, jungle-covered hills. That looked amazing. I asked Jon his opinion, and he said, "Let's do both." *Yes, and!*

We booked two nights at each resort and got a rental car to drive to the resorts and between them. That seemed like a normal thing to do. I realized later that resort people would have just taken a shuttle to the resort from the airport and just stayed in the resort the whole time.

The first resort was amazing! It offered great snorkeling, stand-up paddleboarding, and a bunch of great restaurants. *Okay, resort people, you're not wrong.*

But after the two days, I had moved from relaxed to antsy and was eager to see more of the island. We trundled off in the rental car. Jon drove and I navigated. I've done some left-side driving in our travels, but Jon is by far more comfortable with it and whipped around the roads like he'd been driving them his whole life.

We drove up into the mountains, and of course, we weren't just driving from Point A to Point B. We had to see if we could find a hike—or a climb—somewhere in between. We navigated through towns, behind what seemed to be industrial zones, and wound our way upward. I didn't think tourists had been on those roads in a long time, if ever.

We had a nice drive but couldn't find anything that looked like a trailhead, nor anything suitable for climbing. We started running out of time, so we turned around and headed toward the resort.

On the way back down the mountain, a young woman was walking alongside the road. Jon stopped and asked her if she wanted a ride. "To the bottom of the hill," she said, and hopped in. I don't think it would qualify as picking up a hitchhiker—more like giving a ride to a local. She told us she was walking to the main road where she could get a bus. Of course, Jon asked her about herself while expertly navigating the roads, and then she hopped out and waved at us.

We still had a ways to go before reaching the resort. The distance wasn't far, but the roads were terrible, and we'd spent a lot of time driving around the mountains. On a relatively straight stretch of road, the car hit one of the many almost inescapable potholes.

And then we heard it—the flapping sound that could only mean one thing. We had a flat.

Jon pulled off the road. There were a couple of houses alongside the road, and the other side was a sheer mountain. Before Jon could even pull the spare out of the car, a man came out of the house we had stopped in front of.

He jumped in and helped us change the tire, as expertly as if he worked on a pit crew—or as if it weren't the first flat he'd seen on those roads! The day we arrived in Jamaica, we had stopped at a liquor store on the way to the resort, thinking we should get some local rum. We had a couple of hip flask-sized bottles and gave one to the man to thank him for his kindness.

We made it to the mountain resort with no further mishaps. And, oh! I was so glad we booked it. I liked the beachy resort more than I thought I would. But this . . . this place was magical. Our room overlooked a deep valley, dark green and shrouded in mist.

There were hummingbirds and rainbow-colored salamanders, and lizards or geckos? I'm not sure what they were, but they were beautiful, and they were everywhere. After we dropped off our stuff, Jon wanted to walk the grounds and hit the pool. I wasn't up for a swim, but I was happy to walk around. The grounds opened up onto paths we could hike on—much better than anything we had found up in the mountains—and were incredibly lush. I felt myself truly relaxing and taking deep breaths. I was at home in the mountains, even if they were jungle-covered and hummingbird-filled.

Jon slipped into the pool, and I sat on a bench, refreshed by the view. At first, we were the only ones there. Then, a group of about six or seven arrived and set up on the opposite side of the pool. A few swam, a few stayed on the lounge chairs. They were all adults, and they didn't seem like resort people. There was something about their interactions.

Jon swam over to me and said, "I think that's Idris Elba."

What? Really? Idris Elba, who had just stripped down to his skivvies, not a bathing suit. Not that I was looking. I was very decidedly trying not to stare. But it was hard not to watch. *Was it really him? What in the world was he doing there?*

Filming, we learned by studiously not listening to their conversations, but it was hard not to overhear. It was a small pool, and we were the only other people there. They had been filming nearby and wanted to take a dip to cool down. *Of course they did!*

For us, it was the perfect weekend getaway. We got to see both beaches and mountains, had a bit of adventure tucked in the middle, explored a new country, and even enjoyed a celebrity sighting! No, we did not ask for his autograph. And no, we didn't sneak a picture either, even though I had my phone on me. So I have no proof—you'll just have to trust that it happened.

CHAPTER 27

SLOVENIA & CROATIA:
UNEXPECTED ADVENTURES

I saw images of Lake Bled everywhere that year—especially in my Facebook feed and in travel articles. We hadn't been to Slovenia yet, and Jono was up for traveling with us again that summer, so I started planning our family trip. Game of Thrones was all the rage that year as well, so of course we'd have to go into Croatia to see Dubrovnik while we were there.

While I was trying to fit everything into the schedule, Jon found a hike to the top of Mount Triglav—the tallest mountain in Slovenia and the second tallest in the Julian Alps. *A nice little hike then. Sure.*

We set aside a few days for Mount Triglav, which meant

we wouldn't have time to stay near Lake Bled, but I was hopeful we could at least stop by and see it.

We landed in in Zagreb, Croatia, and spent a day there. Zagreb had everything you'd want in a European capital: streets lined with cafés—not in the Parisian way, but more Prague-style or like a German beer garden—each café filled with people drinking steins of beer. It had narrow cobblestone streets, gothic-spired cathedrals, and European-style architecture. But it also had a few things that tipped Zagreb from quaint to interesting and raw.

There were concrete tunnels that ran under the hills and through the town, a legacy of WWII when they were built as bomb shelters and pedestrian walkways.

There was also a museum unlike any we'd ever seen—the Museum of Broken Relationships. There were rooms filled with various objects such as wedding dresses, necklaces, books, pairs of shoes, and cards. Each was accompanied by a story describing the relationship and its fate. Everything from war and disease to death and infidelity had crushed people's dreams of love. Even Jon, who is not usually the biggest fan of museums, was absorbed by the real-life stories.

We were glad there weren't many tourists in Zagreb, at least not noticeably, and few Americans. Zagreb felt like it was off the beaten path, and we were glad we had stayed a day there before moving on.

After Zagreb, we went to Ljubljana, Slovenia. We rented bikes and rode them through the city and up to the castle. The castle offered views over the city, with its red-tile roofs and the Julian Alps rising in the distance. We rode across stone bridges guarded by winged, snarling green dragon statues, their tails curled as if ready to launch into the sky. Riding along the river canal lined with cafés spilling onto the cobblestone streets, I could have stayed a few more days in Ljubljana. I was again amazed at how few tourists we saw.

On the way to Mount Triglav, we drove through Lake Bled, one of the main reasons I'd wanted to go to Slovenia in the first place. I had visions of sitting somewhere—in a park, on a mountain, or taking a boat to the little church—and enjoying the beautiful view.

Yeah, no!

Lake Bled was a mob scene. We found all the tourists! There was an endless parade of people walking down to the lake with bathing suits, towels, and beach bags. Traffic in the small town was close to gridlock, and there was no place to park. All the slots were full, and several cars in front of us were "sharking" to find a spot. It was clear the town was in no way prepared to handle the swarms of visitors attracted by the idyllic pictures on Facebook.

We kept driving until we got to the base of Mount Triglav, where we were staying at an athletic training center. It was a place where people could stay for the winter and train cross-country skiing or other winter sports. They rented out rooms to non-athletes like us when there were vacancies. It was far from luxury. The dining room looked like a college cafeteria, and the Wi-Fi barely worked, but we were much happier there than among the hordes at Lake Bled.

The next morning, we packed our gear and made sure we had our synthetic hiking clothes, warmer layers, rain shells, headlamps (just in case), water, snacks, maps, and information from the center stuffed into packs. Mount Triglav was not going to be a walk in the park.

With hiking, as with many things in life, expectations are everything. If you expect a one-hour hike and it turns out to be two hours, that second hour will feel like the hardest hour of your life. If you are mentally prepared for three hours, that second hour won't be so bad. I have learned through forced marches and running in formation in the military, as well as hikes with family, that it's best to either set expectations for the whole day or not to know how long the hike will be, especially because some guides are woefully inaccurate in their estimations of time. "A little bit up," or "only a little further" is not helpful expectation-setting!

I knew Mount Triglav was going to be long, so I set my expectations for the hike to last the entire day. The path wound through an alpine wilderness, surrounded at first by pine trees and ferns, then opening into meadows with little flowers and more pine trees. It looked like the Von Trapp family might come over the hills at any moment.

At the beginning, there were some horizontal stretches and downward slopes to offset the climb, so it didn't feel entirely uphill. But since we planned to stay the night at a lodge on top of the mountain, the day would be predominantly uphill. Mount Triglav is at over 9,300 feet, so we would have an elevation gain of around 7,000 feet from where we started— *A big damn up!*

The other thing with hikes is that you always think you see the top well before you actually do. You think you see the top, and then you get there, and it's just a false summit. Another peak rises behind what you thought was the summit, and it's likely hiding yet another. Mount Triglav was like that.

I was still working as a technology consultant, which meant five days of staring at my computer screen or sitting in meetings in the office for 12 hours a day. If I was lucky, I would take a walk around the small lake in our neighborhood once a week. An all-day uphill hike was far beyond my norm. After five or six hours, when I was running out of steam, I thought I saw our lodge—but it was a different hut, and there was still another ridge to climb.

By that point, we had left the lush lower elevations and were above the tree line. The path and the mountains were made of white rock, with streaks of pine green where there were shrubs or where moss clung on the rock. Snow capped the highest peaks. Everything was white and green, not the gray or brown granite I expected.

Finally, the mountain lodge we were staying at came into view. It was triangular, like a ski chalet, with several stories of windows. The roof was white to match its surroundings. It was still quite a ways, all uphill, but I knew I could make it.

When we got to the lodge, it was too early to check into our room, so we went to the lunch and snack bar instead. We ordered some food and flopped down at a table and benches in a corner. It was all hearty hiker's fare—stews, mac and cheese, and pastas—which was fine with us. I ordered the only vegetarian pasta, and Jono got a chili mac and tiramisu.

After we'd polished off the food, Jon said, "I think we should push on to the top now."

Top of what? We're in the lodge!

As a professional climber and mountain guide, Jon is the one who plans the hiking and climbing adventures. I focus on keeping up and taking one step after the other so as not to psych myself out. I didn't realize we still had to climb to the peak, an almost vertical push to the top, using *via ferrata* gear to clip in.

Maybe if I'd expected that from the beginning, I wouldn't have lost steam, but let's be honest—Jon and Jono were both in much better shape than I was. I was darn proud that I'd made it to the lodge, but I had nothing left for a vertical push. My "all-day" expectation setting had been turned off as soon as I saw the lodge. It was now set to "rest."

I told them I'd watch our stuff.

They got their gear on and trooped out.

I dutifully "watched" our stuff—if sleeping with my head on it counts as watching.

When they came back, we checked in. We'd reserved three beds and were lucky to be assigned a room, which had two sets of bunk beds and literally nothing else. It was about 6 by 8 feet, just big enough to squeeze in the two beds. We were each given a stack of blankets to make our beds. There was one window overlooking the mountains we'd just hiked. There was no electricity. The bathroom was back down the stairs near the dining area. It had running, non-potable water for washing hands, and the toilets were some kind of eco-microbial, non-flush jobbers. I've seen a lot worse.

Rustic as it was, I was super happy to have a bed and very glad we'd made the reservation. We—okay, I—wouldn't have made it back down to the car before nightfall if we'd tried to do the round trip in one day, and that would have been a whole different kind of epic adventure.

Since there were no lights, we went to bed early, and I woke up re-energized for the hike back. Knowing it was mostly downhill helped. It was a long hike, still four or five hours, but we had the advantage of enjoying the same beautiful scenery without the pressure of the continuous push to the top and without the exhaustion of the constant "up."

We headed back to Croatia, but this time, our destination was Dubrovnik. We stayed at a Marriott because I had points. It was right on the ocean, with its own beach, and an absolutely gorgeous resort hotel. I honestly hadn't expected Dubrovnik to be a beach town because of the focus on the walled city and *Game of Thrones*.

Jon and Jono took full advantage of being on the beach, and I even joined in a little. They took videos jumping off old walls and jetties into the ocean.

From the hotel, we took a water taxi to get to the walled city, which was amazing. It was a ten- to fifteen-minute cruise in a motorboat along the coastline, the water flanked by high cliffs, with the road we'd driven in on up on the cliffs. No traffic, no congestion, and a beautiful ride! *What could be better?*

The water taxi took us to Dubrovnik's port, filled with boats like ours from other hotels, larger sightseeing vessels, and swarms of confused tourists. It was mayhem. I wasn't sure we'd ever find our ride back.

From the port, there was a large stone doorway that led into the walled city. We walked through it, turned left, and were almost blinded by the main thoroughfare, paved with white, shiny stone like marble. In the midday sun, the glare off the pavement shone directly in our eyes.

There was a church at one end of the thoroughfare. We walked the opposite direction from it, down the length of the vast street that felt more like a giant courtyard. We made our way to the other end, trying to cling as closely to the shady side to avoid both the sun's heat and the glare off the pavement. As we walked, we dodged tourists who were wandering back and forth, darting into the shops, and lining up at the ice cream shop. There were *Game of Thrones* stores and T-shirts everywhere. *Game of Thrones* was too popular for Dubrovnik to be an off the beaten path destination anymore. *I should have known.*

At the end of the thoroughfare was a stairway up onto the city walls, so up we went.

It was August. We managed to get to the old city at noon, and it was blazing hot.

I was never good at dressing for hot weather. Growing up in Minot, North Dakota, where summers were not that hot and not that long, I never really worried about shorts or summer outfits. That day, I made one of my worst fashion choices ever—I wore a black T-shirt and black knee-length capris, and I absolutely melted. The only thing that could have been worse was if I'd worn black jeans and my preferred cowboy boots.

The only good thing about being up on the walls at noon was that there weren't too many other tourists with us. We were able to circumnavigate the whole city on the walls without having to worry about crowds.

The city below was a mosaic of orange-tiled roofs perched atop the stone walls of homes. A few church spires rose up and towered over them. Everything was set against bright blue backdrop, with only a thin line demarcating the sky from the ocean.

We took some jumping pictures that made it look like we were floating above the whole city. Jon is a great photographer, so the shots of me were great, but my face looked like a tomato. EMT squads were positioned around the walls, just in case someone suffered heatstroke. I didn't have to call them over, even after jumping multiple times for pictures, but I was glad they were there.

Walking on top of the walls offered a different view of the city from each angle, and we stayed there for almost an hour—way too long in the heat—but it was all so gorgeous.

The staircase down off the walls was in a tiny back street. It was secluded and relatively shady, so we stayed in those smaller back streets, exploring and avoiding the high traffic zones.

We passed a basketball court tucked into an alley near the top of the walled city, where some locals were playing a pick-up game. There were homes with laundry hanging on lines and children playing, and it felt like we'd found the real Dubrovnik.

It reminded me of our experience in Venice years earlier, when we'd been so overwhelmed by tourists that we kept walking until we got away from everyone and found some quiet back streets. One of our favorite memories of Venice was walking into a tiny grocery shop to buy olives. Jon struck up a conversation with the clerk, whose family had lived in

Venice for generations, and he told us about his life there.

Later that night, after we managed to find our water taxi and make it back to the hotel, we walked up the coastline, away from the walled city. We heard some yelling, so we followed the noise and found a water polo game being held in a roped-off section of an inlet. I'd never watched water polo before. We climbed up on stone steps constructed as bleachers and watched.

It was fascinating to watch people tread water, then leap up like dolphins to hurl the ball or block the opposing team's passes. I wouldn't have lasted two minutes in that sport before I'd get dunked and just sink. It was really impressive.

The interesting part about travel is that no matter what you plan or how well you plan, things always turn out different than you expect.

I expected to love Dubrovnik and Lake Bled—after all, they were the main reason we chose Slovenia and Croatia for that trip. But it was the challenge of climbing Mount Triglav and the unexpected beauty of Zagreb and Ljubljana that stayed with us long after we returned home. Even in Dubrovnik, one of our favorite moments was watching the water polo players, not something we would have ever found in TripAdvisor or in a guidebook.

That's the beauty and the value of traveling. Finding the unexpected. Learning about things you could never truly understand otherwise.

CHAPTER 28

JAPAN:
SNOW MONKEYS AND HEDGEHOGS

For our Christmas travel, I threw out a couple of ideas including Japan. Jono immediately said, "Oooh, let's go see the snow monkeys." We had watched the *National Geographic* documentary on snow monkeys together, and I agreed it would be cool to see them. I wasn't sure how we'd trek through snowy mountains in search of snow monkeys though. I booked the trip to Japan anyway, but I didn't have much faith we'd actually see any monkeys.

I was told by friends that Japan would seem like the "most foreign" place we'd ever traveled. I didn't expect that to be the case, since we'd already lived in Korea. Admittedly, I was schooled almost immediately when I tried to tip the hotel porter after he carried our bags to our room. "You are in Japan now." he said. "We take pride in a job well done." *Ouch, got it. No tips!*

We spent a few days in Tokyo, and once we'd figured out the subway system—with the help of a local woman who explained the different price zones and routes—I loved how each different metro stop felt like popping up into a completely different part of the city, each with its own personality. It was like emerging in different New York neighborhoods: Midtown Manhattan, Upper East, Wall Street, or Greenwich Village.

Our favorite neighborhood was hip and trendy, filled with vintage clothing stores, and Jono found a hedgehog café. Holding a sleepy hedgehog was exactly the thing I never knew I always wanted to do.

On one of our days in Tokyo, we wanted to go to the fish market. Jon and Jono wanted sushi; I just wanted to see everything. The market itself was huge—a full city block of vendors selling every kind of fish and seafood. Fish was displayed with glassy eyes staring at us. There were aquariums filled with lobsters, crabs, and other creatures that could be plucked out and cooked. So *not my thing!*

There were also countless little cafés and restaurants serving a variety of seafood, from sushi to fish soups and stews, and dishes I couldn't begin to name. We picked a sushi restaurant that was tiny—it had just a few seats around a counter. Everyone was required to order a meal to have a seat. Jon and Jono picked out their meals, both sashimi, so they wouldn't fill up on rice. They picked a third plate for "me" to order, which they would share. I had a glass of wine.

The sushi chefs cut, sliced, and rolled everything right in front of us, and even after we were served, the show continued as they prepared everyone else's meals. Jon and

Jono said the sashimi was amazing and fresh. I was glad they loved it, *but no thank you!*

Afterwards, we walked through what felt like half of Tokyo, including the "IKEA of electronics stores," a ten-story building filled with every imaginable gadget.

By dinner, I was starving, having only eaten a granola bar for lunch. I didn't want to stop for lunch and hold up Jon and Jono, who were still full from the sushi feast, especially with so much to see. That was probably a bad decision. I should have eaten some real food.

Jon had gotten a recommendation for a ramen restaurant from a friend who had been to Tokyo many times. We found it on Google Maps and got out at Shinjuku station. Shinjuku station was mammoth, covering multiple blocks with innumerable exits, and we weren't sure where to go. We picked an exit at random and left the station.

Jon navigated us through a neighborhood we hadn't explored yet, with tiny back alleys, gambling and game shops, and tons of stores and restaurants. We must have walked another 45 minutes to an hour. After having walked all day with no food, I was pretty much at the end of my rope.

Finally—hallelujah—Jon found the fabled ramen shop. We must have passed at least fifty similar shops, but no, we had to go to *this* one.

It was closed. Jon double-checked the address, name, and hours.

I turned away from the ramen shop. Next door, there was a little Italian restaurant on the second floor. I started walking up the steps. I said, "I'm eating here."

I was done. I had passed from hungry to hangry, and I wasn't about to go back out into the madness of the district to find another ramen shop. And let's face it, I know it's my problem. I'm the vegetarian who refused to eat sushi and didn't want to stop for lunch because there was so much to see. If we went back out to find a ramen shop, Jon and Jono could eat at the first one, but I'd have to read the menus—and maybe by the fifth, seventh, or eleventh place, there would be some vegetarian options. It was my fault, but I didn't care. I was exhausted, hungry, and tired of struggling to find food that I could eat in Japan.

I got pizza, and so did they. It was a homey little place with excellent food and a great atmosphere, and I'd recommend it to anyone who wanted a good restaurant in Japan. Of course, no one goes to Japan for pizza, but still!

The walk back to the train station was actually really short. We had apparently left from the wrong side of the station, so we effectively had to navigate around it before finding the right path to the ramen shop. It's always easier to figure out the best route after the fact, but it can be confusing while you're still trying to reach your destination.

Next, we headed into the mountains with the goal of skiing—and, yes, seeing the monkeys. Jon and Jono spent the day skiing on a mountain not far from Nagano.

I don't ski. Growing up in Minot, North Dakota, didn't offer many opportunities to ski. If you have never been to North Dakota, it's the flattest place you can imagine. People on the East coast will say, "Like Ohio flat?" No, not like Ohio. Ohio has lovely rolling hills and is not flat like an ironing board. There was a billboard outside of Minot that read, "Welcome to North Dakota. Mountain removal project completed." It was put up by the tourism board. Why they thought that would attract tourists, I'm not sure. They should have put up a sign that said, "We're one of the 50 states."

I was perfectly happy to hold down the fort at the hotel. Our hotel room had a hot spring bath in it. A literal tub filled with continuously flowing hot water from a hot spring.

We stayed one night at a hotel near Mount Fuji earlier in

the week, which had an *onsen* (hot spring bath) on the lower level, but that was an experience I hope never to repeat. That *onsen* had separate men's and women's chambers, and you had to go in your birthday suit. I was there with a whole bunch of elderly, naked Japanese ladies. I suppose I had the better experience, since Jon and Jono went to the men's side together. *Yeesh.* Check that experience off my list—no thank you, never again.

I could use the hot spring tub in the room at my leisure while they were skiing. I admit I stayed in until I turned pink like a shrimp, then got out, read, and dunked myself again. I was on what was probably the hardest project of my career, and there was a lot of nasty office politics, so it was nice to have the day to myself—to decompress, relax, and definitely not think about work.

We had a friend who happened to be in Japan for work in the same general area as we were. He was planning to visit the monkeys too, so we arranged a tour to coincide with his schedule, and we would meet him for dinner afterwards.

At the stop where we visited the monkeys, our tour guide directed us toward the snowy path and told us when to be back at the bus. We hiked through the mountains for maybe ten to fifteen minutes. It felt secluded and hushed with the snowfall, and even though we hiked with our twenty bus mates, it still seemed remote. As we got closer, we started seeing snow monkeys in the trees and along the sides of the path. Of course, we tried to take selfies with the monkeys. Sometimes it worked, sometimes they moved on as we tried to snap a picture.

Passing through a ticket booth, we came around a bend and saw them—so many of them. They were everywhere! Tourists, I mean, not snow monkeys.

There were probably five tourists for every snow monkey we saw. The snow monkeys were swimming in the hot springs, just as we'd seen on the *National Geographic* show, but tourists were practically standing shoulder to shoulder around the pools.

I knew the monkeys were in a reserve of some sort, and I knew that other tourists were going to be there.

But I never imagined the throngs of tourists.

Jon took a picture of the area, including the monkeys in the pools and the tourists in the background. It was chaos.

We met up with our friend Jeremy there and spent the rest of our time in the park with him, each of us taking more pictures of monkeys.

We met up with Jeremy again that night in Nagano, and he took us to his favorite restaurant. Since he had been working in Nagano and had been there a few times before, he knew some Japanese and had developed a relationship with the owner of the restaurant. He ordered for us, and we got what were essentially omelets filled with different ingredients—mine had noodles and vegetables. I was so happy to have a vegetarian option and for someone else to handle the ordering. We had a great night exploring Nagano with our friend, with him showing us some of his favorite spots.

When we looked back at our pictures later, we found Jeremy among the crowds of tourists surrounding the monkeys, identifiable by his hat, in a "Where's Waldo?" moment.

Unlike Jon, when I took pictures of the monkeys, I avoided the tourists in the background. However, if I posted any of *my* pictures, I would perpetuate the myth that these monkeys are remote and unique in the wild. I've seen fewer tourists at the Bronx Zoo in New York. Jon's picture is the one we should have posted to show others what it's really like.

Jono got to see the monkeys, but it wasn't the magical environment *National Geographic* had shown. *Was it remote and magical when they filmed it? Did their film make it such a popular tourist spot? Or was it always that popular, and they just focused on the monkeys and didn't show the tourists?*

Maybe it doesn't matter—we still had a magical trip to Japan: seeing Tokyo's vibrant neighborhoods, seeing more than we wanted to in the baths near Mount Fuji, finding the snow monkeys, and skiing. And we got to spend some time with our friend Jeremy in the midst of it all.

CHAPTER 29

THE PYRENEES:
WHO YOU TRAVEL WITH . . .

I had originally envisioned a trip to Spain and France for one of my best friends and me. Becky and I have been getting together once or twice a year since we met on a mission trip to Peru years ago. She lives in Maine, and since I'm in New Jersey, we usually meet in the middle—which means traveling to Vermont, New Hampshire, Rhode Island, or Massachusetts. We usually hit all the wineries within a two-hour radius of wherever we're staying.

If you haven't heard of those states as top wine-producing regions, well, you're right. Some of the wineries are decent, especially if they fly in grapes from California. Sometimes they'll do something interesting, like blueberry port or spiced wine, which can be very good—or very, very bad.

We talked about going someplace where they make great wine, so I was thinking Spain, because . . . Spain! Rioja is one of my favorite red wines. I also thought if I went to Spain, I might be able to swing through Andorra, adding another country to my list. Plus, I had always wanted to visit Carcassonne in France. A fun trip would be to fly into Barcelona, drive up to Andorra, continue into France to see Carcassonne, and then return.

Nice and relaxing, plus lots of good wine. It had been a stressful time at work, as usual, so that sounded perfect.

Unfortunately, COVID protocols were still in place in early 2022, and Becky wasn't comfortable traveling yet. Jon volunteered to go in Becky's place, but of course we had to add in a few adventures.

"I'd like to check out some climbs in the area," he said.

He added several stops, stretching our route both to the east and west.

We still flew into Barcelona, but we only stayed there one day—just long enough to see La Sagrada Familia. We hadn't been able to go inside the first time we were there with Jono, so we made a point of doing the full visit this time. I was blown away by it. I assumed that the inside would be as intricate and gaudy—pun intended—as the outside. But the outside and inside are day and night. The inside is light, airy, and holy, with none of the ornate decorations I expected. It was truly inspirational and humbling in a way I've never experienced after having visited bajillions of churches throughout the world.

Afterward, we picked up our rental car, a compact SUV by a Chinese company called Lynk and Co., which has not yet been imported to the United States. There was a ridiculous line of people waiting to get cars because the rental office had been closed the day before for a holiday. By the time we got through the line, picked up the car, and drove to Monserrat, it was early afternoon.

Monserrat is a beautiful white monastery with a terra-cotta tile roof, perched high on a mountain overlooking a valley. Jon wasted no time when we got there. We parked, got our gear out of the car, and took the funicular to the top of the mountain.

The view from the top was breathtaking, with granite outcrops poking through the deep greens of the mountains and the monastery far below. There were hiking paths all around the mountain, and a lot of day-trippers and hikers enjoying the cool spring day.

Jon walked along the path, first one way and then doubled back, comparing the trail and the cliffs alongside it to his digital climbing guide. I followed. Finally, he found what he was looking for and dropped his pack on the path, at the base of a cliff.

He started to get out the climbing gear, and I looked up—something I usually don't like to do. In climbing, looking up is often worse than looking down for me. If I look up a cliff, I can psych myself out and wonder whether I'll be able to make it or if I'll hold us back. I couldn't see the top of this cliff, which meant it was going to be a multi-pitch (multiple-rope-length) climb.

Jon had said he wanted to "check out" the climbing. *Oh, master of understatement.* Yes, I had all the gear, but I was mentally still in "check-it-out" mode, which for me would have meant a short climb, or some route-finding for future trips. I wasn't sure I was up for a multi-pitch adventure.

We had lost a lot of the day already because of the delay at the rental agency, so if we were going to make it to the top, we needed to get moving. I got my gear on, stopped looking up, and started climbing.

Jon knows what I'm capable of, so he always chooses routes he thinks I can climb. Despite how high or difficult it looked—though it was challenging—I was able to reach the top. It was three pitches, which takes a while because after each rope length, Jon had to reset the ropes and get ready to climb again.

Of course, once you go up, you have to get back down. Sometimes that involves a multi-stage rappel; other times, you can walk down the back side of the mountain. This time, Jon had to go to the other side of the peak to set up a rappel off the back. I belayed him, and he went around the peak, where I could no longer see him. He pulled the rope until there was no more slack, but I wasn't sure whether he was secure or not. I waited in my belay position, unsure. Minutes ticked past. I yelled but heard no response. I even tried to call his cell phone, but there was no service on top of the mountain. I don't know how long I waited, but finally I heard Jon calling; he told me to start moving toward him. I did as I was instructed.

He had been forced to come back from the rappel position so that I could hear him. As I got near him, he said I should have known to start moving toward him when I felt the rope tugging. I didn't know that. *How would I know that?* My understanding was to always keep him on belay until he told me he was secure. I guess I know now.

By the time I caught up with him and we rappelled down the mountain, it was getting late. The sun was going down, and it was getting chilly. I'd made the delay worse by not knowing to move, but that only ate up about twenty minutes. We'd started later than intended because of the car rental chaos, and it had been a long, multi-pitch climb. We climbed for at least four to five hours.

We got back to the funicular only to realize that we'd missed the last train down. By a few *hours*. Everything was locked up tight. There were stairs by the funicular, but they were fenced off. We tried a hiking path, but after a ten- or fifteen-minute walk, it didn't seem to be going the right way, so we doubled back to the funicular. There had to be a path down. We were starting to get desperate when we ran into a hiker, and he pointed us in the right direction.

There was a nicely graded path that wound its way down the mountain, very obvious once you knew where to look. The hike down was beautiful, with the sun setting over the mountains and a small village tucked in the valley below.

We were focused on the view when we heard a crash. Just ahead of us were two Iberian ibex mountain goats, fighting. They would rear up, crash into each other, charge away, reset, and repeat. It was just like a *National Geographic* show—except it was live. We couldn't have been more than fifteen meters away from them—too close, really. Fortunately, they were too busy fighting each other to worry about us.

We took as many pictures and videos as possible with the sun setting in the background, then rushed to get back down to our car before dark. We still had to make it to Andorra that evening, which was another two hours away.

We spent the morning wandering through Andorra la Vella, the capitol of Andorra. Andorra sits between France and Spain and relies primarily on tourism—including skiing in the winter, since it is nestled in the Pyrenees—and year-round shopping. Andorra is a tax haven. It felt like an outlet mall, with multiple blocks of high-end stores. It had more stores than the country's population of roughly 80,000 could sustain.

We're not into shopping, and we couldn't spend much time in Andorra anyway, so it was time to get on the road again.

Jon wanted to see Roncevaux Pass, the site of a famous battle. It was a crazy addition to the itinerary because it took us several hours to the west and had us essentially circling the Pyrenees before going up and over and back east to Carcassonne. I looked at Google Maps in the hotel, and it was not going to be a quick drive. It seemed to be about a six-hour drive, no matter which way we went.

When we got to the car, we weren't getting good cell phone coverage. We figured out the unfamiliar interface of the Link & Co. SUV, entered the navigation, and then set out from Andorra to Roncesvalles, on the Spanish side of Roncevaux Pass. We left at noon in the hope of getting there by nightfall. The SUV's navigation system took us on two-lane scenic roads winding through the Pyrenees.

We stopped at one overlook where there was an observation point levered out over the valley below. The railings and walls of the observation deck were clear plexiglass, so they didn't obstruct the view. It was so beautiful and seemed to be in the absolute middle of nowhere. We didn't see many other cars on the road.

We followed the GPS until we noticed we still had about six hours left to travel, even though we'd been driving for two to three hours. What was supposed to be a six-hour drive was now going to be closer to eight or nine hours. *Had we been driving backwards?*

I pulled Google Maps up on my phone and found a more direct way to go, then routed us onto the highway. It was definitely not as pretty, but we still had a long road ahead of us. The sun was starting to set when we pulled off the highway to take the small road that would lead us to Roncesvalles.

My cell phone rang from a number in Spain. The hotel asked if we were still coming. Their front desk closed at 10 p.m., and they wanted to make sure we would make it in time. We did make it, but without much time to spare.

Roncesvalles was barely a town, and it was definitely not on the beaten path. There was a beautiful old church, the Real

Collegiate de Santa Maria de Roncesvalles, and a gift store. We stopped in both, took a few pictures, and then we were off to Roncevaux Pass. We would go up and over the pass into France.

The pass had the bluest skies, and the mountains stretched out across the horizon, dotted with scrubby brown bushes, a few trees, and valleys with villages and bright green farms. There was no one around and very little to mark the pass, except for a single stone monument commemorating the Battle of Roncevaux Pass in 778, part of Charlemagne's campaigns.

After the pass, we set the SUV's GPS for Lourdes, France, our first stop on the French side of the Pyrenees. At one point, we hung a right into a residential neighborhood and kept following the GPS up a narrow lane, winding higher and higher up the mountain.

We ended up on a single-lane dirt path winding around and over the mountains. There were valleys far below and no railings. The sky was bright, filled with only the lightest wisps of clouds, and the mountains were covered in green grasses, trees, and shrubs climbing the sides of the lower mountains. We were above the tree line, so our view was unimpeded. I drove, and Jon filmed everything.

We passed horses and bicycles, but thankfully only saw a few other vehicles. Whenever we passed a vehicle, one of us had to pull over to let the other by, because we were driving on what was essentially a rutted horse trail. I was thankful we had four-wheel drive on the SUV! *It was exhilarating!*

We switched drivers after about a hour and a half, but by the time we traded out, the really treacherous bits were already behind us. Jon was jealous I got to do the fun parts. He wasn't wrong. It was stressful, but I loved it!

We finally came down off the mountain and stopped at a small town in France to get lunch.

"The SUV's GPS must be set on 'shortest distance,' which

means it will take us on bike trails if it saves even a mile," I said.

I had the same thing happen to me once while driving in Belgium, and I wondered why I kept ending up on small dirt paths when there were highways nearby. I should have known what was happening after our first day's drive through the scenic roads of the Pyrenees.

If we had realized what was happening though, we never would have taken that "road." We would either have changed the GPS's settings, or we would have looked up better directions on Google and navigated to the highways, missing what became one of the highlights of that trip for me.

We finally made it to Carcassonne—one of my main goals for that trip. We tried to fit so much into our itinerary with the addition of Jon's adventures that we could only stay one night in each location. Carcassonne was the first place where we were going to stay two nights, and I was looking forward to a small break from the hectic pace we'd set for ourselves. Carcassonne is an ancient, walled city—and the name of a game we'd played as a family numerous times—which is why I had wanted to go.

We were lucky enough to have booked a hotel within the town walls themselves, though it took us a while to figure out how to get there, since you can't drive inside the walls. The inner city is entirely pedestrianized except for locals and deliveries. The GPS kept trying to take us straight in through the walls. Finally, we read the instructions on the hotel's website about where to park our car, parked, and found the hotel shuttle.

Inside the walls, the city is filled with restaurants, shops, and hotels, but it still retains the shape and structure from antiquity. From Carcassonne's walls, you can look down on the rest of the town, which sprawls below the hill into the green valley.

In addition to the fortified walls around the entire city, Carcassonne has a well-preserved castle which dates back to the Roman era. We spent several hours exploring the castle and walking on the city walls.

After Carcassonne, we headed to a climbing area called the Calanques, much farther east than I had originally planned, near Marseille, France. I drove, following the GPS on my phone this time, not trusting the SUV's system. The climbing area was on the far side of Marseille.

Marseille is very confusing, with multiple tunnels that lead to different parts of the city and a busy downtown area by the port. Jon was busy looking at the directions to the climb. I took the wrong tunnel, got re-routed by the GPS, and faced the same series of tunnels again. "Will you please help me navigate?" I asked.

"I'm trying to figure out the approach to our climb," Jon responded, not taking his eyes off his guidebook and maps.

"If we don't get through Marseille, we aren't climbing," I said. "These tunnels are killing me."

He put the climbing map down and helped me, but we still made a couple of wrong turns. We ended up at the back entrance of the Calanques park, which would make our hike longer, but I had no desire to drive back out and around to the front entrance. I'd handle the longer hike.

Of course, we did not "check out" the climbing in the Calanques. We didn't have an easy climb—it was another multi-pitch climb. But this time, I had set my expectations for a multi-pitch, long day of climbing. The best part of the climb was the view. Once we got to the top, there was an amazing 360-degree view of both the Calanques park and the ocean.

The trip had definitely not been the relaxing trip I'd planned with Becky. There was far less wine, far more climbing, and a whole lot more driving. Instead of a relatively short trip from Barcelona to Andorra to Carcassonne, we'd circumnavigated the Pyrenees and climbed two multi-pitch routes.

I would have had an amazing trip with my friend, but the trip with Jon was much more adventurous and expansive. The choice of who to travel with has as much of an impact on the trip as the location. Apparently, which GPS you use and how it is set also makes a major difference.

CHAPTER 30

SLOVAKIA & POLAND:
IN SEARCH OF UKRAINE

It was Christmas of 2022, and it was the first time Jon, Jono, and I were able to travel together since the pandemic. Jon and I had been able to get out a few times, but by then Jono was living on his own, finishing a master's degree and working, so he hadn't been able to travel with us.

As we considered where we wanted to go, Jon said he wanted to do something to support Ukraine. The Ukraine war had broken out earlier that year. We had been donating to a charity recommended by a Ukrainian colleague, Razom, but Jon wanted to see if there was something more hands-on we could do.

I went back to my Ukrainian colleague for suggestions; and she asked, politely but pointedly, "Do you speak Ukrainian or Polish?" *Uh, no. Would Duolingo Russian help? Unlikely!*

I had been to Ukraine in 2018 with Michele during our lack-of-visa-induced flight from Belarus, and we were very affected by the invasion. Our lack of ability to do anything meaningful to support Ukraine and its refugees was deeply frustrating.

Although I wasn't convinced we could do anything, I started considering travel options for that part of the world—though we wouldn't cross the border into Ukraine itself.

Several years earlier, Jon had wanted to do a "European train trip" during Jono's spring break. We spent an amazing week taking trains between Prague, Vienna, and Budapest. On the train from Prague to Budapest, we rode through Slovakia, but we didn't stop. Looking back, it seems a terrible oversight, but Bratislava simply hadn't been on my radar then, and it didn't make it onto the itinerary. This trip, I wanted to explore Bratislava and drive through Slovakia to make up for what we'd missed.

And, while Michele and I had been to Warsaw before, we'd only spent twenty-four hours there—via our cheap flight from Milan—and I'd liked it enough that I wanted to see more of Poland.

So, we would go to Slovakia and Poland.

My challenge in planning was trying to balance having a fun family trip with our now-adult son and the effort to learn more about Ukraine and see if there was any way we could support the refugees.

We flew into Vienna—which had cheaper, better flights—and there was an easy one-hour train ride to Bratislava.

As we landed, Jono asked if we could go into Vienna. "I want to see that one church," he said.

While it had been eight years since our spring break train trip, I knew which one he was talking about. The church was relatively unassuming on the outside, right in the middle of Vienna's old town. Inside, it was hushed and magical, like stepping into a completely different world. I had no idea how to find it again.

Jono pulled up his phone and started searching the internet. After a few minutes, he said, "That's it! Peterskirche–Peter's Church."

"Sure, we can go," I said, but I was also thinking through the logistics of it. There were many trains to Bratislava from Vienna, so that wasn't a problem. However, we wouldn't have anywhere to store our suitcases, and I wasn't excited about dragging our bags through Vienna's cobblestoned pedestrian district.

The airline solved the problem for us: our bags didn't make it to Vienna. We had to fill out forms and tell the airlines where we'd be. The airline agent didn't even blink when I told him we'd be in Slovakia. "Yes, we can deliver the bags to your hotel in Bratislava tomorrow," he said.

We spent the afternoon enjoying Vienna. We walked through Vienna, struck by how beautiful it was with all the holiday lighting. Jono navigated us straight to Peter's Church. It was Christmastime, and a service was underway when we walked in, so it didn't have the same hush as before, but it was still magical.

After seeing Vienna, we took the train to Bratislava, a quick, easy trip.

We started the next morning by climbing to Bratislava Castle. The Castle is massive, white, and rectangular, with simple lines. It had been built starting in the ninth century—then occupied, expanded, destroyed, and restored so many times over the ages. The present building was restored again in 1953. It now serves as a museum of Slovakia, with exhibits ranging from Baroque art to displays about the anti-communist Velvet Revolution that helped bring down communism in then-Czechoslovakia.

The Castle stands on a hill overlooking the city. The skyline of Bratislava was dotted by features that spanned the historical timeline. There were several Orthodox church spires that looked like fairy-tale towers and rows of red-roofed, Slavic-style buildings and homes. There were also numerous concrete-gray, square, unadorned, communist-era apartment buildings. The modern era brought a host of new structures, from energy-generating windmills to huge glass-sided skyscrapers still under construction.

The most iconic—and most unusual—feature of Bratislava is the UFO Tower, which spans a bridge over the Danube. It was originally opened in 1972, a marvel of communist-era design. It literally looks like a UFO sitting on a tripod over the bridge. We made a reservation for the restaurant in it to celebrate Jono's birthday later that night.

Bratislava is a modern city and a member of the EU, but its old city still retains its charm. We spent the afternoon walking through it and exploring the shops and restaurants.

When it was time for dinner, I'll admit I didn't have high hopes for the food at the UFO restaurant. I suppose I expected old-style food like goulashes, perogies, and huge cuts of meat like we'd seen in many of the restaurants in the old town.

From the dining room of the UFO, we could see all of Bratislava, including the Danube cutting between green trees on one side, and the Castle on the hill on the other. We could see energy-generating windmills in the distance and the rest of the old town and church spires.

We ordered drinks, and Jono got a cocktail with a smoke bubble perched on top, which broke and blew away as he took a drink.

The menu was eclectic with interesting flavors and

textures—foams, caviar, and a wide-ranging palette of sauces and seasonings. They served us an amuse-bouche of tzatziki, which had been lightened with foam. I ordered a stuffed pasta, similar to a ravioli. I honestly don't know what was in it, but it made my top ten meals of all time. It might've had ginger and saffron—I don't know—but it was rich and sublime. I'm not used to vegetarian food having so much flavor! It was a truly remarkable experience and definitely not what I would have expected from a UFO-shaped building in the middle of Bratislava.

After Bratislava, one of our first stops was Devín Castle, just outside the city and the first of several abandoned castles we saw in Slovakia. It was perched high on a hill and not restored, so the walls were crumbling. We climbed up a path to reach the Castle and took pictures in front of it, the structure silhouetted against the darkening sky as the sun set.

Walking back to our car outside Devín Castle, we saw The Gate of Freedom Memorial, a simple concrete arch, unadorned except for simulated bullet holes. Through the arch, you can look across the Danube and Morava rivers and see Austria. The arch commemorates the Iron Curtain and the fact that the rivers separated the democratic West from the communist regimes during the Cold War. Hundreds died trying to cross those rivers to reach the West; their names are now etched into the monument.

It was a harsh reminder of the Cold War and that Slovakia had been part of communist Czechoslovakia—one of the pieces of the Czech, Yugoslav, and Soviet communist bloc.

As I looked at the Gate of Freedom Memorial, I realized how much we take our freedom for granted. The biggest concern I had going into Vienna the day we flew in was how to manage our suitcases. After spending the afternoon there, we hopped on a train between the countries—no need to reserve ahead of time, no border checkpoint, no hassle. Back in the communist era, people would have died trying to make a trip to Vienna.

It was also a reminder of how far the world had progressed since WWII and the Cold War.

We drove across Slovakia, heading for Spiš Castle, the largest castle in the country and one of the "can't-miss" stops. We arrived at sunset, and the castle was again silhouetted against the darkening sky. Similar to Devín castle, it was abandoned and unrestored, with only the walls remaining to indicate its former glory. It made for some gorgeous, silhouetted pictures, but there wasn't much to do there besides look at it.

We stayed the night in Košice (pronounced ko-si-chay), Slovakia, because it was close to Spiš Castle and on the far east side of the country on the route to Poland. Košice was a super quaint town with a long walking district that ended at a Ferris wheel. There were old gothic churches and numerous shops, and the holiday market was still in full swing.

We stayed in a little hotel right in the old town, so in the morning we decided to take a stroll through the walking district and holiday market before hitting the road.

We stopped at a booth selling pastries. "One," we said, holding up one finger. The man pointed at the menu showing three options, which were written in Slovakian. "English?" we asked. The man shook his head and said, "Slovakian, German, or Russian," (though he didn't say them in English, so they sounded more like Slovakee, Deutsch, and Ruskie.)

With Jon's high school German and my Duolingo Russian, we looked at the options again. The man read out the three options using German and Slovakian. I heard the vendor say "apple" in Slovakian; I knew the word because it was the same in Russian. It sounded the same, but it was written in

Roman letters versus Cyrillic, so I hadn't recognized it right away. Then I saw the word for "cheese," which also sounds the same in Russian. The third option, which Jon knew in German, was sauerkraut.

We ordered an apple pastry and got a paper cup of mulled wine to share. If you ask me, mulled wine at a holiday market is heaven in a cup, and I'm always game to have one. After we finished our pastry, we packed up and headed out of town.

I entered our destination, Zakopane, Poland, into the GPS. We planned to drive through the Carpathian Mountains into Poland, and it promised to be a beautiful drive. It was my turn to drive, and I always love driving through mountains.

Getting out of town was tricky—driving through the narrow, cobbled streets—but I was relying on Google to guide us. We drove alongside the pedestrian zone, heading toward what looked like a main road out of town. A police vehicle came up behind us and turned on his lights. *Oh crap!!*

The last time I'd been pulled over in a foreign country was in Mexico during spring break from the Air Force Academy. A group of us had gone to Guadalajara to work at an orphanage, and we had caravanned in two cars. I was driving the trailing car and had raced through a *very* yellow light to keep up with the other vehicle. The cop in Mexico took my driver's license and told me he was going to take it to the station and that I should come get it the next day.

Someone told me later that the cop was just fishing for a bribe and that I should've just handed him some cash to get my license back. Maybe that's true, but that option didn't occur to me; I'd never been "asked" for a bribe before. So, I just drove off without my license, thinking I could probably just get a new one back in the States if I claimed I'd lost it. I had lost it—I had just lost it to the Mexican police.

All of that swirled in my mind as I pulled over, and I started getting my passport and drivers' license out, while

Jon opened the glove box to pull out the rental information.

The cop spoke enough English to tell me that I wasn't driving "alongside" the pedestrian zone; I was actually driving *in* the pedestrian zone. *Whoops!*

"I'm sorry, I was just following my GPS," I said.

"You have to use your eyes too," he said. Fair point.

"Have you had anything to drink?" he asked.

"No," I said emphatically. It was like eleven in the morning.

"You are not from here, so I will reduce the fine." He asked me to pay ten euros. I handed him ten euros in cash. *Was that normal, or was it a bribe?* I had no idea, but I wasn't going to argue the point, especially since it wasn't an astronomical price.

After I paid him, he gave us another warning to be careful and then let us go.

After we pulled out, Jon said, "What about the mulled wine?"

It took me a minute to understand what he was talking about. We had shared that paper cup of mulled wine. I might have had two ounces. But he was right, I *had* had something to drink.

I laughed and said, "Oh my gosh. I totally forgot the mulled wine."

If I'd remembered when the cop asked me, he would have known. He would have seen it in my expression, no matter what I said. I've never had a poker face. The only thing that saved me was that I had literally forgotten we had it.

Fortunately, we made it out of town, into the mountains, and into Zakopane, Poland, without further incidents.

Zakopane, Poland, is a ski destination, so I booked a night and day there to let Jon and Jono ski. I was happy to hang out in the chalet, catch up on work, and read.

We planned to leave Zakopane the next afternoon and

drive to Krakow for New Year's Eve. Jon found and reserved a Ukrainian restaurant in Krakow where we hoped to connect with the refugee community. I also made reservations at a place right on the main square of Krakow that had a New Year's Eve special.

As it turned out, we had a delay leaving Zakopane due to a misplaced passport. While we found the passport—thankfully—we ended up getting to Krakow too late to make the reservations at the Ukrainian restaurant.

Jon was disappointed, but we were able to make our reservation at the touristy restaurant on Krakow square. Our table was in a plastic bubble with heaters to keep us warm against the chill of the night. There were horse-drawn carriages going past. The square was filled with people strolling. It wasn't packed like Times Square, which is a good thing, but it was busy—and the Square was definitely the place to be on New Year's Eve!

After dinner, it was still early, so we wandered around. The Christmas Market was still running, with booths selling trinkets and clothes—and, of course, food stands with spiced wine and sausages. I loved reading the signs in Polish and being able to understand a few words because they were the same as Russian, just in Roman letters, like *chleb* and *ser*: bread and cheese.

At one point, we heard a commotion and went to see what it was. There was a group of thirty to forty people singing and holding up the Ukrainian flag. They counted down and then started celebrating. It was exactly 11 p.m. They were celebrating the New Year in Ukraine, which is one hour ahead of Poland.

At midnight, the rest of the Square celebrated New Year's with fireworks shooting over it, cheering, and raising paper cups.

We hadn't made it to the Ukrainian restaurant for dinner,

but we still got to see a small impact of the Ukrainian war and some of the Ukrainians who had fled their homeland because of it, ringing in the New Year!

After Krakow, we went to Rzeszów (somehow pronounced Zhayzhouf) because it's the closest town in Poland to the Ukrainian border.

Jon looked up a couple of aid and refugee organizations in Poland that we could stop at and potentially offer aid. We tried to go, but it was challenging. There were no "Refugees, come here" signs. We would go to one address only to be told that they had moved to a different location. We did eventually find two refugee centers, but as my colleague said, we didn't speak Polish or Ukrainian, so there wasn't much we could do.

Rzeszów is a small town—not really a tourist center—but it still had a nice walking district, and its holiday market was still running. In the holiday market, Jon stopped at a few wine-tasting stalls, which I'm always happy to check out. I tasted the wine while Jon peppered the proprietors with questions about refugees and got them to reveal that there was a U.S. military presence in Rzeszów to support NATO and serve as a backstop if Russia tried to continue westward.

We stopped in a restaurant for a drink and dessert afterward, and Jon again chatted up our server, trying to get a read on Ukrainians in the area. Our server said, "The Ukrainians are sometimes rude. The ones who were able to make it over the border into Poland are the rich ones, rich and arrogant, and they aren't nice. The ones without means are still in Ukraine."

We ordered a piece of cheesecake, and it was terrible—tasteless and chalky. Thinking it was an anomaly, we tried a different dessert, and it was just as bad, if not worse. Jono said, "It tastes like Jell-O with fingernails in it." We laughed and wondered if the Ukrainians were just "rude" because the food was so bad.

We stayed at a local hotel just off the walking district. In the morning, there were U.S. soldiers in uniform at the breakfast buffet. Having been in the military, it was at once familiar and also completely unexpected. We were in Poland! There definitely hadn't been a military presence there back in our day.

Jon walked up to a couple of the soldiers and thanked them for their service. He told them he'd served in Hungary in support of Bosnia and understood the sacrifice they were making by being away from their families over the holidays. Jon waved Jono over and introduced him to the soldiers. He said Jono had been a baby when he'd been in Hungary supporting NATO in Bosnia.

As we left Rzeszów on the way to Warsaw, we drove past the airport where we were told the Patriot missile battery was located—all the intel we wanted for the price of a bottle of a wine at the holiday market! Jon pointed them out, tucked behind fences and hidden unless you knew what to look for. It was reassuring to know that the U.S. was in Poland, supporting NATO, and keeping watch in case Russia decided to make a move.

Michele and I had been to Warsaw previously, and we had walked through the Old Town. At the time, it was winter and absolutely freezing, so while we tried to see as much as possible, we kept having to duck into souvenir shops to warm up and didn't linger as long as we would have liked. This time, when Jon, Jono, and I went to the Old Town, it was still chilly, but fortunately for us, Poland was unseasonably warm that year, so it was reasonable. We found a free walking tour in English and joined in.

I had never really done a walking tour before. Where Michele and I had looked at the architecture and seen the signs marking where the old Jewish ghetto had been, this time our guide showed us old photos of walls that had been built during the war as a barrier to keep the Jewish population on one side. He said that 80–90 percent of the city had been destroyed by the Germans, a fact hidden by the beautiful restoration work that had been done. He made the war and the destruction come to life, so that you could almost see the scars beneath the beauty.

The tour was even more impactful because we knew that just across the border, Ukraine was going through their own war. Towns were being bombed and blasted by tanks—something that hadn't been seen since World War II. *How many towns in Ukraine will be left destroyed as Warsaw was? How much rebuilding will need to be done?*

The tour was sobering and inspiring. Afterwards, we returned to our hotel, located in one of Warsaw's newer districts filled with shiny malls and office buildings.

That evening, in front of the mall near our hotel, we saw a whole line of refugees queuing up for food provided by the World Central Kitchen. It was yet another reminder of the presence of the nearby war.

While we never found a way to actively contribute when we were in Poland or Slovakia—because we couldn't speak Polish or Ukrainian—we certainly felt surrounded by Ukrainians and people who were supporting them. From the Ukrainians in the square in Krakow celebrating their New Year, to the refugee agencies and World Central Kitchen providing food, to the U.S. military presence serving as a NATO backstop to prevent further Russian advances.

We returned home, inspired to continue to donate to World Central Kitchen, Razom, and other organizations that support refugees and Ukraine.

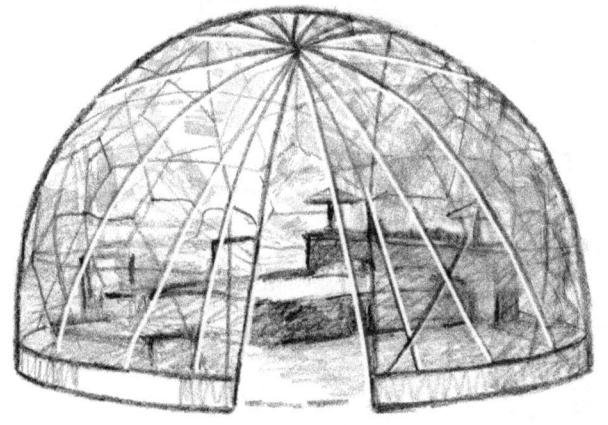

CHAPTER 31

JORDAN:
GOLDEN TRIANGLE

Jon's view on traveling is that the best trips incorporate people, places, and activities. When I suggest a travel destination to Jon, he automatically asks, "What's the adventure? Who can we see? Who can come with us?" Jon is an extrovert—a community-builder who is always looking for ways to connect with others. I've dubbed his philosophy "The Golden Triangle of Travel."

I don't disagree with the Golden Triangle, but I believe a place can be an activity, too. Walking around a new city like Belgrade or Copenhagen is enough "activity" for me, and as an introvert, I'm perfectly happy being alone. *I can be "people."*

When Jon's brother Pete and sister-in-law Michele (my travel buddy!) invited us to Jordan where they were dropping off their son—our nephew—for a semester abroad, we were in.

For me, you just have to ask, "Would you like to come with me to <insert name of country>?" and I would probably say yes. Jon was on board too, since two of the points of his triangle—people and place—were already met. But, of course, he still asked, "What's the adventure?"

At the time, we were watching *The Climb* on HBO Max, a climbing competition hosted by Chris Sharma and Jason Momoa. Two of the episodes were filmed in Wadi Rum, Jordan. If you've never heard of Wadi Rum, I'm with you—I hadn't either. But you've likely seen it in films ranging from *Star Wars* to *Dune* to *The Martian*. It's a red desert, with rock outcroppings and mountains jutting up through the sand. It's stunning in a barren sort of way, like the Moon.

Once Jon saw there was rock climbing in Wadi Rum, all three points of his triangle were checked, and he went from "in" to psyched.

He went online to find a climbing guide in Jordan. "Do you want to climb?" he asked me.

He is a far better climber than I am. I consider myself an "advanced beginner"—the same designation I have given myself for the past thirty years. I climb a few times per year, whereas Jon, a professional climbing guide, climbs thirty to forty times a year—maybe more. *Who can keep track?*

He also loves climbing far more than I do. I like to go climbing as an outing and climb one or two routes, then find a nice dinner. If he goes with a climbing buddy, they'll climb all day from sunrise to sunset. Asking me if I wanted to climb was a legitimate question.

"Yes, as long as the guide can find something that I can do," I answered, meaning an easier-grade climb. He knew what I meant. I didn't want to miss out on an opportunity for a cool adventure, but I also know I'm not a rock star climber.

This was the first time we traveled with both of our families. Michele and I had finished our fifth trip together just a month earlier, but we'd never had our husbands with us. Our nephew Elijah was dropped off on the first day of our trip for his semester abroad, but his younger brother, Nano, joined us on the rest of the trip; he was eighteen at the time.

The day we dropped off Elijah at his school, Jon and I had taken the morning to see Amman. Once again, I was reminded of how far the Roman Empire had extended. Michele and I had visited Athens a few years earlier and saw the Acropolis and Roman ruins in North Macedonia and Bulgaria. Jon, Jono, and I had been to Rome and had seen the Colosseum.

Amman, Jordan, seemed worlds away from Rome, yet Amman's second century Roman theater was extremely well-preserved and every bit as Roman as the Colosseum in Rome. It had three tiers of seats carved into stone, with super steep steps going to the top.

After we dropped off Elijah and got some travel tips from his professor, Professor Dan, we decided to split up for the day. Pete, Michele, and Nano visited Amman. Jon and I planned to see the Dead Sea en route to our hotel near Petra.

The Dead Sea looked like a long lake—no ocean currents or waves like one might expect from a sea. It was narrower than I thought it would be. At one point, I received a text message from my cell phone carrier that said, "Welcome to Israel." We were still on the Jordanian side of the Dead Sea, but apparently close enough for the cell signal to get confused.

At the start of the Dead Sea, there was a mile-long stretch of high-end hotels. We weren't staying at any of them, so we kept on driving, looking for public access to the sea. We finally pulled over on the side of the road. There wasn't a parking area or a trail, but it looked like we could make it down to the water.

We scrambled down gravel slopes dotted with sharp spines of tufted salt which kept snagging the hem of my sundress. The crystals were everywhere, and it was like walking through a mine field trying to avoid them. There was no way to walk all the way out into the Dead Sea, so we turned around and headed back to the car. I was wearing cowboy boots and a sundress. I probably should have changed into better shoes, since boots were not ideal for scrambling uphill on loose gravel.

From the Dead Sea, we drove over and through the mountains to Petra. We stopped frequently to take pictures because the mountains were so remote, so barren. The sun was setting, huge and red, right over the ridges of the mountains. We kept trying to capture pictures of the mountains with the sun flaming in the background.

We stopped at one overlook, and our car was immediately surrounded by a pack of wild dogs. We decided not to get out and take pictures there.

We've all seen images of Petra in *Indiana Jones*, and I was so excited to see the pink façade carved into the stone. Honestly, I didn't know what to expect beyond that one iconic image from the movie. After we met up with Pete, Michele, and Nano at the hotel, we tried to research what we'd see and plan for the next day's visit. Professor Dan had advised us to go straight to the end of the canyon and then work our way back. He also suggested taking a donkey ride to the end, since it was a long and strenuous hike.

We really didn't know what to expect, but we all agreed to go early in the morning so we could see as much as possible before it got too hot.

We took the hotel shuttle to the visitor center, and then

walked down a long, dusty road. We said no to offers to ride horses because the professor told us those would only take us to the start of the canyon and weren't worth the cost.

After the road was a long slot canyon where the walls rose up and almost closed over the top of us, similar to Antelope Canyon in Utah. There were small carvings in the wall of the slot canyon, similar in style to the Indiana Jones wall but smaller and less detailed, as if half erased. We stopped at each new carving, equally fascinated by each one, not realizing that we hadn't even reached the main attractions yet.

After about twenty minutes of walking, the canyon opened up revealing the famous façade called "The Treasury," just as it appeared on *Indiana Jones*. This was the façade that everyone wanted to see—there were tourists everywhere, despite the fact that it was still off-season and early in the morning.

There were camels everywhere, and their handlers offered to let us ride one or take a picture with them. We said no or ignored them, but they were persistent. "You dropped something, madam," one said to get my attention. When I looked at him, he added, "Your smile." A different camel handler tried the same thing on Jon, telling him he'd dropped his heart. *Geeze!*

We took a few pictures and selfies but were eager to move on, away from the camels and high-tourist zone. We also knew there was still a lot left to see. We certainly hadn't been going straight to the end of the canyon as we'd been advised by Professor Dan, and it became clear just how big the place was. After the Treasury, the canyon opened into a wide valley. On the left were walls and carvings, a wide road down the middle, and other edifices and ruins dotted the hills—but it was no longer tightly enclosed in like a slot canyon. The area was massive!

Petra was built by the Nabateans in the 4th to 2nd centuries BCE and had served as a regional marketplace. With vendors selling souvenirs and snacks along the road and tourists wandering through the area, it was easy to imagine it as the commercial hub it once was. The canyon walls would have made it defensible while also funneling people in to buy wares during their journey across the desert.

Despite the professor's advice, we kept getting distracted—wanting to take a closer look at every façade and ruin we saw. After the Treasury, there was a whole row of façades that of course required more pictures. Then there were steps up to what might have been an old temple with columns around the edges. Of course, we had to go up there and explore too.

I took the opportunity to sit on an old stone step, take off my shoes, and pour the sand out of them. The sneakers I wore that day had a loose-weave fabric that let sand in. Not ideal for an entire day in the desert!

At the end of the canyon is the hike up to the monastery. We could see the stone steps cut into the canyon winding up and up. Just like the professor said, there were donkeys everywhere, and their handlers offered to give us a ride to the top. The price was crazy low, around five dollars.

We ignored the professor's advice and walked up, too proud or too embarrassed to get on a donkey. It was straight up 800 stone steps, with vendors lining the way, displaying trinkets and T-shirts. One vendor sold beautiful goblets hewn from rock. Did she really expect us to buy rock goblets and carry them to the top?

It was a tough slog up the steps to the top, with a few stops along the way to take pictures—not to rest! It was getting hotter, which certainly reduced the pace as well.

Once Jon and I got to the monastery, I sat down on a rock to rest. Our nephew Nano came up shortly after, and he and

Jon went to explore some of the other view points. I stayed on the rock, drank some water, and waited for Pete and Michele. The monastery was similar to the Treasury, with an intricately carved façade. *Was it worth the hike? Maybe. Maybe not.* I wouldn't have wanted to miss it, but it was a long hike for one façade.

There were a lot of other people resting or taking pictures. One couple in particular caught my attention. The woman was standing on a rock, wearing a slim, long skirt that looked entirely inappropriate for the hike we'd just done. She primped her long hair and posed like a model while her boyfriend took multiple shots. She stepped down off the rock, looked at the pictures, and then berated him for how they turned out. She gave him more instructions, hopped back up on the rock, fluffed out her hair, and tried again. They switched after a while and she took a few shots of him, but then she was back on the rock. I watched them move to another spot and go through the same routine.

Pete and Michele arrived, and Michele sat on a nearby rock. We watched the Instagrammers do their thing. Pete went to see if he could catch up with Jon and Nano.

After we regrouped and started back down the hill, at least thirty minutes later, I could still see the couple posing to get the perfect shot in yet another spot. They were not the only people spending hours to get the perfect Instagram shot at Petra; they were just the most obvious. I'm sure they had some beautiful shots. I'm sure it made their trip to Petra look magical and gorgeous. But I question whether they enjoyed their time there. Did they really even see anything?

After seeing the Monastery, it was still early, so we were able to take a more leisurely pace going back through the canyon. There were a few side areas that we wanted to see. The men split off to go see the Church. It was on a hill exposed to the sun and looked too hot, so Michele and I visited the Tombs, which turned out to be my favorite part of the entire area. You could actually go inside some of them and see the ceiling and carvings. Since they were off the main trail through Petra, there weren't many tourists, and we had the whole place to ourselves.

After the men joined us at the Tombs, we split up again. Jon, Nano, and I climbed up another side area, while Pete and Michele walked back along the main road.

The hill we climbed offered the best view of the valley and the road winding back to the Treasury. There was hardly anyone else around. It was almost like we'd found our own private part of Petra. There was a small shop selling trinkets and water up there, so we were definitely not the first people to explore that hill! We scrambled down the cliff on well-worn steps.

By the time we finished, we were exhausted. We'd walked seven to eight miles through the canyon—me dumping out piles of sand every few miles—and we hadn't ridden any of the donkeys, camels, or horses along the way. Petra was nothing like the single image of the Treasury I had emblazoned in my mind from *Indiana Jones*. It was really so much more, so much bigger. A whole city's worth of ruins and façades.

Jon and I waited at the Wadi Rum visitor center for our guide. Numerous people approached us and asked if we had a guide or needed one. We turned them away, saying we were waiting for Ali. *Surely, there could only be one Ali!*

The night before, we stayed at a bubble camp after taking a tour of Wadi Rum, riding in the back of a truck through the desert with its striking rock formations. In the evening, since we were the only two families in the camp, we sat around a campfire with the whole night sky on display above us.

Pete, Michele, and Nano left that morning to go to the Dead Sea and then into Israel.

We saw a Jordanian man wearing a traditional ankle-length robe (a *dishdashah* or *thawb*) with Sportiva climbing approach shoes. This was our guy.

It was 9 a.m., and he said, "We should have started earlier if we're going to do Jabal Umm ad Dami." At more than 6,000 feet, it is the highest mountain in Jordan. Ali measured us up, trying to figure what we could do.

"How long will it take?" Jon asked. "We have a flight out of Amman tonight, so we have to leave by 8 p.m."

I raised my eyebrows, thinking, *Holy cow, I don't know if I'm ready for an eleven-hour day.* It gets dark by six or six-thirty, so finishing a climb by eight would be on the *very far* side of when we'd want to finish a climb.

As a guide, Jon must do the same assessment of all his climbing clients in order to take them on routes that are challenging but not so hard that they're discouraging, dangerous, or impossible. Although he's certified for just about every kind of rock and mountain climbing, he didn't know Wadi Rum and wanted a guide who knows the local area. It turns out that to enter Wadi Rum National Park, you must have a licensed tour guide—not necessarily a rock-climbing guide, but someone licensed to be in Wadi Rum.

We finally settled on Jabal Ram, the second-highest mountain, which Ali estimated would take six to eight hours. *Jabal* or *Jebel* means "mountain," which is why the names sound similar.

As we drove through the ramshackle Wadi Rum village and into the national park—riding in the back of Ali's pickup while he and his cousin rode in front—we realized that the bubble tent where we had stayed the night before with Pete, Michele, and Nano was adjacent to Wadi Rum National Park. There are also bubble tents within Wadi Rum itself, but when booking online, it can be hard to tell which are inside the park and which are outside.

Wadi Rum National Park was wider, wilder, and enormous, making where we stayed the night before look like its tamer little brother. Wadi Rum was an infinite landscape of sand and rock, like you might find on the Moon or Mars. It was easy to see why it was picked as a filming location so often.

We stopped in front of a mountain of stone that rose straight up out of the sand around us. Ali hitched his *thawb* up to his waist, revealing his white cotton pants beneath, and belted his backpack around his waist to keep the robe in place.

Jon and I had small day packs filled with water, snacks, and our climbing shoes. Ali had a rope but told us it would only be used for rappelling down—"abseiling," he said, using the British term, which I only learned when I asked Jon what he meant.

I know better than to look up, but I couldn't help myself. I admit I looked up, and knowing we had no climbing gear—except the rope to rappel—I thought, *Are they kidding? I don't know if I can do this.*

Ali's cousin drove the truck away, and I had no choice but to follow Ali up.

He was like a mountain goat, effortlessly walking up the rocks. It wasn't vertical, but it was steep. Ali pointed out a rock that he and his sister had carved their initials into when they climbed up there with their goat as kids. This was truly his backyard.

Ali was also wearing the right shoes. Jon and I had approach shoes at home, but we hadn't brought them to Jordan. We thought we'd be doing more vertical rock climbing, so we had sneakers and climbing shoes. Approach shoes are somewhere in the middle. Jon and I started out with our sneakers, and they definitely didn't have as much friction as Ali's shoes.

Section by rocky section, Ali led us up the rocks while he and Jon compared notes on being climbing guides and discussed *The Climb* show, for which Ali had helped set up climbs. I just focused on not falling too far behind.

Ali adjusted the route he'd planned to take, accommodating my skill level, and stayed back on the harder scrambles to make sure I could make it up.

Whenever we took a rest break, I drank as much water as I could. It wasn't that hot, since Ali constantly guided us to climb on the shady side of the rocks, but it was still warm, and I felt constantly parched. Ali would recline and smoke a cigarette.

There was a short vertical section, maybe six to eight feet, and I wasn't confident in getting up it. Ali was on top, holding his hand out as if to help me up. That made me feel even less confident. There was no way he could pull me up, and I'd need to hold onto the rocks to make it. I said, "Hang on, I'm putting on my climbing shoes."

Ali and Jon both tried to encourage me to just go, but I stopped and put on my climbing shoes, stuffing my sneakers into the small backpack. I scrambled up with no problem—the extra grip from the climbing shoes made a difference and gave me the confidence to do it. I think I earned a measure of respect from Ali, both for making it up the vertical crack and for insisting on taking the time to change my shoes.

However, the thing about climbing shoes is that they're great for climbing up vertical rock—designed to catch even the tiniest bump or crack—but they're worn tight and not made for hiking. Frankly, they're painful if worn too long. Whenever it was vertical or steep, I wore my climbing shoes. On the longer, less vertical stretches—there was nothing flat—I switched back to my sneakers. Jon managed in his sneakers, but he's a climbing guide, and I'm not.

At one point, when it seemed like we were getting near the summit, Ali offered to make tea. "Tea?" I asked. We were on a pile of rocks in the middle of the desert. "How would you make tea?"

"I always have a teapot," he answered. "And I can use small sticks to make a fire."

In his backpack, he had a freaking teapot—and tea. Jordanians are extremely hospitable, and at every hotel we'd stayed at, we had been treated more like family than guests. We were usually given welcome drinks, and at the Petra Marriott Hotel we received branded mugs as gifts. So of course he would have a teapot ready to whip out at any moment.

It was warm out, and I wasn't sure how far the summit really was. I was getting nervous about getting back down and back to Amman for our flight home.

I've been hiking enough to know that usually when you think you're nearing the summit, the real summit is still a ways off. In Wadi Rum, I thought I saw the summit but knew that would be too easy, so I asked Ali how far we had to go. He tried to do the guide thing and say, "Not far, only a little bit up," but I pressed him.

"Probably two hours," he said.

Ugh! Maybe I would have preferred, "a little bit up!" Definitely not time for tea then!

We had to go down, around, and back up before we even saw the summit. After about five hours, we finally made it to the top. We rested in a shady spot—Ali was a master at finding shady spots. He went off to do his midday prayer, his iPhone having signaled the call to prayer earlier, at a time when we couldn't stop.

We took all the selfies and photos we could while he finished his prayers. We had time to take in the amazing red-sand desert, littered with craggy rock mountains sprawled before us. There was no sign of civilization—not even any bubble tents—for as far as we could see.

And then it was time to go down. Honestly, my heart sunk as we started to walk down. I had my hopes set on rappelling, but you can't just rappel down a mountain. You can only rappel down vertical faces, and we had climbed a mountain shaped like a dome. A mountain, not a cliff.

Although the descent wasn't as exhausting since we weren't going against gravity, it was far freakier. When you're going down, you have to look to see where you're going, and it's impossible not to see the bottom of the climb since you have to look for steps and handholds beneath you. Climbing down backward while facing the cliff is just as awkward as descending forward while looking out. Either way, you must find footholds and handholds and not fall. Down climbing isn't done that often in rock climbing because it's just hard, and rappelling is so much easier.

On top of that, my feet were killing me. I wore my climbing shoes as we approached the summit and kept them on because some of the down-climbing was spooky enough that I wanted the extra grip. I wished—like I had so many times on that climb—that we'd brought our approach shoes.

Ali always went down first to show us the path and support us—mostly me—if we needed help. Some of the slab rocks were steep and slippery enough that Ali crouched down on his butt, feet in front like a crab, and told me to do the same. He didn't have to tell me twice. I scooted down on my butt so many times that I ripped through my pants, ending up with a huge hole in the butt by the time we reached the bottom.

We did find a few places to rappel, and whenever it was time to set up a rappel station, I sat by and waited while the two of them discussed the best way to do it. Jon was happy to show Ali a few different techniques. Ali usually rappelled first, leaving Jon to hook me and himself up to the rope. Jon made sure I was set up to rappel before he went down. I know rappelling can be scary to some people, but I enjoy it—it's just going down a rope, and it saves me hundreds of feet of down climbing. I'll rappel any day!

We rappelled, and then we had more down climbing. We ended up rappelling about five times, with significant down climbing between rappels.

And then, miraculously, we were on level ground!

It was about eight hours by the time we finished the climb—maybe nine. At the base of the climb, Ali pulled out the teapot. He found some sticks, lit a small fire with his lighter, and started to boil water for tea. Jon and I didn't have any water left; both of us had finished off three or four liters each. Ali drank maybe a liter over the entire climb and still had plenty left for tea.

Ali settled down in front of the fire, clearly in his element, reclining in the sand as comfortably as if he were on his couch. Ali's cousin drove up in the truck and joined us in front of the fire. Ali recounted the climb to his cousin in Arabic while Jon and I took off our climbing harnesses, and I switched back to my sneakers.

Jon and I shared a styrofoam cup of tea. Ali and his cousin drank theirs from a plastic water bottle cut in half with a knife, the top and bottom each serving as a cup.

The best part of having a guide like Ali isn't just being able to climb a mountain, though we never would have found our way up without him and certainly not back down. It was getting to know Ali and becoming a team to overcome the obstacles. Ali became part of the "people" leg of the Golden Triangle, as well as leading us through the "adventure" leg.

We'd only been in Jordan for a few days, but they were days packed with activities. We felt so happy to have been invited on the trip with Pete and Michele.

ON TO THE NEXT PHASE

CHAPTER 32

PORTUGAL & MOROCCO:
MINI SABBATICAL

I was on a mini sabbatical from work. I had two weeks to decide if I wanted to stay in my company or if it was time to exit. I had been there for almost twenty-five years and had the chance to take early retirement. I'd been planning to retire and travel within the next couple of years anyway, so when the opportunity came, I should have jumped at it. But it was too sudden, too fast, and I didn't know if I was ready for it.

I was between projects, and I needed to think. It seemed like every time I settled on an answer, my mind would juggle all the thoughts, and a new answer would pop out like a Magic Eight ball: *Signs point to Yes. My reply is no. Ask again later.* I always think best when I travel. It gives my mind new input and problems to solve, so I started planning a trip.

I wanted the "comfort food" equivalent of travel, something easy and friendly. I had been to Portugal before, but only to Lisbon for a few days. I'd always wanted to see more of the country, so it seemed like the perfect spot. I told my husband my plan and asked him if he wanted to come along.

"You should add in some adventure. What about adding on Morocco?" he asked. He declined to go—he knew I needed time by myself to think.

I flew to Porto and planned to drive through Portugal into Spain and then ferry across to Morocco.

The hotel I reserved in Porto was a bit of a splurge, but I chose it to use up the last of my AMEX points so I wouldn't lose them if I gave up my corporate credit card—if I decided to leave.

Vincci Ponte de Ferro was built into the hills overlooking the Douro River. The lobby was at street level, while all the rooms were on the lower floors, aligned to overlook the river. There was also an exit at river level, providing a great introduction to Porto's many hills and tiers.

After I checked in, I asked the hotel clerk where to go for breakfast. He recommended a pastry shop a couple blocks away, tucked down a side street. I never would have found it or chosen it myself, but it was the place to be. There was a constant stream of locals coming in and going out. There was no English on the menu, nor did they speak it. I mimed a square with my hands to get a menu. Some items on it I couldn't understand, even with my knowledge of Spanish and using Google Translate. I picked a pastry I thought had eggs, like an egg sandwich, but it turned out to be a pastry filled with custardy cream—still eggs, just not the scrambled-type I was hoping for. I would've never chosen it if I'd known what it was, but it was tasty.

It was raining and gray out, but I wasn't going to let that deter me from exploring. I layered up with a Patagonia rain jacket and started walking the city, letting myself get lost in the streets. There were churches, narrow streets winding into even narrower ones, stairs, funiculars—level upon level to get lost in. There were some must-sees like the blue tiles in the train station and on other buildings, but mostly I enjoyed wandering the streets, discovering little shops and cafés.

The only thing that was slightly challenging is that I don't eat fish. Some vegetarians are fish-eaters—pescatarians—but I never liked fish in the first place. When I became a vegetarian, it was easy to say no to fish as well. I stopped to look at the menus of some cute cafés, and it seemed to be fish, seafood, fish, and some fish thrown in for variety. It reminded me of the *Pitch Perfect 2* movie, where Anna Kendrick's character asks about Copenhagen, "Is there anything to eat here besides fish?"

Her friend says, "I saw a KFC."

Anna says, "Nope, I checked. All fish."

I had signed up for a port-tasting tour—it is Portugal, after all. We were supposed to meet at the base of the bridge; and while I thought I knew where that was, after just one day I was hardly an expert on Porto, so I entered the address into Google and followed its walking directions. Google did a terrible job handling Porto's verticality. It told me I had "arrived," and while I might have been able to drop a rock down to the meeting spot, I was about 300 vertical feet above it—and there was no direct staircase.

There was a funicular and one staircase that was pretty direct from the top to bottom of the city, but I wasn't near either of those. Everything else was winding, curving streets, and stairs. I called the tour operator and told them I was running late. Pocketing my phone, I followed any street that went downward. I found the group only a few minutes late.

There were about ten of us on the port tour, and the guide asked us to introduce ourselves with our names, where we were from, and why we were in Porto. In my introduction, I said I was on a mini sabbatical from work.

One of the Europeans asked, "For how long?"

"Two weeks."

There was an awkward silence. To a European, I might as well have said two minutes. That doesn't even count as a summer vacation, much less a sabbatical.

The most interesting part of the tour for me was learning how the land has been engineered over the years, with layers of rocks forcing the grapevines to fight harder to grow. That struggle makes the grapes sweeter and produces better port. It also makes me think that's why I don't like Portuguese wine as much—it has a slightly sweeter note to it, like port. I like port, but I never liked Portuguese wine as much as wine from other places like Italy or Spain. Now I know why.

After Porto, I picked up a rental car and hit the road. There is something magical about a road trip through a country you've never seen. You have the power to stop and see whatever you want, and there is a freedom in that. And of course, with a wide-open road, I was left with my own thoughts again.

The whole "early retirement" thing came up because my last couple of months at the job hadn't gone well. I was thrown onto a job I didn't want to do—a job that was too messy to save—and I felt like I was taking the fall for it. The day I found out I was being released from my project, my boss asked me what project I wanted to do next, and I told him I wanted a retirement package. I didn't know if that was possible, but something had to change. I was in Dallas for the week. My boss told me the news around noon, and although my flight home wasn't until the evening, I was a mess. Staying at the office while I was upset would do no good for my team or my project. My boss encouraged me to leave early, and I did.

It was too early to go to the airport, so I went to the Fort Worth Stockyards, where one of my favorite boot brands had opened a flagship store. They'd been marketing to me throughout the few weeks I'd been in Dallas, and I'd been hoping to visit—but I had been working until 10 p.m. every night. I called Jon in the Uber on the way to Fort Worth to let him know what was going on and that I'd be home later that night.

The Stockyards are still in use, still smell like cows, and are surrounded by a few blocks of old-timey western shops and restaurants. The area reminded me of Deadwood, South Dakota, where my mother grew up and where I spent a lot of time as a child with my grandparents.

I found the boot store, but they didn't have any of the boots I liked in my size. There were multiple other boot stores, so I wandered between them, browsing and dragging my suitcase behind me, but I really wasn't in the mood to shop.

I must have traveled to Dallas twenty to thirty times as a consultant, and every time, I worked the whole week and then left, seeing little of the city. I had never been to the Stockyards, never shopped for boots, never taken a moment for myself. How much had I poured into that company—and now, this might be it? *Just like that?*

That night, when I pulled up in front of our house, Jon had lined the driveway with candles, guiding me home and reminding of the ones he'd arranged for me in Korea. He knew how upset I was, and it meant so much that he welcomed me home that way.

When I talked to Jon about the potential early retirement,

he said he'd support me no matter what I decided. It was the best stance he could take. I needed to make the decision. I was the one who was going to have to either keep working or leave, and I needed to be at peace with my decision.

When I talked to my son about it, he asked insightful questions that helped channel my thinking. "What are you trying to achieve in your company that you haven't already?"

I had been pushing for the next promotion, but in reality, I probably would have hated it. Sounds like sour grapes, I know, but that next level gets super political, and I'd be a step removed from leading teams, which I enjoyed. My company always favored salespeople, and I just never liked sales. Landing the next level was unlikely—and I'd probably have hated it if did. So, nothing. His questions made the answer sound so simple. Yet, why did I still feel so conflicted?

My first stop outside of Porto was the town of Aveiro, dubbed the Venice of Portugal. I found a parking garage near the center of town and pulled into a slot. I went into reverse to straighten out my parking job, and the car lurched forward. I tried to put the car in reverse again, but it went forward. I looked down at the six-speed stick shift and tried again—once more, it lurched forward. By then, I was only a few inches away from the concrete wall of the parking garage. I locked the car and walked away, knowing it wasn't going to help to keep trying the same thing over and over.

Aveiro had canals with little boats and bridges, as well as cute shops and winding streets. The Venice of Portugal though? That seemed like a bit of a stretch. After walking through the town, I got a cup of coffee and a chocolate pastry, my mind still churning over how to get out of the parking garage.

By the time I finished my coffee, I had a plan. I went to my car, pulled out my soft-sided suitcase, and put it between the car and the concrete wall, hoping it would serve as a buffer if the car still refused to go into reverse. I had Googled how to get the car into reverse, but I couldn't find the specific answer for the model of car I had. However, there were a few helpful options. I found a ring in the leather casing around the stick shift, pulled up—and bingo: reverse! I stopped, grabbed my suitcase, and was on my way, feeling renewed by both caffeine and the adrenaline of solving a problem.

As I drove south from Aviero, the sun finally poked through the clouds—the first time I'd seen it since I landed in Portugal. I felt like the whole world was opening up to me. Portugal was one country, in one small corner of the world. Yet, it looked so wide, so expansive. It was beautiful and green, and I thought, *It's a big world. It's just one job. You can do anything you want.*

When I left the military, I found a new career, and it had worked out well. There were thousands of other jobs I could apply for. I had experience and skills. And if I really regretted my decision to leave my company, I could always apply to be rehired. While it wasn't guaranteed I could get back in, it was certainly less final than it had been when I left the military.

I know it sounds cliché, but that moment of sunlight and freedom gave me peace about my decision. It was time to leave and see what the rest of my life—and the world—had in store for me.

If my life was a movie, I wouldn't have had that revelation until the last scene, until the last stop on my journey. But that's not how life works. For me, it was that moment of sunlight and seeing the open stretches of Portugal where I made the decision.

Now, I had to start the healing process. I was at peace with my decision to leave, but after all the messiness of my last job, I was far from at peace.

My next stop, Óbidos, felt like a renaissance fair, toppling over the edge from quaint into touristy. Instead of walking through the town—which I could see was filled with people in medieval garb hawking their menus or wares at souvenir shops—I hopped straight onto the stone walls surrounding the city.

Walking the walls let me circumnavigate at least half the city before I had to descend into the streets below. From up there, I could see cheesy Renaissance Fair-style games and more shops, but also houses with small vegetable and flower gardens, and laundry hanging out to dry. The walls were thick and nearly vertiginous, with no railing on the inside overlooking the city.

I stayed at a Marriott near Óbidos, only to discover it was a golfing, seaside resort. "Golfing, seaside, and resort" being three of the words *least* likely to entice me to choose a hotel. But it was a Marriott, and I had points, so there I was.

My room had a back patio that opened onto sand dunes, and I hiked through them as the sun went down, covering the land with a diffused light. It reminded me of the sand dunes along the coastline in Skagen, Denmark. I walked until it was too dark and the wind too chilly.

I had a couple more days in Portugal, and it did feel like the "comfort food" of travel that I'd wanted. I passed through the surfing capital, Nazaré, now famous for the *100 Foot Wave* series on Netflix. I walked up and down the shoreline and watched the waves crash. It was off-season, so there weren't any 100- footers, but the waves would still have been more than I could handle—though, to be honest, so are the waves in a wave pool!

I stopped in Coimbra, another town built vertically like Porto, with great shops and restaurants. Evora, another walled city, felt less touristy than the others I had visited. From there, I crossed into Spain near Badajoz.

Once I got to Spain, I felt like a weight had been lifted. The landscape opened up—Spain is wilder, bigger, and more rugged than Portugal. I enjoyed Portugal, but I love Spain. I like the wine better in Spain, and they speak Spanish in Spain. As someone who devoted so many years of my life to studying Spanish, Portugal was one of the most tantalizing places. I can almost—kind of, sort of, mostly—understand everything, but I can't speak it. I asked at every shop, restaurant, and hotel in Portugal—Spanish or English?—and they all preferred English. In Spain, the Spanish is as smooth and sweet as caramel flan.

I spent a day in Sevilla. I hadn't been to Sevilla since I was fourteen, and I felt a sense of almost déjà vu all day. Of course, the historic plazas were mostly the same, but Sevilla is a modern city, so much of it felt new. I've traveled to many places, and Sevilla was one of the few where I ever thought, *I could live here*. It just felt so comfortable. I could have stayed for another week—or a month.

But I didn't have a month, and I needed to journey on. The next morning, I was going to Gibraltar, dropping off the car at Algeciras, and then taking a ferry to Morocco.

I couldn't count Gibraltar as a new country, since it's part of the UK, but it's always fun to see something new. As I was driving toward Gibraltar, a car in front of me kicked up a rock. It hit the windshield with a crack that made me duck down like I was being shot at. Instantly, I watched a line grow from side to side across my windshield. *Crap!*

When I was a teenager, my father and I were driving to the Air Force Academy for an orientation weekend. We were coming from North Dakota, and there's a whole lot of nothing between North Dakota and Colorado Springs, Colorado. Somewhere in the middle of Wyoming, in the dead of winter, a rock kicked up by a passing car shattered the driver's side window into a spray of safety glass—I was driving at the time.

I stepped on the gas.

My dad, in the most calming voice possible said, "What are you doing?"

I said, "I'm going to catch up to that car."

"Why?" he asked, again calmly.

"They did this to us."

"What are you going to do if you catch up to them?"

Finally, my "fight" response and adrenaline started to level out, and I realized he was right. If it had been accidental—like kicking up a rock, which was probable—then there was nothing catching them would accomplish. And if it had been intentional—like shooting at us—then I definitely didn't want to pursue them. It was Wyoming. People have guns in Wyoming. I slowed down to a normal driving speed, and we had to drive through the winter with the window out until we could get to a town big enough to fix it. In Wyoming, that took hours.

I realized there was nothing to be done about my windshield and continued on to Gibraltar, though it took a while for my heartbeat to slow and for the adrenaline to process out of my system.

The funny thing about the windshield is that my Volkswagen SUV at home had an almost identical crack, caused by a rock while driving home from my client's office in Connecticut. However, that crack had been there since 2019, pre-pandemic, and I'd never taken the time to get it fixed. It had been there for almost four years. The crack was another reminder that my life was out of balance and, once again, made me realize it was time to leave my company.

I did some research on Gibraltar the night before to figure out the best places to park and the best ways to enter, but I had limited time before dropping off the car and getting to the ferry. The thought of dropping my car and hopping on a bus made me super nervous: *what if it took a long time to get back to my car?* I decided to drive into Gibraltar. This was post-Brexit, so there was a full border between Spain and Gibraltar (the UK), and a long line of cars waiting to get in.

I started sweating, thinking I might have made the wrong decision if I was going to be stuck in the line for too long; but it moved pretty quickly, and within about twenty minutes, I drove into Gibraltar.

Gibraltar is only 6.7 square kilometers, with fewer than 35,000 people. The rock of Gibraltar, which one would think is a rock, is really a huge mountain looming over the city. I really had no idea it would be that big. Big enough that you can take cable cars to the top. I didn't have time for the cable cars, so I drove into and through the town.

In reality, I was whipping around on the super narrow, mostly one-way roads as if I were on a racetrack. Not that I was speeding . . . I don't think. The streets were just so tight and curvy, with nowhere to pull over, and the traffic moved fast. I zipped through the town following the flow of traffic—twice since I missed a turn—before basically driving right back out again.

I realize it sounds weird that I would spend twenty minutes in a *queue*—it is British, so I must say queue—just to drive through the town and back out. However, it was totally worth it just to see the town and the "rock." And, with my six-speed stick shift, I felt like a race car driver. My adrenaline surged, and I loved it.

I was nervous to turn in my car, knowing I had a cracked windshield. Michele and I had already been grilled once—on our first trip together—when we returned the car in Italy. We'd done nothing wrong, but they accused us of a dent we hadn't caused, and it took Michele months to get it resolved. This time, the windshield was cracked, and it was definitely on my watch. Would there be a lot of paperwork? Would I have to explain what happened?

I found the rental agency and handed the agent the keys. I told him there was a little problem and my windshield was cracked. He didn't even walk out of the office to go look at it. He just said, "It happens. You have insurance, right?"

I couldn't believe it was that easy, and yes, I had insurance through Expedia that covered it with no headaches when I got home.

Hopping on the ferry to Morocco, I felt light and free again, no longer having to worry about the rental car. As much freedom as rentals give me, it's so freeing to turn them back in. As the ferry started moving, I watched the rock of Gibraltar fall away, the continent of Europe fade into the distance. I was heading toward the rest of the world. I left the questions behind and started to face forward.

I was a little uncomfortable about what I would find in Morocco. I had gotten mixed reviews from people who had been there. One friend said it was the only place that had made him nervous, but it had been many years ago. I think being a solo woman in a Muslim country was a factor as well. I planned to spend just a couple of days there. If I loved it, I could always go back. If I didn't enjoy it, I wouldn't have to be there that long.

I had assumed Tangier would be sketchy. It's a port town, and it's the city I'd heard the most mixed reviews about. I was pleasantly surprised to see that it was shiny and clean, and I walked on the boardwalk alongside the water, up into the old town and back. I stopped at a tea house for a mint tea—a glass stuffed with a handful of mint leaves made the most refreshing drink.

I took a day trip to Chefchaouen, the famous "blue town" that fills Instagram feeds. It was undeniably lovely, but I was disappointed to learn that the blue was less an ancient tradition and more a clever marketing scheme designed to draw in tourists. There wasn't really a historical reason for it, they just wanted to make the town stand out and painted it blue about forty years ago. Now it is "the" destination in Morocco. My favorite part of Chefchaouen were the cats that seemed to be everywhere. I dedicated myself to taking pictures of them versus trying for the perfect Insta-selfie.

After Chefchaouen, I took a day trip to Marrakech. Marrakech is what I picture when I think of Morocco. On the drive there—and even earlier on the way to Chefchaouen—I was struck by how green the landscape was. It wasn't all desert like I'd imagined.

Marrakech looked exactly as I'd expected. My guide had been working for years and seemed to know everyone and all the hidden stops (though of course everyone may go to those same stops; how would I know?) We saw bread baking in a community oven, the fires heating the Hammam baths, Bahia Palace, and explored the winding streets of the old town.

Our last stop was the market—huge and winding, easy to get lost in. There were the snake charmers I had expected (you can take pictures for a fee!), along with every trinket, souvenir, spice, and tea you could ever want. It was overwhelming and huge. I said said no to every vendor trying to sell me their wares before finally caving and buying a couple of small tea glasses that were painted bright turquoise.

After the market, we were supposed to go camel riding. I told the guide, "No camels. I don't want to ride a camel." It had already been a long, hot day. My flight left the next morning, and my mind was shifting to what awaited me—and how my decision would be received—back at work. He said, "You already paid for it."

I repeated, "No camel ride." He nodded at me.

I settled in for the drive and called my husband. It was morning in the U.S., and he'd just be waking up. I told him where I was and that I'd just told the driver I didn't want to ride a camel.

"What? You have to ride the camel," he said.

"I'm not riding the camel. I'm tired, hot, and I don't know if the poor things are well taken care of."

"Ride the camel for all of us who aren't traveling with you."

"I'm not riding a camel."

At about that time, the driver pulled over right in front of a field of camels. "No camel ride," I told the driver. "I gotta go," I told my husband and hung up.

"You already paid for it," the driver repeated.

I stepped out of the car. One of the camel herders came over and pulled a robe over my head like I was a toddler and expertly wound a scarf around my head. He walked me to a kneeling camel.

I got on. What else could I do? The camel stood up, and then we were walking around the field. The handler knew his business well and I got a great selfie with the camel. If you rode a camel and didn't get a selfie, did you even ride the camel?

I sent the picture to my husband and all my close friends and family who were following my journey and knew the decision I had to make.

The picture of the camel was a great reminder that "It's a big world" out there. It was yet another indication that it was time to move on from my job and do something different.

My mini sabbatical had accomplished what I needed: it helped me make up my mind, gave me peace about the decision, and set me on the road to healing.

I got the windshield on my VW fixed when I got home.

CHAPTER 33

KASHMIR:
WHERE ARE WE?

I was reclined in a Shikara boat with a canopy overhead, next to my friend Kalyani, with a gondolier rowing us around. This was not Venice, and the boatmen probably weren't called gondoliers, but that was the only name that fit. We were on Dal Lake in Srinagar, Kashmir, India. The lake was surrounded by mountains. It was a warm evening, and the sun was just setting.

I couldn't help but think, *What the heck am I doing here?*

Kalyani and I had worked together for the past year and a half, and she lived in Mumbai, India. We'd only met once in person the previous year when I'd traveled to meet the team. Still, she and I had a connection, lived through some crazy times at work together, and she was a good friend. When I told her the news that I was leaving our company, we both cried, and it felt like I was losing a friend.

I promised to see her the next time I came back to India. I'd already been to India four times for work, so India wasn't high on the list, but you never know.

She said, "Let's do a girls' weekend."

I loved that idea, and we stayed connected after I left the company, texting back and forth with possible date options and locations. For locations, she offered Mumbai—where she lived—Goa, Kashmir, or Kerala.

Mumbai: I'd been there twice for work already—nope.

Goa: beaches, nope.

Kashmir: YES, YES, YES!

Kerala: I don't know anything about it, but it's not Kashmir, so . . . nope.

I'd wanted to go to Kashmir forever! I had bought an India travel book back when I was at the Air Force Academy and was always fascinated by the region, but it had never been safe to visit. Jammu and Kashmir, the northernmost state of India, had been contested between India and Pakistan for years. When the British left back in 1947, they divided the region: the primarily Hindu areas became part of India, and the primarily Muslim areas became part of Pakistan. That may have looked good on paper, but it triggered mass migrations of millions and violence that claimed the lives of another million people. Kashmir is now primarily Muslim, but it is part of India.

To this day, India and Pakistan are hostile to each other. When I was filling out my electronic visa request to come to India, there were a ton of questions related to Pakistan. Am I Pakistani? Was my mother Pakistani? Was my father, my husband? Have I ever been to Pakistan?

I asked Kalyani if it was safe to travel to Kashmir now.

She said, "The area has gotten safe over the past few years after a crackdown by the Indian government." Jammu, farther north, is still not safe. (Important sidenote: This was in 2023, prior to the terrorist incident in April 2025 that killed 28 people and injured many more, which has caused tensions to increase between India and Pakistan. I would not recommend traveling to Kashmir currently).

Of course, flying to India for a "girls' weekend" doesn't make sense. From the U.S., it's about an 18-hour flight, with a ten-and-a-half-hour time difference—and flights aren't cheap. Kalyani only had four days for our "weekend," so I decided to add on a few additional days in India and a side trip to Sri Lanka to round out my journey. We decided to meet up in the airport in Mumbai for our flight to Srinagar, the capital of Kashmir.

And so there we were—right in the middle of Srinagar, Kashmir, on Dal Lake.

I couldn't get over how beautiful Dal Lake and the boats were. We floated past stores that you could only access via boat, and there were also floating shops where a boat would paddle up alongside us and offer little carved boats, jewelry, or tea. I shook my head no to all the offers. Kalyani bought a little wooden boat for her kids.

I had been somewhat nervous about how we would get along. We were friends, and we were excited by the trip, but traveling with someone and talking on the phone once a week were vastly different. We had agreed on separate rooms, giving each of us space—to talk to our families, to work (in her case), or just to do whatever. But I was still nervous.

After the lake, Kalyani and I were in an auto rickshaw (three-wheeled moto-taxi) on the way back to the hotel when we spotted a French café that looked great. We both decided to ask the driver to stop—and we'd only gone about 100 feet.

Over dinner, we looked at TripAdvisor and Google Maps to decide what we wanted to see—which was just about everything!—and caught up on work and family. It felt as natural as if Kalyani and I had been traveling buddies and friends our whole lives.

By the time we got back to the hotel, it was dark. As we got out of the taxi, I saw that there was a line of white lights going up the hillside. "Look," I said to Kalyani, thinking they looked beautiful. We were told the lights were hung on the fence of a local Army garrison, set up to defend India. *Right.*

At breakfast the next morning, I wondered how close we were to Pakistan. I pulled up Google and mapped how long it would take to get to Islamabad. It showed me two days to walk. No options for driving or mass transit. I showed it to Kalyani, and she all but looked over her shoulder and wiped the map from my screen.

We reserved a taxi for the day and drove to the Chashme Shahi Gardens. There was an obvious security presence along the way, with police on every street, checkpoints, and armored vehicles I hadn't ever seen anywhere else in India. We had to get out of the taxi and walk past some barricades before proceeding to the Gardens.

It was a bright, cool morning, and the Gardens were in full bloom. There were mountains all around us, and it was the perfect place to start our day.

We were approached by people with racks of traditional Kashmiri outfits that we could put on and get pictures in, for a price (of course). It was like one of those old-timey pictures you might get in Deadwood, South Dakota, or Tombstone, Arizona. I would have said no, but Kalyani asked, "When are we ever going to be here again?" She negotiated with them in Hindi.

Before I knew what was happening, I was getting a headdress and scarf tied around my head, with the same impersonal efficiency as when I was outfitted for the camel ride in Morocco.

They asked what color robe I wanted, and I pointed to a turquoise one. We posed around the garden, both separately and together, doing traditional Kashmiri poses that they demonstrated for me to copy. I have to admit, for the six dollars or so we paid, the pictures are pretty cool. Kalyani was right, when would we ever be in Kashmir again?

After the Gardens, we jumped in the taxi to go to the Jama Masjid Mosque, which is Kashmir's central mosque in the middle of old Srinagar. During the 30-minute drive, we pointed out examples of the unique architecture to each other. Kashmir's homes and buildings combine almost Tudor-style façades—like those you might find in the Alps of Austria or Germany—with intricate, Arabic-style geometric designs. They're unique, and we kept trying to capture images of them as we drove past.

At the Jama Masjid Mosque we were asked—more like told—to put on robes and headscarves. I was wearing long pants, so I was a little surprised that I had to wear a robe over my slacks, but I know better than to protest when it's not my country. Kalyani was wearing a *kurti*, a long tunic with matching pants underneath. Her outfit was deemed appropriate for the mosque, but she still had to put on a headscarf.

The mosque featured the same intricate blend of Alpine and Arabic-style woodcarvings. When we stopped to take a few pictures, Kalyani said, "It feels like we're in a different country."

"*I am* in a different country," I said.

Kalyani was right that it didn't feel like the rest of India. It was its own culture and style, and it was unlike anything either of us had seen.

After the mosque, we decided to stop for lunch. Kalyani found a tea house online that looked cute. I ordered a breakfast dish with eggs and a local bread, along with something called "noon chai." I assumed it was a strong tea that you might have at noon. Boy, was I wrong. "Noon" means "salt" in Kashmiri, and the tea was a pink, milky concoction that reminded me of vomit. Apparently it's very popular—but I thought it was disgusting.

Kalyani said I should order something else. I asked the waiter for black tea, and I was told they didn't have any. *How could they not have black tea?* Kalyani suggested English Breakfast. I agreed, and the waiter walked away with my order.

Apparently, black tea is a very specific thing in India. I would consider English Breakfast in the category of black tea, but that's not the way it works in India. Maybe it's like how there are over fifty different words for snow in Inuit. Also, some teas automatically come with milk unless you specify otherwise. After that, I let Kalyani order tea for me. It was too complicated, and I didn't want any more of the pink-vomit tea.

It was not the first time I'd relinquished control to Kalyani that trip, and it was only day two. She handled most of the costs since she had access to pay through the local Paytm app, which worked for everything from tickets to auto rickshaws to snacks. She even bought the little boat carving from the floating vendor on Dal Lake using it. I kept track of costs so that I could balance out our spending in the hotels where they would take U.S. credit cards.

It was also immediately apparent that English wasn't the lingua franca, and Kalyani had to use Hindi for most of the negotiations. My Hindi, on the other hand, is a bit rusty—or rather, non-existent.

Apparently, foreigners had not yet realized that Kashmir was safe to travel to, as I was one of about six foreigners that I saw during the four days we were traveling in Kashmir. The vast majority of the tourists were from India and could speak Hindi as a common language even if their native Indian language was different. If I had not been traveling with Kalyani, it would have been significantly more difficult to navigate and negotiate.

The next day, we reserved a taxi again and headed for Gulmarg to take gondolas up the mountain. From there, we planned to double back and continue on to Pahalgam for the night. If you look on a map, the route was a zigzag—west first, then looping back east. We had initially planned to go straight to Pahalgam in the east, but Kalyani really didn't want to miss Gulmarg. I agreed right away—I always want to see everything—and Kalyani seemed just as aggressive as me with her list of touristic to-do's.

Kalyani found an artisan market selling quality handicrafts and rugs. Since it was on the road to Gulmarg, we stopped en route. She was interested in buying a rug, she said. They had the most beautiful rugs. Kalyani and the seller looked at several rugs, the vendor spreading them all out on the floor in front of her.

I must have looked longingly enough at a more modern one, woven in blues and purples, because suddenly I was getting the hard-sell too. In learning the price, I learned a new word, *lakh*. One lakh is 100,000 rupees, and this rug was four lakhs. I quickly pulled out my phone to convert the price to dollars. The beautiful rug I was looking at was almost $5,000. *Are you kidding me?*

I shook my head and said, "No, that's more than I was planning to spend."

Instead of understanding that as the "no" I intended, he took that as an indication of the need to bargain. "How much would you offer, madam?"

"No, I'm sorry," I said. "No, thank you."

"Please, madam. How much were you planning on spending?" the vendor pushed.

After attempting to decline politely a few more times, I finally said "Zero! I was planning on spending zero. I was not planning on buying a rug. No, thank you."

He took the hint at that point and got a double whammy when Kalyani decided against buying a rug as well.

Still, the vendor was a professional and took us to the next stop on the tour of the shop, which was to the room with silk shawls, scarves, pashminas, saris, and anything else you could imagine made of fabric. Kalyani engaged with the vendor and looked through stacks of silk scarves and saris.

I wandered around the room in case anything caught my eye. I found a wool jacket in red and black, with a high collar. I reached to pull it off the rack, and a clerk in the store said, "No, madam, that's not your size."

I ignored him and pulled the jacket off the hanger and tried it on. It fit like a glove. It was absolutely perfect, and my plan of spending nothing at that store was dashed. It was fortunately a *lot* cheaper than the rug, so I didn't mind. Kalyani found a couple of pashminas and a sari, and then we were on our way to Gulmarg.

At Gulmarg, our driver dropped us off in front of the gondola which would take us to the top of the mountain.

"*Where am I?*" I wondered as we ascended. It looked just like Colorado. Did I just travel halfway around the world to be in Colorado? But then I saw the homes of the local villagers dug into the side of the mountain, and that wasn't something I could see in the U.S. We were in the Himalayas, so of course I was expecting the mountains to look more like what I'd seen in Nepal. Bigger, snowier. We were approaching 14,000 feet, so these mountains were still big, they just weren't Nepal big. They were Pikes Peak big.

The view was breathtaking—pine-covered mountains stretching as far as the eye could see. But I couldn't get over how much it looked like Colorado. We circled the hill taking pictures of all of the different vistas, but it was chilly, and we weren't planning to hike around the top. We hopped the cable car back down, found a nearby resort to get some tea—I let Kalyani order for me again—and then we were back on the road to Pahalgam.

I was excited about the hotel in Pahalgam. When we were planning the trip, I wasn't sure how to broach the topic of budgets. Kalyani is an executive at my former company, so I knew she earned a good salary, but since it is based on the Indian economy, I wasn't sure what her travel budget would be.

I solved the question by letting her pick the hotels. She would be smarter about the area anyway, and then she could pick places that would meet her budget. When she picked the hotel in Pahalgam, my jaw dropped—it was twice what I'd planned to spend. She'd picked a stunning mountain chalet. I told her I was looking forward to sitting on the deck with a glass of wine or tea, looking at the gorgeous views of the mountains.

The previous night, she'd chosen a sprawling resort hotel near Srinagar for dinner. It was outside of town, nestled in the foothills. We saw a wedding in progress, and it was clearly a location for special events.

I thought that Kalyani didn't drink wine. We'd only had one dinner together the previous year, and I had been afraid it might be awkward if I was drinking wine and she wasn't. But she did drink, and we ended up spending a very pleasant evening drinking wine and enjoying a few Indian dishes she picked out for me—I'd given up all control by this point!

When we got to the hotel in Pahalgam, it wasn't quite what we expected. It was a quaint mountain hotel—cozy, with stuffed chairs and nooks to hang out in. However, we didn't have balconies, and it was pouring rain, so there were no mountain views.

We went down to the dining room. I decided to wear the red wool Kashmiri jacket that I'd bought earlier that day. With a black shirt underneath, my black jeans, and black cowboy boots, I thought it was a striking combo. As Kalyani and I stood at the entrance to the dining room, it felt like every head in the place turned toward us. I realized I was the only non-Indian in the dining room, proudly sporting my new Indian jacket. Cultural appropriation or just cultural appreciation? I rocked the jacket and loved it, so I'm going with appreciation.

After we were seated, Kalyani ordered our meals and then asked for the drink menu. The waiter turned over the menu and pointed to the drinks. It had a variety of teas, juices, and sodas.

"No, the drinks. Like wine," Kalyani said.

"I'm sorry madam. We don't serve alcohol."

We stared at him.

"Kashmir is a dry state," the waiter clarified.

That didn't make any sense. We'd shared a bottle of wine at the gorgeous hotel in Srinagar the night before.

"There are only three places that sell alcohol," he said. "Two in Srinagar—a hotel and a wine shop. And one wine shop in Pahalgam."

We had just happened to stumble into the one place in the whole state that served alcohol the night before—and hadn't realized it at the time. Kashmir is a predominantly Muslim region, so I guess it made sense.

It was a Sunday night, and the wine store in town would already be closed, and we didn't really want to go back out in the dark and rainy conditions anyway. The next day was a holiday—Gandhi's birthday, a famously dry holiday—so the wine shop would definitely be closed. We laughed, and Kalyani ordered our tea.

On our last day together, it was super rainy when we woke up, so I was content to drink tea and write. She was already talking to the hotel concierge to look for activities. "Do you want to ride horses?" she asked. I couldn't imagine riding horses in the rain, so I shook my head.

"We can get a taxi to take us to the surrounding valleys," she offered instead. That sounded better, at least until it cleared up. We spent the day driving between different valleys, trying—and, of course, failing—to capture the beauty of the area. By the time we returned to the hotel around 3 or 4 p.m., I was ready to relax until dinner. Not Kalyani! "Do you want to go horseback riding now?"

I was known for scheduling trips wall-to-wall. Michele liked to travel the same way, which is why she and I got along so well. My family demanded I added in more rest days whenever we traveled. I didn't expect Kalyani to out-activity me. Yet, she was the one who kept pushing for one more thing. If she was up for it, I wasn't going to say no. We ran back to our rooms to add a few layers and then headed to the stables next to the hotel.

We got on our horses, and a handler walked alongside each of us, making sure the horses stayed on course. It was supposed to be forty-five minutes up, and forty-five minutes back. We walked along the road and gravel roads before finally walking on mountain paths. The destination was an open meadow in the middle of the mountains, called Little Switzerland.

To be honest, every other tourist on a horse tour was brought to the same spot, making it overcrowded. We preferred being on the horses, enjoying the beauty of the mountains, and the peacefulness of the ride there and back.

The mountains around us again reminded me of Colorado. Just a dusting of snow on the mountain tips, but mostly alpine, pine-covered mountains. Just like Colorado. By the time we got down off the mountain and were walking on the roads back to the hotel, it was pitch dark. It must have taken two and a half, maybe three hours—there was no way it was forty-five minutes each way.

As we walked up the final incline to the hotel, the horses must have gotten eager to be back and get their rations. I was in front and almost to the top when I heard Kalyani scream. I looked back, and she was on the ground next to the sidewalk, and both handlers were rushing to her side.

I tried to get down to help her, but I wasn't sure how to get off the horse by myself. I felt like I was stranded on an island. "Are you okay?" I yelled.

Finally, the handlers got her up, and then one of them came to get me off my horse.

"I'm okay," she said. "The ground was soft where I landed."

Fortunately, our horses were short. I don't know what breed they were. They weren't ponies or mules, but they were short. Luckily, her fall wasn't as bad as it could have been.

We went back to our rooms, changed, and met for dinner. I asked her again how she was feeling.

"I'll have some bruises tomorrow, but I'll be okay."

I felt bad for her, but then she added, "I'm so glad we did that. It was the highlight of the trip for me."

I enjoyed the horses, but the highlight of my trip was getting a new like-minded travel buddy and seeing a fascinating part of the world.

We agreed to do another girls' weekend, though she assured me we'd pick somewhere that would have wine next time!

CHAPTER 34

INDIA:
BACK TO INDIA

The trip to Kashmir, India with Kalyani was my fifth trip to India, and it would have felt like a major oversight if I still hadn't taken time to see the Taj Mahal. Like going to Paris and not seeing the Eiffel Tower or New York without seeing Times Square. So, after our "weekend" in Kashmir, I signed myself up for a Golden Triangle tour, which included the Taj Mahal, plus sightseeing in Delhi and then Jaipur.

A driver would take me to each of the cities, drop me off at lunch stops, and then take me to my hotel each night. He handed me off to a different tour guide in each of the cities to see the major attractions. He was very nice, but he didn't speak a lot of English, so we didn't do much chatting between stops.

My tour guide in Delhi was young, the same age as my son—twenty-seven at the time. As we traveled between three different sites, we talked about life and family, and the historical places we were visiting were more like a backdrop for our conversation. He told me he was still unmarried, and his parents were giving him until thirty to find his own wife before they'd arrange someone for him. His older brother was getting married soon, having found his own wife before the clock ran out—which, my guide said, took the pressure off him for a few more years.

At one point, he pointed to the Presidential Palace, where the President lives, but she wasn't there at the time. I was startled when he said "she." I'd never heard of a leader of India outside of Narendra Modhi. Modhi's picture is everywhere in India and a frequent feature in the news cycle in the U.S. Who was she?

Apparently, since 2022, the President of India is Droupadi Murmu. There is both a President and a Prime Minister. He showed me a picture of Murmu as we drove to the next spot.

I enjoyed the tour in Delhi, not necessarily because of the sites we saw, but because of the guide and our conversation.

The guide handed me back to the driver, who quietly drove several hours to Agra, stopping along the way at a rest area and lunch stop. Without Kalayani's guidance, I tried to order my favorite paneer dish—cubes of cheese with a tofu-like texture in a red spicy sauce—but I botched it and got barbecued paneer instead. It wasn't bad, but I already missed Kalyani's gentle control of my travels (and meals) in India.

Once we got to Agra, the driver dropped me off at the hotel, which was booked as part of the tour. I was told to be ready for a 5 a.m. pickup to avoid the lines and see the Taj at sunrise. No bags—just my phone for pictures.

I had been a little nervous about the quality of the hotel since it was included in the package tour and I hadn't picked it myself. But it was actually amazing, with extensive gardens surrounding the palatial hotel. It must have been off-season because there was almost no one around, and it felt like I had the whole place to myself.

At O'dark-thirty the next morning, the driver picked me up and introduced me to my guide for Agra. I had dressed in the bright-red Kashmiri jacket that I'd bought with Kalyani. She actually told me I should wear it so that I would stand out in the pictures against the backdrop of the Taj Mahal. Even though she was no longer there to help me order food, I was still living in Kalyani's world!

I had set my expectations low for the Taj Mahal, which is crazy to think. I'd heard some negative reviews, like "smaller than I expected" or "too touristy."

But I loved the Taj Mahal! The guide was very efficient and knew exactly where I should pose for the best pictures. He knew the story of the Taj Mahal very well. It wasn't a conversation—he was clearly reciting a well-rehearsed set of facts. It was also clear how proud he was of the Taj Mahal and his country. He wanted me to know as much about it as he could tell me.

"The Taj Mahal is a love story," he said. He explained that the king loved his wife—albeit his second wife—so much that he built the entire temple as a tomb for her after she died giving birth to their 14th child. At the palace next door to the Taj, we visited where the king would sit and look at the Taj and remember her. After he passed away, he was buried next to her in the Taj Mahal.

The Taj looked exactly like I expected it to, but better. Beyond the iconic image of the Taj always shown in photos, the grounds included an entrance gate, a mosque, and a large garden with a reflection pool.

The Taj itself was simply gorgeous—made of white marble intricately carved in geometric and floral patterns. There were inlaid semi-precious stones of various colors—green malachite, blue lapis lazuli, turquoise, red garnet, and multi-colored agate. Everything was intricate, hand-carved, and carefully placed. It took over seventeen years to build the mausoleum, with another five years to complete the surrounding structures. It looked like it had been built with love and craftsmanship.

In Jaipur, I had the third of three guides. Like the guide in Agra, he delivered a prepared monologue. Maybe it was the different history he had to tell compared with the Taj Mahal's love story, but it put me on edge right from the start. Our first stop was to look at an ornate façade where women could hide behind the screens and watch the street below. Five stories of intricate shuttered windows with screens were carved in pink and white stone. Its intricacy is absolutely mind-blowing, but I couldn't get past the idea of women having to hide behind the screens. It was like a monument of repression for me.

When we got to the Amber Fort, the misogynistic narrative continued. The guide told me about the king and his many wives and concubines. There were rooms for the wives and the concubines, rooms where women could look over the plaza in the palace and not be seen.

The guide was also treating me like an ingenue, warning me about people offering to take photos for money or selling trinkets. I told him I'd traveled a lot, including multiple trips to India, but he stuck to his routine, guiding me through pathways and doorways as if I were a porcelain doll.

Then, he showed me where the women could bathe while the king watched and decided whom he wanted to be with that evening. I shut down and stopped responding to him. After listening to talk of women's repression and misogyny—and being treated like a fragile flower myself—I just wanted the tour to be over.

Finally, he sensed something was wrong. "Ask questions," he said. "What's your feedback?"

I said, "I know it's history, but I don't want to hear about concubines anymore. I don't want to hear any more about how women are treated like second-class citizens."

He told me about Indira Ghandi who was Prime Minister forty years ago and also mentioned the current president. He tried to tell me some of the advances being made for women while we finished the tour.

Maybe it wasn't fair of me, but is it so hard for people to look at their audience and adapt their speech accordingly? Did he really think I wanted to hear all about concubines and men getting to spy on them while they bathed? Couldn't he have summarized some of those parts quickly and told me about other parts of the history? There were so many other things to focus on—glorious battles or beautiful architecture.

After the Amber Fort, we were supposed to stop at a restaurant for lunch—where I would eat by myself, and which wasn't included in the tour price—and then go to a jewel shop. I had already been to many jewelry shops and knew that I didn't want to do that again, so I said, "Can we please just go back to the hotel?" I was done with that guide and with my day in Jaipur.

On my last day in India, I had time to explore Delhi on my own before heading to the airport. I had two goals: Chandni Chowk and Lodhi Gardens.

Chandni Chowk in Delhi is a street market covering several blocks and a zone of utter chaos. There are spice markets, gem shops, food markets, and just about anything imaginable.

I took an Uber from my hotel and was surprised when the Uber driver stopped and pointed at a sign that said Chandni Chowk with an arrow. On my Uber app, there was still another ten minutes left in the ride, but he pointed at the sign, so I got out and started walking.

I almost immediately turned around and got back in the Uber. I'd just hit my 74th country, traveled dozens of countries on my own, and this was the first moment I felt truly overwhelmed. My purse was already hung across my torso, but I clutched it to my chest as I started to move. Moving was difficult simply due to the sheer crush of people.

People—100 percent men—kept walking alongside me, calling out, "Madam, where are you going?" "Taxi, madam," "Madam! Madam! Madam!"

I literally side-stepped and doubled-back, like a football player, to avoid the hawkers. I'd resume walking, and another person would fall into step beside me. I crossed the street and dipped down a side street selling lamps, lighting, and lightbulbs. I wanted to see the spice markets, not lighting, so I doubled back to the main street. Unfortunately, I couldn't walk a single step without people wanting to take me somewhere or offer me a ride.

I'm sure most, if not all of them, are legitimately trying to get my business, but my policy is still to say no to anyone who approaches me. I would rather approach a taxi that is idling and ask them a price—or nowadays go through Uber. If I pick someone out, it always seems safer than saying yes to someone who approaches me.

But Chandni Chowk was beyond anything I'd experienced. It was just so much!

The reason the Uber driver dropped me where he did is because the main road was off-limits to motorized vehicles.

Instead, the street was packed with bicycle rickshaws—not even the ever-present tuk-tuks—just good old-fashioned pedal power. Several of them shadowed me as I walked along the main street, asking if I wanted a ride. I shook my head and didn't look at them.

Then, one rickshaw driver drove up alongside me and said, "Walking is very hard." It was such an unusual line that I looked at him. He was young, maybe in his twenties.

"No," I said, shaking my head. Like the others, he pedaled alongside me for a few more steps, then waited patiently.

Finally, I turned and looked at him. He said, "Fifty rupees for one hour. I'll take you to the spice markets."

I looked at his face, and he seemed trustworthy. Fifty rupees was about sixty cents. I caved.

"Okay."

He helped me into his rickshaw and then he took off, and we rattled along for several blocks. I watched the streets flow past and thought, *I don't know if I ever would have made it this far, through all of those people.* I think I would have turned back if I hadn't agreed to hop in the rickshaw.

I settled back, watched, and felt the breeze in my face. I was so thankful for the ride.

We stopped, and he parked his rickshaw and said, "Follow me, we'll walk to the spice markets."

At this point, he was my lifeline. He was tall and young and knew those streets like the back of his hand. I was none of those things. I scrambled to keep up. He'd turn back occasionally to make sure I was still following, then continue on. We dove into some back alleys where they were selling every variety of spice—cinnamon, peppercorns, and turmeric. There were porters walking through carrying huge boxes. There were boxes and bins on the ground, and people were going every which way, like a living obstacle course.

Winding our way through the back alleys, we came back out onto the main street, where he walked me into a spice shop and into the hands of a spice seller who gave me a whole spiel on their spices. The shop wasn't that large, but it was wall-to-wall with foreigners—the only foreigners I'd seen all day. Yes, this was part of the "tour." The driver received a commission from the shop if he brought tourists by. I'm not sure if he got paid for bringing people or only if they bought something. I wasn't in the mood to buy, so I looked around and took a moment in the relatively calm atmosphere to breathe while the driver got a drink of water.

When we got back to the rickshaw, I said, "Can you take me to where I can get a taxi?" I didn't want to tour around for the rest of the hour that my fifty rupees bought me.

"Yes, but there is one more place I want to show you on the way," he said.

"Okay," I agreed.

We bailed out of the rickshaw, and he once again dashed through back alleys until we ended up in a small, quiet alley with nine traditional Jain houses and a Jain temple at the end. Some—maybe all—of those houses had been converted into jewelry shops, which the shop owner told me had been passed down for generations, with jewelry still made in the old style.

This was not the first jewelry shop I'd visited during my trip, and each one began with a traditional introduction from the owner. I looked around politely, with absolutely no interest in buying anything. When I felt enough time had passed to be courteous, I gave the rickshaw driver a "Let's go" look, and we left.

Thankfully, he took me to the street where I could get a taxi, as promised. He told me I should cross the street to make it easier for the next driver to take me to the Lodhi Gardens, where I'd said I wanted to go next. I gave him five hundred rupees instead of the fifty he'd asked for. It was only six dollars, and I was able to see the spice markets and the back alleys I would never have reached on foot.

Lodhi Gardens was my last stop in Delhi—and my last stop in India. I considered skipping it, but I didn't figure I'd be back in Delhi anytime soon, and it was still early, so I went. Compared to the crush and chaos of Chandni Chowk, it was an oasis of peace—like Central Park in the middle of New York: large and green, and all the more precious because of the contrast with the world outside its borders.

Lodhi Gardens is also magical because, unlike the temples I'd been escorted through with my guides—so restricted that I couldn't even bring in a granola bar—these temples were unprotected, unguarded, unguided. Built in the fifteenth century, they added a sense of peace, mystery, and history to the atmosphere.

I sat and watched a parrot hunt for insects, watched families stroll by, and climbed up and down the temples, renewed after the onslaught of the market.

After my fifth trip, I certainly hadn't seen all of India, and I would likely be back again. At least I felt like after the trip to the Taj Mahal that I had filled a major gap in my knowledge of the country.

I'd also gained a better understanding of the culture, history, and politics after spending time with three different guides in three different cities, in addition to my "weekend" with Kalyani in Kashmir.

CHAPTER 35

SRI LANKA:
THE BEST PART OF TRAVEL

What in the world had I done? It was pitch black and raining cats and dogs. I'd checked my iPhone weather app before the trip, and it showed rain every single day for the six days I'd be in Sri Lanka. Since the trip was tied to the trip with Kalyani and her schedule, the dates were pretty set. I just hoped it wouldn't be as bad as it looked—maybe just a light tropical rain in the afternoons?

The moment I looked out the window, I realized this was no light tropical rain. This was a monsoon.

I had a cooking class scheduled for the next afternoon, and WhatsApp notifications were already rolling in, asking if I'd be willing to reschedule or do a private class since my original session had been washed out. The roof had caved in on the location we would've used. *Yeesh!*

I wasn't 100 percent confident my driver knew where he was going. I didn't use Uber at the airport because it was still tied to an old credit card, and I didn't want to load the new one while standing in the arrivals hall. Instead, I walked to the taxi stand, told the driver "Courtyard by Marriott," and showed him the address on Google Maps. There was a lot of hand waving and gestures from my driver, several other drivers, and the cab stand manager. How did they not know where a Courtyard was? I watched our progress on Google Maps to make sure he stayed on course.

As we drove through the city, I saw the lights reflecting in huge puddles forming on the road and laughed at myself. I know how to check ahead for weather conditions and pick the right places for the right seasons, but that's not real life. Some of my best travel adventures happened when things didn't go as planned—like being run out of Belarus because we had no visa or standing at the architectural dig in North Macedonia in 107-degree heat.

I had wanted to write a travel memoir for a while and had been encouraged by some of my friends. I'd even put pen to paper—more like fingers on keyboard—but nothing sounded right.

And then, in the dark taxi on the rainy night in Sri Lanka, I finally had a vision for what and how I needed to write. The best stories were the unexpected adventures and trials that made travel both challenging and rewarding.

By the time I got to the hotel, (which was so brand new the drivers were not yet familiar with it), I felt completely uplifted. I finally saw a path forward for how to write about my travels.

I was looking forward to my days solo in Sri Lanka, regardless of the monsoon. Solo travel is when I have enough peace and freedom that I can think and create, and there is nothing that compares to that feeling for me. My Golden Triangle tour in India didn't feel completely solo because I'd had guides everywhere. In Sri Lanka, I was on my own!

I agreed to change the cooking class to be a private session, so the next morning I took an Uber to the meeting point, which was essentially on the side of the road. It was crowded with pedestrians weaving around me on the sidewalk and buses, taxis, cars, and moto-taxis (or tuk-tuks) flying by on the street. I had no idea how I was going to find my tour guide-chef.

I need not have worried. It was not a touristy section of town, so I stood out like a sore thumb. The guide walked straight up to me and introduced himself. He handed me a shopping basket—an actual wicker basket—and walked me a block to the market.

I've been to fresh markets dozens of times in dozens of countries, but I've never seen quite such an assortment of local produce, spices, and fish. There was no meat, bread, or household goods like cleaners or plates in this market. It was all produce, spices, and fish. Meat, the guide explained, is sold in different markets.

We saw lotus roots; coconuts of all varieties, from small and hairy to smooth and hairless; wood apples, which are woody on the outside with a soft, squishy black interior; green oranges that look like limes but are actually oranges, he assured me; pomegranates; avocados; tamarind that looked like baby mice; and mangoes—mangoes, mangoes, mangoes. He told me there are thirty-six varieties of mango in the country.

The market was relatively small, covering only a single square block. There were seven similar produce markets around the city so that people wouldn't all have to converge in one spot, which I thought was smart. From what I'd seen so far, Colombo was very spread out. I had taken an Uber for thirty-five minutes to get to the meeting point.

We wandered through the market, and as he picked up spices and herbs, he held them out for me to smell. I'll be honest, no matter what he held in front of my nose, it smelled like fish. That entire market smelled like fish, and I had to keep my nose closed to deal with it. I do not like fish—and I never did, even before I became a vegetarian. *Why is it so stinky?*

He asked what looked best to me after we wandered through, and we picked a small pineapple and a pumpkin—or maybe it was a squash. The vendor carved off about a sixth of the pumpkin and plopped it into my basket.

After we had everything we needed, we hopped in a tuk-tuk. The trip to his house, which also served as a cooking studio, took another twenty minutes. When we got there, he ushered me out to his little balcony and told me to relax.

The house was surrounded by trees, and all I could see was the jungle and a few other houses. I could hear cars on the highway off in the distance. I could also hear monkeys chattering and the plunk of coconuts hitting the ground occasionally.

When he joined me on the balcony, he pointed out some flying foxes in the trees. Flying foxes are not foxes; they're bats. Huge dang bats, which I'd only seen previously in the night zoo in Singapore.

He served me wood apple juice. Since I had a rule *never* to touch any juice or fresh produce while traveling in developing countries, I asked if it was safe to drink. Of course, he said yes, explaining that Sri Lanka is not like India and that the homes have a tap for clean drinking water. I drank a little of the juice, which looked like chocolate milk but tasted like mango-citrus juice. It was tasty, yet that brown color was disconcerting, and I couldn't get past the contrast between how it looked and how it tasted.

While he showed me how to chop and cook Sri Lankan curries, there was ample time to talk about Sri Lanka and the culture. He also asked me where I was headed next.

I said I was taking a train to Ella the next day and staying for two days, then taking the train back. He all but rolled his eyes. Apparently, I was about to do what all the tourists did. I had become a cliché.

I'll be honest: one reason I wanted to ride the train was that Anthony Bourdain's show featured him riding it—both in the episode itself and in the intro. The train in Sri Lanka is iconic. The views are supposedly amazing, and the train apparently sells out fast, so you have to book early. I had reserved my ticket a month in advance—the earliest the site allowed—so I could experience the train.

But I'd barely been in the country twelve hours at that point, most of it sleeping. What did I know?

"What do you think I should I do?" I asked him.

"If you're only here for six days, you don't want to eat up two whole days—nine hours each—on trains. You should go to Sigiriya and Galle. Ella is too touristy—go to Haputale instead."

"How should I get there if not by train?"

"Just Uber."

On one of our cooking breaks (which he used to smoke), I sketched out a possible itinerary based on his recommendation, looking up the various places on the map.

As far as the food we cooked, if there were no coconuts, I don't know what Sri Lankans would eat. We used ground coconut in the rotis—small, pancake-like, crispy bread. We used coconut milk and coconut oil in the pineapple and pumpkin curries. Then we made something like a Sri Lankan guacamole, with garlic, onion, and tomato, but using ground coconut instead of avocado.

It was all delicious and all cooked from fresh ingredients. The chef said that most families still cooked that way, getting produce from the markets like we did and cooking from scratch. He said he made the coconut rotis several times a week. He had prepared a vegetarian menu for me. With such an abundance of vegetables and such flavorful curries, I don't think anyone would miss meat.

After our meal was eaten and cleaned up, I left with my new itinerary–scratched out on some Post-its I'd dug out of my purse.

The next morning, I slept in and did not get on the 5:55 a.m. train to Ella. I was actually happy about that, as I had been stressing about getting to the train station early enough—it was a good twenty to twenty-five minutes from the hotel, and I would have had to take an Uber at 4:30 or 5:00 a.m.

It was also nerve-wracking because I'd just torn up my itinerary, and I didn't know where I would be staying each night. I was traveling solo, so I could be flexible. I took a deep breath, and at 8:00 a.m., I clicked "confirm" on my Uber app, requesting a driver to take me to Ella.

About five minutes later, I climbed in the back of the Uber, and we set off for a five-hour trip for a cost of about sixty dollars. It was crazy! Ironically, my driver worked full-time for the railroad in a technical role but drove for Uber as a side hustle. It was Sunday, a day off for him.

Whether Uber pays its drivers well enough I can't say, but as a rider—especially a female solo rider—I'm all in on Uber. I feel safe with an Uber that has been designated to pick me up, where there is a record of me getting in the car. If I hopped in a random taxi or or tuk-tuk, I could disappear and no one would ever know—there would be no trace of me.

There are a couple of added safety features in Sri Lanka and India that I'd never seen before. First, there is a PIN system: I am given a PIN, which I give to the driver verbally. The driver must input the PIN before the ride can be completed and before he gets paid. In India, the PIN had to be provided before the driver was given the destination to ensure I was in the car with the correct driver.

Secondly, after about two and a half hours of driving, the driver wanted to stop for coffee and a bathroom break. We stopped at a little coffee shop, and Uber popped up a notification saying, "It looks like you've stopped. Is everything okay?"

Some might think that's big-brother creepy, but I found it to be very reassuring. After the stop, the driver handed me a small box of tea. I'd watched him buy it but assumed it was good local tea for his family. I was so touched by that gesture, especially after he'd paid for our coffees.

After our coffee stop, we still had three hours to drive. It seemed silly to sit in the back, so I moved to the front where I had a better view and we could converse more easily.

While we drove, I thought through the travel memoir I wanted to write. Occasionally, I would tap out a one-liner email to myself about a chapter or a way of focusing a topic.

We drove through Haputale on our way to Ella. The chef had recommended Haputale the day before, but we only stopped briefly to take pictures. The town was perched on green-covered mountains, and it was definitely not touristy. I didn't see any foreign tourists, and while I found some hotels on TripAdvisor in the area, prices varied widely—from $7 to $280.

While I like a good travel bargain, I will pay more for a hotel that I know is safe and clean. Tera and I had paid two dollars for a room in the Alojamiento La Plata hotel in Quito, Ecuador, and after a day with a shared toilet that didn't flush, we learned that lesson well.

I had a room booked in Ella and I didn't want to lose the money on the room, so we pushed on. I told the hotel in Ella I would stay one night instead of two, which they agreed to, allowing me to continue to Sigiriya along the route the chef recommended.

My chef friend was not wrong about taking an Uber. We arrived in Ella in five hours, and I was there early in the afternoon versus arriving close to dark.

My driver and I had discussed where I was going next, and before he dropped me off, he asked me how I was going to get to Sigiriya. "Uber, I guess," I said.

The driver nodded and said, "Maybe I could take you."

I didn't want to get him in trouble with his railroad job, and since the next day was Monday, I assumed he'd need to be back at work. I said, "I would love that, but if you need to return or have a rider to take back to Colombo, I don't want to hold you up."

Here's where the economics question comes in for the drivers. In theory, he could have picked up someone who wanted to Uber back to Colombo that night—though how likely that was, I have no idea. If he didn't, then the entire five-hour return trip, including his time, gas, and some tolls, would have been at his cost. Should the one-way fare have covered his two-way expenses? Maybe? Did it? I don't think so.

He said he had to call his boss and would let me know. We traded WhatsApp information. As soon as he left, I thought, *Would I get as lucky with another Uber to Sigirya the next day? It was another four-hour drive. Would there be a driver in Ella willing to take me?*

I was in the middle of the country, so I'd either have to find one or negotiate with a taxi driver—or maybe there was a bus. But within ten minutes, the driver texted me and said he'd stay and take me to Sigiriya. I looked up the Uber rate for a drive to Sigiriya, and we agreed on that price, though

I'd pay him directly. I also tipped him well, outside the app. The view was so gorgeous from my hotel, overlooking the mountains surrounding Ella. Everything was covered in bright green vegetation. There was a waterfall on the mountain just to my right. The valleys and hills stretched on forever, with mist swirling around them.

I made myself a cup of tea, sat out on the deck, and opened my laptop to write a few thoughts about the travel memoir. Mostly, I just enjoyed sitting on the deck and drinking tea.

I initially planned to be in the hotel for two days, but now I had just one night, so I had to make it count. There was a placemat in the hotel room featuring some tourist destinations in the area. The Nine Arches Bridge—a famous railway bridge in Sri Lanka, featuring, yes, nine arches—was supposedly only a forty-five minute walk away. The driver had mentioned the bridge too, so that seemed like the place to go.

The railway passed right by the hotel, so all I had to do was follow it. It was a railroad bridge after all. I asked the hotel clerk which way to go. "This way?" I asked pointing left.

He said, "No that's the wrong way. You should take a tuk-tuk. There isn't time to make it walking."

It was 4:00 p.m., and the sun set around six, so I figured I should have plenty of time. I left the hotel and walked to the right.

I walked on the railroad ties some but found it easier to walk alongside the path. I also kept stopping to take pictures over the valley and the mountains, which were beautiful, green, and lush. There were very few people on the railway—a few locals here and there, but it was mostly quiet.

I also stopped occasionally to dictate an email to myself about chapters I wanted to add into the travel book. I took my time, soaking in the landscape and enjoying the freedom to think, even though I knew I had limited time before the sun went down.

I walked past the Ella town station, where the train would have dropped me off if I'd taken it.

About twenty minutes into the walk, I started feeling like I was pretty isolated. And there was a man coming down the tracks toward me. I can handle myself, so I wasn't afraid, but I also like to be prepared. I reached down and grabbed a small rock and stuck it in my pocket.

A minute later, I reached down again because I felt a stinging pain on my foot. I had changed out of my cowboy boots into sneakers for the walk, and three little black leeches, each about half an inch long, were trying to latch onto me inside my sock. I picked them off with my hands, and the little suckers attached to my fingers. I grabbed another rock and used it to scrape them off my hands.

By that time, the man I'd seen coming toward me was very near, and he asked, "Are you all right?"

"I have leeches all over me!" I said.

"You have to walk in the center of the railroad." He made a sweeping motion to indicate the middle of the tracks. "Some people are allergic, like a bee sting, but they're not poisonous."

"Thanks," I said. I hadn't even thought about the possibility that they'd be poisonous or that I would be allergic. I just wanted them to stop biting me.

He kept walking, and once I made sure there were no other leeches, I started walking again, this time carefully down the center of the tracks.

I felt foolish for having picked up the rock when he was nice enough to stop and ask if I was okay and explain how to avoid the leeches. As I walked, I kept checking my socks for leeches and found them on me several more times. I'm not sure if I missed them from my earlier check or if they were still finding me even in the center of the tracks.

The second time I tried to remove them from my legs, I

used a rock so they couldn't attach to my fingers. But they were wily, trying to squirm down into the little shoelace holes, so I had to use my fingers to dig them out and then scrape them off my fingers with the rock. They were vicious little guys.

After about thirty more minutes, I came to a railroad tunnel and knew the Nine Arches Bridge was on the other side because I saw dozens of people milling around and taking selfies. *Sigh.*

The railroad tunnel was one more adventure. It was about 100 feet long and teeming with bats. I couldn't see them because it was too dark, but I could certainly hear them.

The bridge was beautiful, with nine arches as promised, but it was just a bridge. The walk had been by far the best part of the journey, leeches or not. I took a few pictures and selfies, then turned around. I definitely didn't want to be out after dark, and time was getting short.

On the way back, I walked down the center of the tracks to avoid the leeches, but I kept bending down to double-check my feet just in case.

As I approached Ella station, the lights were on, and it looked like the train might be coming. I waited, but when it didn't appear, I kept walking. I did walk on the side of the railway, just in case. The train seemed like a bigger threat than the leeches at that point.

I passed by a lady who was waiting on a path by the train tracks. She asked me where I was going, and I told her I was going to my hotel. The lady said the train was coming. I walked a few more feet and saw that the tracks ran between two hills. There wasn't much clearance between the hills and the tracks, so I turned back and waited with the lady. The train came by a few minutes after that. Clearly, she was a local and knew the train schedule.

Even standing where we were, the train passed by so

close. People were hanging out the windows, waving and smiling. I could almost have reached up and high-fived them. *Would that have been my train if I hadn't taken the Uber?*

The next morning, the driver came to pick me up, and we were off on another journey. It would take four hours to get to Sigiriya. I sat in front that day, feeling more like a passenger than a "ride." I asked where he had slept and he pointed at the back seat. He did have a change of clothes, though, so this may be something that he did occasionally. I still felt bad, as the hotel I had stayed at was comfortable—verging on luxurious—with the most amazing views.

He said he'd been getting pings all night to take other Uber jobs, but locals had damaged his car on previous trips when he took jobs because of intense competition. There had been economic protests in Sri Lanka a few months before I came. I still went because things seemed to have calmed, and tourism was one of their top three industries—tea, unsurprisingly, was number one—so I figured it would be good to support the local economy.

On the drive, we talked about his job, family, economics, and politics in Sri Lanka. He stopped whenever we saw monkeys on the side of the road so I could take pictures, which was often. He agreed monkeys are cute but said they can be a road hazard. Like deer in the U.S., I supposed.

Once, when he needed a break, he stopped at a little stand selling coconuts. The vendor hacked off the top of two coconuts and handed me one to drink. It was refreshing but too much for me to drink while standing on the side of the road. I handed the coconut back to the vendor, assuming she'd sell the coconut meat separately.

The driver dropped me off at Sigiriya Fort, which was the most amazing and unexpected thing. A king back in the late 400s AD built a palace shaped like a lion from an almost

600-foot-high granite mountain. Much of the fortress on top had crumbled, but you could still see the foundation, the lion's paws at the base of the mountain, and frescoes honoring the king's many concubines. *Ah, more concubines.*

The top of the mountain— a giant flat-topped plateau where the palace had been—was so high and so exposed, with so few railings, that despite all the rock climbing I've done, I felt nausea and vertigo in a way I don't think I ever had. The view from the top was amazing, with a 360-degree panoramic view of the surrounding jungle, but I had to sit down in the center of the mountain top, away from the edges. *I can see just fine from over here, thank you very much!* I was happy to get back down to the base of the mountain, to walk back through the palace grounds and take pictures of more monkeys.

When the driver dropped me off at my hotel—another lovely place with serene, beautiful grounds and even more monkeys—I told him the same thing I had before: if he got a job that would take him back to Colombo, he should do it. By then, however, he was committed to taking me back and told his boss he'd work a half day and come in the afternoon the next day.

We left early the next morning, and true to his word, he dropped me off at the hotel around noon, already starting to take work calls as we drove.

Back in Colombo, I had a free afternoon, and I wanted to walk through Galle Face Green— a boardwalk and park area in downtown Colombo that faces the Indian Ocean.

There was also a Burger King in a mall in that same area. After five days in Sri Lanka eating only Sri Lankan vegetable curries—as well as my time in India with Kalyani and on the Golden Triangle tour—I was dying for an Impossible Whopper. I planned to get my burger first, then walk along Galle Face Green.

I walked rather than taking a tuk-tuk or taxi because it was only a thirty-minute walk, and I was tired of being in a car after three days of Ubering through the country. I was walking through what seemed to be an upscale part of the town with high rises, hotels, and a university. There was a lot of construction going on, so I made my way over broken concrete and around barriers.

A middle-aged man started walking alongside me and said, "I'm a policeman."

Tera once told me, "If you have to say you're hip, you're not." I also remembered the scam back in Bogotá with the fake policeman trying to "help" me. This man had no badge, nor did he offer to show me one. I didn't ask for one because I already knew he wasn't a policeman.

"I am with the tourist police. This area is very safe," he said.

I said, "Nice," but I didn't break my stride or even look at him. I had checked the GPS on my phone a few minutes earlier and knew I had several blocks on this stretch of road before hanging a left.

"It's a nice day," he said. "Where are you going?"

I thought for a few seconds before answering, but I didn't think I was giving away any secrets by telling him my destination. "The mall."

"The mall is closed," he said.

Right! Totally believable that the mall would be closed in the middle of the afternoon on a Wednesday. I increased my pace and started scanning for shops or restaurants to duck into.

He said, "You need to go to the gem shops downtown. That is much better for shopping."

Magically, a tuk-tuk pulled up alongside us. "Only fifty rupees and he will take you to the gem shops."

"No," I said, and kept walking.

"Do you know how much fifty rupees is?" the not-policeman

asked. "It is less than one quarter of a dollar. Take a quarter and cut it down into small pieces."

It was such a ridiculous statement. Even if the ride was free, there was no way that I was going to get into that tuk-tuk. Who knew where I would be taken?

The tuk-tuk driver now added his own pleas to the not-policeman's. "Only fifty rupees."

I said no and kept walking, eyes straight ahead, not looking at either of them.

The policeman eventually peeled off, but the tuk-tuk kept driving alongside me for another block or two. I didn't make any further eye contact with him and just kept walking.

Finally, the tuk-tuk driver sped off, looking for an easier mark.

I took the left turn and made it to the mall, which, unsurprisingly, was open and packed with people.

After lunch—my Impossible Whopper was perfect and hit the spot!—I walked along the boardwalk fronting the ocean. When I got to the end of the waterfront and had to turn left to go back to the hotel, I debated whether to hail an Uber or not. I decided to walk. I kept going, stopping only to put on a windbreaker and a hat on when it started sprinkling.

When the sprinkles turned into a monsoon downpour, I was only about two blocks away from the hotel. I could see it across the lake, but it was pouring. I stopped under the branch of a tree and waited a minute to see if it would pass. It didn't, and I was getting drenched standing there.

Finally, I started running. Tuk-tuks slowed down as they passed, yelling and offering me a ride. Though these tuk-tuks were most likely genuinely interested in helping me not get doused (and picking up a small fare in the process), I didn't want a ride. I was having too much fun. I kept running. I felt like a little kid out playing in the rain and running through puddles. I only had two blocks to go, and it was a warm rain. I was soaked by the time I made it to the hotel, but it was amazing.

Sri Lanka is one of my favorite trips ever, partly because I needed the time to rejuvenate and think after my precipitous retirement and partly because being there gave me the vision on how to write about my travels.

But mostly because Sri Lanka was so friendly. I cannot think about Sri Lanka without thinking about the Sri Lankans who became such a part of my trip. The chef who taught me about Sri Lankan cuisine and culture and recommended that I change my itinerary to see a lot more of his country. The Uber driver who became my personal driver and friend as we traveled across the country—someone I was able to talk to about the economy, the monkeys (they were everywhere!), and who made me feel safe while I saw as much of the country as I could.

After Sri Lanka, I not only felt at peace with having left my company, I felt committed to what I was going to do with my future.

Ever since I'd gone to Spain as a fourteen-year-old, travel was part of who I was. Travel was how I understood the world and understood myself. I always knew I was going to continue to travel, but now I was excited to write about it as well.

CHAPTER 36

People always ask me what's next. The truth is, I don't know.

I always have lots of ideas for places I'd like to go next, but it depends on who is available to go with me or if I'm going solo, and what other commitments I have.

I would like to go to anywhere that inspires me or anywhere I feel like I can learn something. In this world, honestly, that's just about everywhere.

I'd love to go back to some of the countries that I don't feel like I saw enough of, and there are still a lot of places I haven't been.

Wherever I go, I will keep writing about the experience and hopefully share the journey with anyone who wasn't able to travel with me.

As my husband said to me in Morocco, "Ride the camel, honey! Ride the camel for all of us who aren't with you."

ABOUT THE AUTHOR

Tauni Crefeld, a graduate of the United States Air Force Academy, served as a Security Police Officer, leading troops and learning leadership lessons. After her military service, Tauni joined a major consulting firm where she spent 25 years, rising from entry level to Managing Director.

As a consultant, she was known as a fixer for leading large teams and turning around underperforming projects. Throughout her career, she applied the same solution-orientation to uncover the hidden obstacles holding women back, and helping them advance into leadership positions.

Tauni and her husband have one son and a cat and live in New Jersey. An avid traveler, she has visited over 75 countries and enjoys outdoor adventures with her family, including hiking, paddleboarding, rock climbing, and bikepacking.

OTHER BOOKS BY TAUNI CREFELD

The Fixer   *Own Your Path*

www.ingramcontent.com/pod-product-compliance
Lightning Source LLC
Chambersburg PA
CBHW032146080426
42735CB00008B/608